The Origins of Oxford Street Names

Ann Spokes Symonds
and Nigel Morgan

Robert Boyd
PUBLICATIONS

Published by
Robert Boyd Publications
260 Colwell Drive
Witney, Oxfordshire OX28 5LW

First published 2010

ISBN: 978 1 899536 99 3

Printed and bound by
Information Press, Southfield Road
Eynsham, Oxford OX29 4JB

Contents

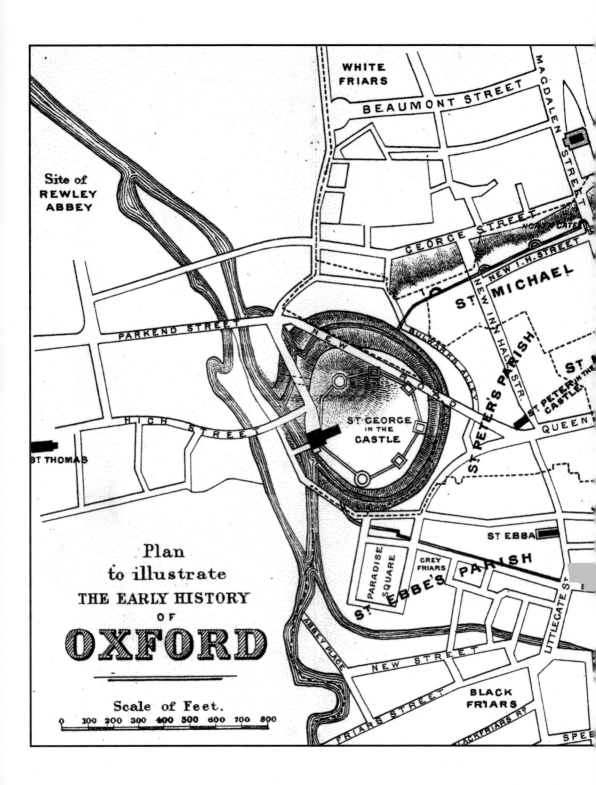

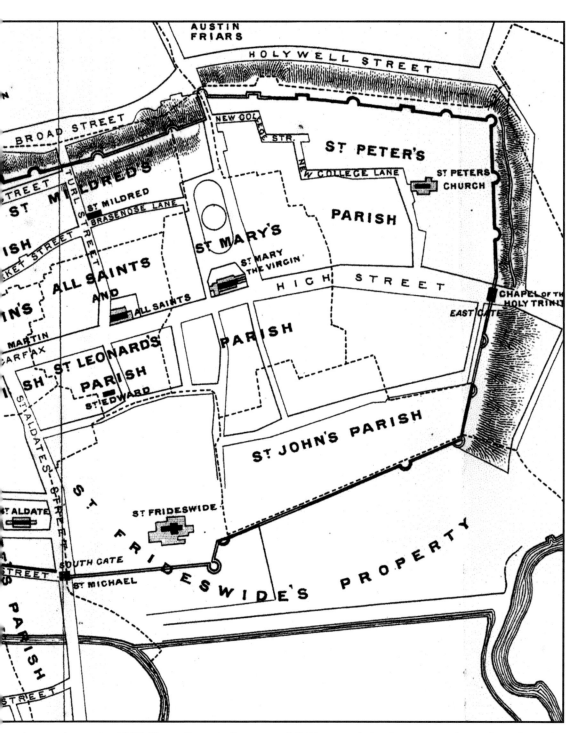

A map drawn in 1887 (from *Historic Towns* ny C W Boase ed. By Freeman and Hunt) to show the parishes and streets of Oxford in the eighteenth century.

Old hyphenated street signs in Oxford taken by David Ludlow in 2004. Most of these have now been replaced.

Acknowledgements

Our grateful thanks go to all those who have kindly lent us photographs and/or provided us with the information we needed. Most of the captions to the photographs include the names of those who kindly agreed to allow them to be published.

We should particularly like to thank the *Oxford Mail* and *Oxford Times* (Newsquest), especially Chris McDowell (Librarian) and John Chipperfield ('Memory Lane'). Others whose help and advice was invaluable are:

Ron Alcock, Jean Arnatt, Elizabeth Boardman, Andrew Burchett, Mrs Phylis Bursill, Robin Darwall-Smith, Richard Dick, David Butler, Maureen Chatterton, Cathy Coelho, Caroline Cooper and Miriam Knight of Oxford City Council Building Control Services, Chris Gilliam, Dr. Malcolm Graham, Professor Stephen Harrison, Lucy Hughes, Stephanie Jenkins, Phil Mercer of BBC Oxford, Carole Newbigging, Councillor Bob Price, John Richards, Marie Ruiz, Susanne Shatford, Dr Eric Sidebottom, Hilary Silk, Councillor Dee Sinclair, Josie Smith, David Townsend, Marie Vickers, and Dorothy Woodward. There were many others who took an interest in our search for some of the missing origins and who gave us hints which eventually led us to a successful find. We thank them too.

Our grateful thanks go to the Greening Lamborn Trust for their generous grant towards this publication. See section on E.A. Greening Lamborn.

We have made every effort to trace all the copyright holders but if any have been inadvertently left out we hope they will get in touch with us.

Foreword

I first became interested in street names in the 1960s when, as a member of Oxford City Council and its Highways Committee, I was asked to help select names for the new estates springing up round the City. I was lucky in the fact that my father was interested in local history and in his extensive library were all the books I needed to learn about the streets of Oxford in earlier times.

One of the most formidable tasks at that time was to find names for the new roads on the Blackbird Leys Estate. The site had previously been a sewage farm which meant that it was very fertile ground. The earliest roads to be developed had already been given the names of birds. In its second phase there were some twenty or so roads leading off a spine road. Because there had been many wildflowers on the site, I decided that the main road should be called Field Avenue and that the roads leading off it should be named alphabetically so that anyone new to the area would be able to find the roads more easily. We started with Andromeda and ended with Vetch. (See Index).

There was also a steady stream of new roads and streets which needed new names in the rest of the City. Like Robert Bridges (See Naming Streets in More Recent Times) I hoped that some of the old names could be revived. Old field names can sometimes be appropriate and are still popular today. For example, Pound Way at Cowley Centre is apposite for a shopping area. In 1961, I also chose Pony Road on the Horspath Road Trading Estate, pony being the slang word for £25.

After the gasworks had been demolished and St Ebbe's was redeveloped no one wanted to retain the old name of Gas Street although perhaps the name 'Gaslight' would have been more romantic. I consulted old maps and found that Gas Street was almost on the line of the old Preachers' Lane. Oxford was the home of many friars at that time. Because old names are, for convenience, included below on the new street name plates, this one read 'Preachers' Lane, formerly Gas Street'.

I was interviewed by the *Oxford Mail* in December, 1977 on the subject of street naming and the article was headed 'Streets Ahead'. I said that I hoped that when I retired from local politics I could convert all my researches into a book as full of interest as that of Salter, the author of the first book on Oxford street names. Writing six other local history books has rather delayed my intention.

One of the ways in which I learnt a lot about the names of existing roads was when I did a live weekly programme on Radio Oxford in the 1970s with the late Andy Wright. People would telephone in to know why a particular street was so-named (Squitchey Lane was asked the most often) and I would consult my boxes of index cards in the studio. When the broadcasts finished, people would write to me, often with helpful information; this was before the days of emails. I still have the four-inch thick pile of correspondence.

The first book of reference for Oxford Street Names will always be that of The Reverend H.E. Salter whose book, published in 1921, was *The Historic Names of the Sreets and Lanes of Oxford.*

Salter (1863-1951) is recognised as the leading Oxford historian since Anthony Wood (see Missing Names) who wrote or edited 36 books which were published by the Oxford Historical Society.

In 1977, Paul J. Marriott self-published an index of street names and consulted me about some of the entries. It was an intensively researched basic guide and a useful little booklet. However, not only have many more new estates and developments been built in the last thirty years, with hundreds of new names, but more information has come to light.

I have a newspaper cutting preserved by my grandfather (undated) on the subject of the street nomenclature in London, describing a debate in the London County Council of which my great uncle Russell Spokes (1865-1906) was a member. There was discussion about changing the name of Elizabeth Place to Iris Place. Imbat Place had originally been suggested by the local vestry but the Press reported that Russell had called this a 'senseless name'. Russell was reported as saying that they were beginning 'to explore the fine list of names afforded by the rural villages associated with the early lives of individual members' (laughter). Mr Smithers said: 'The Committee would have been glad to have selected the name of 'Spokes' but so insignificant was the thoroughfare that they thought the compliment would be a doubtful one' (laughter). Perhaps this shows that the interest in street names runs in the family.

My co-author, Nigel Morgan, and I believe that the index to this book should give full information about the origins of the streets and that it should be as up-to-date as possible. The index is the most vital part of this book and it could not have been undertaken without Nigel's help.

To paraphrase H.E.Salter who wrote in one of his many local history books:

This book is published, 'not because it is completely finished but because delay would be unwise'. There is the temptation to wait until the last 24 origins become known. However, 'risks must be taken if there is to be progress'.

Ann Spokes Symonds

My own interest in Oxford street names is from the 1980s, when as a young surveyor in an old established practice then based in Cornmarket, much of my time was spent in preparing mortgage valuations and building surveys. I found a copy of Paul Marriott's excellent booklet, *Oxford Street Names Explained* and used this regularly for many years; it is often useful for a client to know the date of construction of their house and interesting too, to know the origins of the street name.

The rate of increase in the development of Oxford will not have escaped many, now that the 1100 street names in Marriott's time have increased to over 1500, all in thirty years or so. Having waited hopefully for much of this time for the book to be upgraded, I had to decide that if I wanted an updated version, I would have to write it myself. Happily, I discovered almost at once that Ann Spokes Symonds was already on the case, with a number of thoroughly researched articles already under her belt – but not much wanting to take on the Index – which was the part I wanted to write!

I have been lucky to have collaborated with Ann, whose knowledge, research skills and databases have of course been a huge help throughout what has turned out to be a properly enjoyable writing process.

Nigel Morgan

Street Names in the Early Days

Nine hundred years of history are bound up in Oxford's street names. In the Middle Ages there were no name-plates and the roads and lanes changed their names depending on who lived in the chief house or who traded there. Others were named after the inns or pubs in the street.

Nowadays, to avoid confusion, street names are rarely changed. This is not the case in some cities on the Continent when roads change their names according to the regimes which come and go. On the whole, Oxford residents do not like change. It is said that the British resist it because it is associated with decay, recalling the words of the favourite hymn Abide With Me: *Change and decay in all around I see.*

At times when other parishes have been absorbed into the City of Oxford it has been necessary to find new names for duplicated ones. At one time, for instance, Oxford had six Church Streets (See that section).

Carfax, the central point of the City from the Middle Ages, takes its name from the four roads leading to the gates in the City wall which came in from all points of the compass. The name is probably derived from the Latin word *quadrifurcus* meaning four prongs.

The Bear, from Bear Lane.

The reason so many towns have a High Street is that in olden times it meant a highway. All four streets which met at Carfax probably bore this name at one time but as the years went by they needed to be identified more clearly.

The High Street in 1834.

The North end of Cornmarket with the old Bocardo prison at the North Gate.

Cornmarket once had half a dozen names to identify the various stalls from which people traded.   One stretch, for instance, was known as *draperia,* as in drapery, another *le surie* (shoemakers) and, further north, *lorneria* (harness makers).   It was later called Northgate Street, after the city gate near St Michael's Church.   Its modern name comes from a building with a leaden roof supported on pillars which was used to store corn.   (See Claymond).   It was pulled down in the Civil War in 1644 when royalist soldiers used the lead to make bullets.

Catte (or Cat) Street with old houses (demolished in 1823) in front of Hertford College in 1821, by J.C. Buckler *(Ms. Don.a 3 (85)* Courtesy of Bodleian Library, University of Oxford.

Catte Street, off High Street, was known by this name as early as 1210 and was also known as the street of the mousecatchers.   The name was made 'respectable' and changed to St Catherine's Street (after St Catherine's or Cat Hall situated there) until the old name, with its early spelling, was revived in 1930.

Magpie Lane, also off the High Street, was named after the inn which was there in at least 1662 and the street was Magpie Lane in 1772.   However, in the 13th C it had been known as Grope Lane,   This was a common medieval word for a dark and disreputable passage.   It later became known as Winkin Lane, because the printing press there was owned by Wynken de Wode.   By 1838 the name had reverted to Grope.   Resistance to this name soon resulted in it being changed to Grape Lane at one time.   Then by 1922 it was Grove Street, a name which continued until at least 1935.   Soon after this it fortunately reverted to its earlier name of Magpie.

Magpie Lane with Merton college in the background in 1812. *Ms. Don. A 2 (49)*
Courtesy of Bodleian Library, University of Oxford.

Broad Street with the Sheldonian (right) and the Clarendon Building.

Broad Street was first known as Horsemongers' Street after a horse fair which was held there from about 1235. By 1379, it had become the high road of Canditch after a stream of clear water which ran into a ditch north of the City wall. It was unusual to find a clear ditch because in those days, people would throw their household waste out of their windows into them. It later became White Street because of the unusual shining whiteness of the stream. This was corrupted to Wide Walk and finally in the 18th C to Broad Street.

The South end of Turl Street with the old All Saints' Church (now part of Lincoln College) *Ms Don a (46)* **Courtesy of the Bodleian Library, University of Oxford.**

The Turl takes its name from the revolving or twirly gate in the old city wall at that point. A 1590 description of it was 'the hole in the wall called 'the Turle''.   Like many old street names which were not written down there are rival claims to its origins.   Peter (or Edward) Thorold (or Torald) lived by the gate and some claim that he might have given his name to the street.

Queen Street was known from about 1260 as the Bailey and included Castle Street as well.   By the 17th C it was Great Bailey.   The word means special jurisdiction which was probably because the nearby castle was under the law of the Sheriff of the County as distinct from the town which was governed by the Mayor and Bailiffs.   By 1556, butchers were allowed to have their stalls in the road and it became Butcher Row or sometimes 'The Shambles'.   In early 19th C Queen Street, probably after Queen Charlotte, wife of George III, began to replace Butcher Row.   The map in a guide book to Oxford of 1823 called it 'Butcher Row Street' but it also said that 'the post office is in Queen Street, or as it is often called Butcher Row'.   By 1830 it was definitely Queen Street and a local historian of the time was able to write 'A street which formerly bore the vulgar name of Butcher Row is now distinguished by the more courtly Queen Street'.   As time went by people assumed that the street had been named for Queen Victoria.   Now that so many towns have this name there have been those who in more recent times have suggested that the name of the Great Bailey be reinstated.

New Inn Hall Street in 1836. The house on the right was demolished in 1891.

New Inn Hall Street was once known as the Street of the Seven Deadly Sins.   Although sins may have been committed there, since the two lanes which led off it were often described as the resort of malefactors and felons and a receptacle for filth and rubbish', in fact it comes from the old word 'synne' meaning a small cottage, of which there were seven.

St Ebbe's Street (formerly Little Bailey) is named after the local church.   Pennyfarthing is not, as is generally thought, named after an old bicycle but after an old family of that name.

St Aldate's, probably Oxford's oldest street, was known in the 13th C as Great Jewery (or Great Jury) Lane after the number of Jewish people who lived there.   In the 14th C it became Fish Street because fish was sold there.   Although there was a saint called Eldad, St Aldate is probably not a saint at all but a corruption of Aldgate or Old Gate.   That part of St Aldate's from the South Gate to Folly Bridge was once Grandpont.

There were many attractive names of streets and lanes in Oxford which are now extinct, changed for a variety of reasons as the centuries went by.   These include All Hallowes Street, Barbican Lane, Bocardo Lane, Coach and Horses Lane, Hammer Hall Lane (now enclosed in New College), and Love Lane.

St Aldate's in the early 20th century.

Naming Streets in more Recent Times

Rules for the naming of streets in Oxford have evolved over the years. The Oxford Corporation Act of 1933, Section 56, included the words: 'The Corporation may name any street or any part of a street which is without a name or which bears two names, and may from time alter the name of any street....and may paint, engrave or otherwise describe and place the name of any street....on a conspicuous part of any building or other erection at or near each corner or entrance thereof'.

The Reverend H.E. Salter, a distinguished Oxford archivist and historian, was the first person to write about the subject in his *The Historic Names of the Streets and Lanes of Oxford,* published in 1921. The poet, Robert Bridges wrote the Preface and in it he pointed out that having street names absolutely fixed was 'a modern convenience of extreme utility'. He wanted some of the old street names revived. For example, he thought that St Catherine's Street was a 'silly modernism' and that it should be replaced by the original Cat Street.

Salter went back to the original sources such as the Cartulary of St Frideswide and that of the Hospital of St John, Antony Wood's 17thC *City of Oxford* and his *Life and Times* and the 1772 Survey of Oxford published by the Oxford University Press in 1912. He agreed that if changes were made it might annoy the Post Office and the tax-gatherers but, on the other hand, they were probably more inconvenienced by the number of duplicated streets in existence.

In May, 1935, a Harold Lovegrove of Windmill Road, Headington, formerly of Reading, sent to the Mayor a printed list of names which he thought could be used; he sent this list to Councils all over the UK. He even reserved some of them for Oxford, such as Grace, Wisdom, Understanding, Unity, Peace and Concord. Some of these he also reserved for Cambridge although they were given Happiness, Justice, Religion and Virtue as well. There were 759 suggestions in like vein. 'Gifts of the Spirit Mind and Body' section, ranged from Ability to Zest, including such names as Gentility, Hustle and Bustle, Intimacy, Merriment, Monopoly, Probation, Tragedy, Unction, Whimsical and Wireless. Imagine living in Intimacy Lane or Whimsical Way. It is hard to believe that anyone would have taken these suggestions seriously and it is not surprising that none of these names was ever used in Oxford.

Mr Lovegrove did, however, put forward some good ideas as to which streets should be called lanes, avenues, gardens, squares, terraces, courts or crescents. He pointed out that the name Close or End should indicate that there is no through way. He also did admit that the best names were those of its 'distinguished citizens, male or female, alive or dead (perhaps better dead) to perpetuate their memory'.

At one time when names of roads were required for new Council estates this was carried out by the Housing Committee. However, once the Highways (later Highways and Traffic) Committee set up its Street Names Sub-Committee all street naming came under them.

In about 1955, the Committee had agreed that if street names which were duplicated had to be changed then the road with the greater number of houses or businesses would be the one which could keep its old name.

In December, 1992, the Highways and Traffic Committee endorsed their existing policy about street names. They confirmed that the names of living people should not be used. For exceptions to the rule see the section on Commemorating Curent Celebrities. The Committee also agreed that women's names, including their first names, should be used wherever   possible and that names should not be used which would duplicate or be similar to existing names.

For some years now, the naming of streets has come under the Building Control Department of Oxford City Council. When a new name is required they consult the Royal Mail, the developers, the Parish Council (if there is one), the Residents Association, (if there is one), and the Ward Councillors.

When the department hears back from any of these people the preferred name(s) go to the members of the Council's relevant Area Committee who are asked for their views. If the Councillors agree on a name then the Building Control Department goes ahead with it under delegated powers. However, if the Councillors on that Area Committee do not agree on a suggested name it will go to a meeting of the Area Committee for discussion before the Building Control Department goes ahead. Members of the public may attend Area Committees and speak but only the Councillors can vote. The decision of the Area Committee is final.

Duplicated Names

As early as 14th July, 1932 there had been an article by *Omricon* in the *Oxford Mail* advocating the elimination of duplicated street names. However, not much was done at that time. Over the years, parishes and areas which had been outside the City boundaries came into the City and the need for change became more urgent.

In 1960, the Street Names Sub-Committee of the City Council, aware of the confusion caused when streets of the same name existed within the City, invited the Head Postmaster to meet with them to discuss the issue. He then promised to look at these streets and produced a list, divided into three groups. These were :

1. Those in which the need for change is urgent,
2. Where changes are desirable but not essential and
3. Those where changes were not necessary.

This was in the days before postcodes had been introduced and unless the locality (e.g. Headington or Cowley) was included on the envelope mail often went astray. St John's Street and St John's Road were particularly mentioned as needing change immediately.

It happened that not long after these lists were produced St Ebbe's was redeveloped and therefore some of the roads there, such as Pensons Gardens, Princes Street and Union Street (all duplicated in St Clement's) were demolished.

St John's Road, mentioned above, became St Bernard's Road at the suggestion of St John's College. The residents there had been asking for change as early as 1946 and were only too happy to accept the change. St Bernard's was the foundation prior to St John the Baptist College on its present site.

Charles Street, St Ebbe's (confused with Charles Street off Iffley Road) became Turn Again Lane (see Evolving Names) and Albert Road, Summertown (although not on the urgent list), which was confused with Albert Place, St Ebbe's and Albert Street (Jericho) became Hobson Road (see Index).

In 1967, Lakeside was the name given to a new road off Linkside Avenue. In time, as new houses were built, only about half of them had a view of the lake. Because of the similarity in the sound of the name, letters were often going astray, especially in the days before postcodes. Soon after people moved in, a man who lived in the road asked the Chairman of the Street Names sub-committee if she would consider a change. She suggested that he take round a petition; this he did but in the morning when, in those days, it was mostly the women who came to the door. Charmed by this tall and good-looking man, they almost all signed for a change. When the husbands came home that evening they were furious, saying that they would have to pay for their deeds to be changed and have to print new notepaper and so on. In fact there is no payment required for changing the name of a street on deeds

St Bernard's Road in 2010.

but even so their disapproval was enough for the change never to have taken place. Linkside and Lakeside both remain. On the whole, residents do not like change unless they feel it is absolutely essential.

Alexandra Road in Headington (named after Queen Alexandra) was changed because there was already one in Botley. But what to call it? Queen (or Saint) Alexandra was thought to be too similar. Alice, another girl's name was suggested because of Oxford's connection with Lewis Carroll's *Alice in Wonderland*. However, residents complained that that was too 'childish'. Henry Taunt, the well-known Oxford photographer, had no road named after him and his name was put forward. Unfortunately, this was apparently also the name of a minor politician and was not wanted by the residents. In the end it was agreed that the well-known and popular surgeon, Professor Gathorne Girdlestone (1881-1950), the pioneer of surgery at the Wingfield, now the Nuffield Orthopaedic Centre, should be commemorated. No one seemed to mind that he already had one road named for him – Girdlestone Road - and Alexandra Road was renamed for his second name Gathorne.

A writer of an article called "Street Wisdom" in *The Guardian* of 14th April, 1990 praised Oxford City Council for what it did when there was a need to change the name of one of two Pitt Roads. Because they re-named one of the roads "Chatham" (William Pitt being the first Earl of Chatham) he wrote: 'There, perhaps, is the wit and intelligence, combined with dignity and pride'. In fact, it was suggested to the Committee by one of their members, the Master of Pembroke College, who was a University member of the Council.

Evolving Names

Some roads acquire their names because of their position or even their shape. First Turn, Wolvercote, for instance, was nothing more than the creation of the Bus Company as a fare stage. The service which ran from Carfax to what is now First Turn, was begun in 1910. There was also a second turn at Godstow Road but unlike First Turn this was never formally adopted.

Banjo Road, Cowley Centre is one of the most interesting of evolving names because originally it had no official name, being a back way in to the Centre with only the backs of shops and no houses in it. Often delivery drivers became lost and asked passers-by where they should go. People described it as it looked which was like a banjo with its circular turn-around at its end. Finally, its name became official in April, 1965.

Five Mile Drive is another example of an evolving name. It was named after a walk or drive undertaken when there were few other through roads between the Banbury and Woodstock Roads other than St Margaret's Road in the south. The road was in existence from 1820 but was then called Horsemonger, Horsemanger or Horsefield Road. The dull 'Five Mile Round' or 'Stingy Drive' was the one exception to going beyond the turnpike gates at the north entrance to Oxford. The ride was made daily by, among others, the Warden of Merton, Dr Marsham. In about 1820, when the main roads often became muddy and flooded, a few senior members of the University raised the money to make a dry walk which started from St Giles' Church and continued up the west side of the Woodstock Road as far as Wolvercote. It then led via Horsemonger Lane down the east side of the Banbury Road as far as St Margaret's Road (then Rackham's Lane) and on via the Plantation back to St Giles. Because this was about five miles long it was called walking or riding round the five mile.

It was still being called The Five Mile in 1934. Mr V.C.P. Scott recalled, in 1971, that he made the journey in 1918 when he was nine years old in a pony and trap accompanied by his mother, brother and sister. He said that they called the road Green Lane in those days. Reg Piper, of Cowley, remembered in 1971 that he had a friend called Reg Gillams who worked for the coach builders, P.J. Jones who had several ponies which he kept in a field off the Banbury Road. He took them out for exercise round what he then called the Five Mile Drive.

The first of a new type of sign which was erected in about 1968. Admiring the new sign are Inspector Daff, Oxford City Police, Councillor Ann Spokes, Chairman, City Council Highways Committee (who lived in the road at that time) and Mr J. Wall, Road Safety Officer.

Part of the raised path made by members of the University still exists on the Woodstock Road just past the junction with First Turn.

The raised
path in
2009.

This lane in St Ebbe's is suitably named as the photographer, Henry Taunt, wrote to H.E. Salter, the Oxford historian, in March, 1912:

'It was well-named Turn Again Lane [because] when the old river gate was standing, there was no outlet excepting the one entrance at Littlegate. Wood Street and Orchard Street (right side) were built in about 1825. Wood Street ended at the Trill Mill Stream and there was a little flight of steps down to the water'.

There being no bridge, everyone had to turn again the way they had come. At one time the lane was called 'Charles Streeet, known as Turn Again Lane'. The name Charles Street persisted, however, and it was not until 1972 that the old name of Turn Again Lane was revived.

Oxford's Lost Church Streets

"The foolish appellation 'Church Street' has directed hundreds astray"
(Robert Bridges 1921)

Oxford once had six Church Streets but today not one remains. However, it was not until the mid 1950s that Oxford City Council acted to meet the needs of those who might be led astray. Their sympathy was such that they overdid things and as a result not one Church Street remains.

In the early days there were no official street names but names were handed down from one generation to the next. Churches, unlike residents and traders, after whom many roads were named, were solid fixtures built to last and there was less chance of them disappearing overnight. By the 19th C, Church Street, Road or Lane became a popular name all over England. In London it became the second most used name after Station Road.

One of the reasons that there were so many Church Streets in Oxford was that the City grew and absorbed within its boundaries what were once small villages on the edge of the town. Cowley, Hinksey, New and Old Headington and Summertown all had their Church Streets. Once these roads became part of the City the confusion began. Letters were delivered to the wrong houses; the fire brigade turned up where there was no fire, while summonses to another part of Oxford were unanswered. Police and ambulance drivers often found themselves at the wrong address. Action needed to be taken and residents, who do not usually like change, were in this case ready to accept it.

Church people in the five former villages were invited by the City Council, in 1954, to submit suggestions for new names in their particular Church Street.

In Cowley, the name of the Reverend M.H. Beachamp was suggested. He had been Vicar of the Church of St James there between 1928 and 1939 and it was under his leadership and inspiration that the chapels, now churches, of St Francis of Assisi and St Luke's were built. He also restored the School and the Church Hall and had been a popular figurehead in this growing area of the City. Mr Beachamp gave his consent with delight and Church Street became Beachamp Lane in February, 1955.

In New Hinksey, the Vicar of St John the Evangelist Church, the Reverend W.B. Lander, in a letter to the City Engineer, suggested that 'as the street looks straight down to the Vicarage, why not call it Vicarage Road?'. His idea was taken up.

In Church Street, New Headington, there had been a Chapel of Ease which had been built in 1870 to serve the needs of the growing population. In 1901, Frances Paget became Bishop of Oxford and appointed the Reverend H.N. Perrin and gave him the job of founding and building a new church in Highfield parish responsible to the Bishop. This was on the understanding that the services reflected the Church of England. Perrin thus played an

Church Street, St Ebbe's as it was before 1967.

important part in the early life of the Parish and it was his name which the Vicar there chose, in 1954. This Church Street became Perrin Street in 1955.

In Old Headington, where there had been a church since the 12th Century and which is dedicated to St Andrew, the Vicar, the Reverend C.E.C. Markby, suggested what seemed to be the logical name of St. Andrew's. This was agreed and this Church Street became St Andrew's Road.

Summertown was to select the only non-ecclesiastical name for its Church Street. Alderman Rogers had been Mayor of Oxford and his house had backed onto this street. The house itself had recently been pulled down to make way for the new building called Prama House on the corner of Banbury Road and South Parade. The Church in Rogers Street no longer existed and had been replaced by St Michael and All Angels in Lonsdale Road in 1908-09. Rogers Street therefore replaced the Summertown Church Street.

Thus all these five former Church Streets were given their new names. What then of Oxford's sixth and last remaining Church Street named for St Ebbe's Church in the centre of Oxford? Although its disappearance was perhaps more accident than design, anyone who has seen the changes taking place in Oxford over the last forty years or so can guess what happened. St Ebbe's was redeveloped. Church Street had included among its buildings not only the church but the Oxford Technical School later the College of Technology which became part of the Polytechnic, now Brookes University.

After demolition and before rebuilding took place, archaeological excavations were undertaken. Her Majesty the Queen, on a visit to Oxford in 1968, was taken to see the excavations in what had been Church Street. It was thought appropriate because her son, Prince Charles, was studying archaeology at Cambridge at the time. Gradually, the Westgate Centre took the place of the street and only a short length of it remained. Even this remnant was renamed Pennyfarthing Place.

H.M. The Queen looks at excavations on the site of the former Church Street in St. Ebbe's left to right: Tom Hassall (Archaeologist), H.M. The Queen, Councillor Frank Pickstock, Lord Mayor (and behind him) Councillor Peter Spokes (Chairman, Planning Committee), Douglas Murray (Architect), 1968.

Although nowadays no one is led astray by a 'foolishly' named street there are one or two thoroughfares which still bear the name of Church.   The most important of these is Church Way, Iffley which has been in existence since medieval times and runs through the whole village ending at the 12th C Church of St Mary the Virgin. Also, there is Church Walk in North Oxford, a quiet path which takes its name from the neighbouring church of St Philip and St James which is now no longer a church but the home of the Oxford Centre for Mission Studies. Wolvercote's Church Lane is a footpath which connects St Peter's Church and First Turn with Wolvercote Green.   It has never been thought necessary to alter any of these; it is Oxford's six Church Streets which have been lost and forgotten after over fifty years.

Snobbery and Street Names

Oxford in Victorian times probably did not differ very much from any other City as far as snobbery was concerned. However, it is fair to say that it was rife and there were many occasions, even in more recent years, when the existence of snobbery had an effect on Oxford's street names.

Middle Way at the beginning of the 19th C when it was still called George Street (looking north).

Middle Way in Summertown was formerly known as George Street. When, to avoid confusion with the street of that name in central Oxford, the City Council named it Twining, there was uproar. The furious residents of the street protested and 62 of them in a road of about 75 houses signed a petition against the name.

Alderman Twining, a member of one of Oxford's oldest families, had been a member of the Oxford City Council for fifty years. He was not only responsible for much of the development of 45 acres of land on the east side of Banbury Road, but he gave the land for the new church and school. But Twining was connected with trade and Twining's grocer's shop, purveyors of a fine and well-known tea and other provisions was what most people associated with the name. The feeling was that no one wanted to live in a street named

Twining Brothers

FAMILY GROCERS AND PROVISION MERCHANTS,

Telephone 215.
Telegrams—
"Brothers, Oxford."

OXFORD.

TWINING'S SUMMERTOWN STORES,
294, Banbury Road (Tram Terminus).

NEW SEASON MARMALADE.

1 lb. Jars	..	4½d. each.
2 lb. „	..	7½d. „
3 lb. „	..	10½d. „
7 lb. „	..	1/10 „

Made from an

OLD ENGLISH RECIPE.

after a man who sold tea. As trade was not thought to be good enough for them the residents had proposed that the name should revert to one it had held in earlier years and the street became Middle Way in April, 1955. On the auctioneer's map, drawn for the sale of the land in 1821, it was described as Centre Road. On a 14th C map the land between the Banbury and Woodstock Roads was called 'The Furlong Twene the Ways' and a piece of land in the vicinity was known as Middle Field. In about 1830, Crews Dudley, a developer, planted an oak tree where the present road joins Squitchey Lane and when this well-loved tree grew large the street became Oak Lane. To everyone' regret the tree was cut down in 1919.

We do not know the occupations and professions of the people who were living in Middle Way in 1954 but the correspondence connected with another proposed change of road in Headington still survives.

An advertisement showing Twining's Summertown Stores - Francis Twining when Mayor of Oxford.

The by-pass, also known as the Northern By-pass, is for part of its length also known as North Way.   A short stretch of houses parallel to it near the Headington roundabout also has this name.   The City Council thought that it should be renamed to avoid confusion.   In 1938, they suggested it be called Alden Avenue after the late Mayor, Alderman L.H. Alden, JP, who had died in office two years earlier.   An angry petition from the residents claimed that this would reduce the road to the status 'of any old side road on a third-class estate instead of a road flanking one of the finest main roads in Oxford'.   'In any case, they continued, the name Alden may apply to any of the printers, butchers, grocers or hot-water fitters in Oxford'. The petition stated: 'We as purchasers of the various high-class residences suggest that the name is inappropriate and would be more suitable if used on one of the council's estates'. (There is now in fact an Alden Crescent on the Barton estate). With heads in the air, 14 of the residents suggested the name of Northern Heights.   If the records had not been preserved, we would never have known the occupations of the objectors living in these 'high-class residences' but they included a fruiterer, a railway boilersmith, car deliverer, commercial traveller, the combustion engineer at the generating station, a postman, a post office clerk and an outfitter at Elliston's department store. Two residents worked at Morris Motors and one at the Pressed Steel factory.   In response to these people, who no doubt believed that because they had gone up in the world their road necessitated a prestigious

The Cutteslowe Walls, when the City Council bulldozed the walls down with steamrollers, 1938. Courtesy of Newsquest, Oxford Mail and Times.

Different and adjoining name plates, Wentworth and Aldrich.

name, Alden was dropped and the road remains North Way to this day. It is interesting that people who could be considered to be 'in trade' themselves were not exempt from these feelings of antagonism.

It was not surprising, in the circumstances, that there was also resistance to change in the vicinity of the notorious Cutteslowe walls. These were a monument to snobbery which separated a City Council estate and one which was built by the private Urban Housing Company.

The Council had suggested that the roads which passed through the two estates should be called Wolsey Road and Aldrich Road for their whole length, beginning at the Banbury Road. The developer, and presumably many of those who had purchased their houses on the Urban estate, wished to have nothing to do with the Council's Cutteslowe estate. Under pressure from the developer, it was therefore agreed that different names would be allowed on either side of the walls. The company suggested Carlton and Wentworth for theirs.

The Highways Committee, however, had other ideas and in January, 1934, recommended that the roads be called Cardinal and Sawyer. Seeing through the Council's plan that one of the roads would neatly become Cardinal Wolsey Road, the Housing Company refused. Deadlock ensued, neither giving way, and for many years two pairs of road-name plates could be seen at the junction of Banbury Road, namely Carlton and Cardinal and Aldrich and Sawyer. It was not until 1948 that the City finally bowed to the inevitable and the name plates of Cardinal and Sawyer were taken down from the Banbury Road end.   Despite the fact that on 9th March 1959 the walls came down the separate road names still survive.

It is not always easy to predict which names are likely to win the approval of developers or residents.   The reasons given for refusal may not be connected with snobbery.   One of these was Leyland Close, given to a road close to what was then known as the Leyland car factory.   Nevertheless, solicitors acting for the developers suggested that Leyland Close would be an invitation to young vandals to add a 'd' to make it 'Leyland Closed' in view of the frequent strikes there.   In July, 1973, therefore, the place became Berry Close, derived from Blackberry Lane which had been an extension of the nearby Roman Way.   An Alderman who was fond of puns said that he would give it his vote as it was 'Berry close to the Works'.

In the days when snobbery played a big part in whether road names were acceptable or not, this might have been the reason why developers chose made-up names like Beechcroft and Oakthorpe.   Royalty or peers such as Wellington or Peel or prestigious names such as Dorchester or Cavendish were also often favoured in the past.   (See also the section on Commemorating Current Celebrities).

Apostrophes and Spaces

In recent years there has been a practice of omitting the apostrophe from street name plates. This can cause confusion especially when it relates to the names of people. For instance, in Littlemore the road named after Bessie Ledger is spelled Ledgers Close without an apostrophe, making it unclear how she spelled her name.

In 2009, a new sign was erected in Sheriff's Drive, Upper Wolvercote, opposite the sign on the other side of the road which had the apostrophe. The new one had not. However, as the place is named after the annual Sheriff's Drive on Port Meadow and the nearby Wolvercote Common, it is important to show that this annual round-up of the cattle is undertaken by the Sheriff who holds that office at the time and not after a number

Bessie Ledger

The Sheriff's Drive in 1943 when the cattle were led to the ruins of Godstow Abbey.

of Sheriffs. The cattle are herded into a pound and those who do not have rights of grazing are fined.

The photograph shows the Sheriff's Drive in 1943 when the cattle were led to the ruins of Godstow Abbey. In more recent years, after a pound was built next to the old bathing place at the edge of the common, the cattle are herded in there.

As the originator of the idea to name this City Council development, (on the site of a large house called Church Croft), after the annual Drive, one of the authors of this book raised the matter of the missing apostrophe at a North Area Committee meeting. This monthly meeting is made up of Councillors, including those repesenting Wolvercote. One of the Wolvercote Councillors, Mike Gotch, who happens to live opposite Sheriff's Drive, took the matter up with the City Council Works depot and within four days they had painted an apostrophe on the sign.

In August, 2009, two ex-army men, who lived in St John's Close, Tunbridge Wells, had an argument when one of them could stand it no longer because every day he had to look at the road signs indicating that it was St Johns Close with the apostrophe missing. Deciding that 'enough was enough' he painted apostrophes on the road signs.

However, another resident in the road, also ex-army, called him a vandal and said that the Post Office would not deliver to the road if it had an apostrophe. However, the man with the paintbrush pulled rank on the objector. The Borough Council, in reply, said that the

Sheriff's Drive
with and without
the apostrophe.

St Margaret's Road has several name plates some with an apostrophe and some without. This is one of them.

developers had made the mistake and that if the signs were ever replaced they would spell the name correctly.

In early 2009, Birmingham City Council decided that they would no longer put apostrophes on street signs. They gave the example of Acock's Green, saying that as the Acock family no longer owned the Green there was no reason for the apostrophe any more. Despite angry complaints made by defenders of the apostrophe in Birmingham, the Council did not relent. They said that, above all, there was the cost of reintroducing the apostrophe and that if the Council gave one road an apostrophe then 'countless others would want one'.

There is an Apostrophe Protection Society (founded in 2001) whose headquarters are in Lincolnshire and it is chaired by the founder, John Richards. His fame has spread as far as the United States and *The Washington Post* recently wrote an article about him. There are, of course, many people who say that we must move with the times and that often the apostrophe is not necesssary.   However, it is important that it does not alter the sense of a name which, in many cases, may be ancient and historic.

Another problem which can occur is whether a road is spelled with two words or one. Beech Croft (or Beechcroft) Road in Summertown is one of these. In order to hedge their bets the City Council has a pair of signs at each end of the road, one of which spells it with two words and the other not.   In the City Council's own Highways list for Spring, 1984, it is with two words as it is in the A-Z map of Oxford. In the 1966 *Kelly's Directory*, for instance. it has two words. However, Ruth Fasnacht, the historian of Summertown, writing in 1977, says: 'In 1894 the Council passed the plans for Beechcroft and Thorncliffe Roads'. She never spells it in two words. In the 1992 Post Code book , for instance, it is in two words. On the City Council's Register of Electors it is in two words.

Another example is Dovehouse (Dove House) Close in Upper Wolvercote. It was named after a local field name which was spelled as one word, in 1961. (See Gelling p 34).   In the 1970, 1984 and present City Council Highways lists it has a hyphen.   However, on the City

Council's Voters List it is one word. A resident of number 2, for instance, spells it in two words whereas one at number 9 spells it as one, and says that it does not really matter. Perhaps, nowadays, that should be the right approach.

Sylvia Worswick left) and Una Rees (who has lived in the road for 54 years) stand by Beechcroft Road.

The Beech Croft Road sign on the opposite side of the street.

The Perils of Pronounciation

The Cherwell

There always has been considerable confusion about how the Cherwell river is pronounced. It is an ancient name which was recorded as Ceawwellan in 864; then Cerwelle in 904. There were then variant spellings up to 1496 such as Charewell and Charewill. The 17th century Oxford antiquary, Anthony à Wood spells it both as Cherwell and Charwell and writes: 'The streame is clere and well stored with fish whereby the market is sometimes partly supplied'. In 1797 it was written as Charwell. In Leland's Itininerary, published in 1744, is written: 'The Cherwell river riseth out of a well or a little pool at Cherwelton village (County Northampton) about 7 miles above Banbury by NNE and boyleth so fast out from the head that straight it maketh a streamlett'. Today, the village is now spelled with an 'a' as Charwelton. The problem about how to pronounce the letters 'cher' as in Town Clerk is a national one. The Town Clerk of Oxford pointed out that the surname 'Clark' originated from that occupation; it came from the old word Clerk which meant a member of a religious order or clergyman; in other words someone who could write, who was a secretary or a recorder. One of the difficulties is that one never can prove how something was pronounced in the days before tape recorders. As few people could write there were always variable spellings. When more people began to read the word written down they realised that the pronunciation might be different from how the word had once sounded.

It is not surprising that in Oxford one can hear two pronunciations. The river, as it runs through Oxford, is usually pronouned as in 'char'. Undergraduates used to refer to it as 'the Char'. However, it is less likely to be pronounced that way north of Oxford and Cherwell District Council is usually pronounced as in 'Cher'. Two roads in Oxford derive their name from the river, namely Cherwell Street, St Clement's and Cherwell Drive, Marston. The Cherwell School in Summertown was definitely given the name as pronounced Charwell but nowadays one can hear it pronounced both ways and the 'The' tends to be forgotten too.

Magdalen

The college is pronounced as 'Maudlin' and so, usually, is the bridge. In the 17th century the bridge was often referred to as Cere Willa Briega. Anthony Wood spelled it both Maudlin and Magdalen (1661-6). For instance, he writes: 'Without the East Gate of Oxon is situated East Bridge, commonly called Maudlin Bridge because of the college so called adjoining'.

Magdalen Road in East Oxford is usually pronounced as it is spelled. Magdalen Street and Magdalen Street East which lead into St Giles are pronounced both ways. However, the Church which lies between the roads, is dedicated to St Mary Magdalene and is affectionately known 'Mary Mag'.

Punting on the Cherwell under the rainbow bridge in the 1990s.

In more recent times when Blackbird Leys was developed there was discussion as to whether it should be pronounced Lees or Lays. The former prevailed.

It is important when selecting a new name to make sure that there is no doubt how it is pronounced in order to avoid confusion.

Demesne Furze

Despite strong opposition from Councillor Spokes, who had at one time chaired the Highways and Traffic Committee and its Street Names Sub-Committee, the City Council, in December, 1991, insisted on saddling a road in the new development off Roosevelt Drive, Headington with the name Demesne Furze. She believed that this name would inevitably cause problems with its pronunciaton.

The then Chairman of the Highways Committee, on the other hand, thought that the name would 'quickly add a couple of thousands to the prices [of the houses] and everyone will want a name that's unpronounceable'. He thought that it would soon become a 'prestigious address'.

The Oxford English Dictionary says that the word demesne is from the Anglo-French which has become the modern English word 'domain'. To cause even more confusion one set of City Council papers (see minute of the Highways and Traffic Committee of 3rd October, 1991) spelled it with a second 's', Desmesne. Councillor Spokes opposed the suggested name in Council, saying that she was sure that the residents would pronounce the road how it was written and not 'domain' or 'demain'.

Magdalen College from the Botanic Garden in the 1930's. Valentine's postcard.

Although the road name is supposed to remember the land which was there at the time of the Enclosure Act and the name has been given to the main road running through this development it might have been more sensible to call the road after the distinguished Dr Acland (see separate section) who did more to improve the health of Oxford than many others before or since. He just has a small close named after him.

In a recent survey of residents one said that although when he bought the house the solicitors told him that it should be pronounced 'domain' nearly all the residents now pronounced it as it was written. Others who were interviewed confirmed this.

One of the rules for people who name racehorses is that their names should be pronounceable by the bookies. Perhaps Oxford City Council should have a rule that street names should be pronounceable by the residents.

The Demesne road sign in December, 2008.

Commemorating Current Celebrities

From time to time there are calls for roads to be named after living celebrities such as sporting heroes or people who have made a name for themselves locally or nationally. In 2008 (See *The Times* of 22nd December) coverage was given to a report by a James Hulme in which he said that we should do more to celeberate contemporary British icons. He thought that it would be 'great for local democracy and local pride'.

Oxford City Council, on the other hand, has always been wary of this idea and it has been a tradition, and now a rule, that roads should not be named after people who are still alive unless there are very good reasons for exception to this rule. The City Council's Highways and Traffic Committee confirmed this rule in January, 1993, stating that their existing policy is that the names of living people should not be used. It was at this time, recognising that there were many more roads named after men than women, that they added the rule that women's names, including first names, should be used wherever possible.

The policy of not naming steets after living people is probably wise. In Headington, for instance, at one time the name of the man who owned Oxford United football club could easily have been given to a new road. Perhaps they are now glad that they did not name a road after Robert Maxwell. In June, 1986, a Councillor had suggested that streets should be named after Oxford United players but the Committee reiterated its policy of not naming streets after living persons. There was a very good and popular Oxford United football player who might have had his name given to a road but, years afterwards, he made a racist remark on television and became less revered. A footballer has been remembered in Hodges Court (named in 1993) after the scorer of the first goal when Oxford City Football Club won the Amateur Cup; they were safe there because this was in 1906. The Court is on the site of the club in White House Road. Even some sportspeople have had to give their medals back if found guilty of some misdemeanour.

There have, of course, been exceptions to the rule. When new housing was built in Marston near to Milham Ford School, off Harberton Mead, there were three roads which needed names. The school was asked by the Councillor who chaired the Street Names Sub-Committee to put forward ideas and it chose Moody and Prichard. Moody was the founder of the school. The school particularly wanted to name the third road after Alderman Mrs Prichard, a Governor of the school, because of her long and outstanding work in the interests of the school. This was on the condition that she gave her approval.

Although the City did not usually agree to name a road after someone still living they agreed to make an exception in this case because Mrs Prichard was a distinguished Oxford figure. She was for many years a University member of the City Council and had been given the special honour of the Freedom of the City. Mrs Prichard then gave her consent. Some people have, in fact, refused to have a road named after them. One of these was Lord

William Kimber playing the concertina for the Morris dancers.

William Kimber 'christening' the Crescent with a tankard of beer at a ceremony in June 1958 when he was 83. Although this broke the Committee's rule, it meant that he could be there for the occasion and he played his concertina at the event. He died three years later on the anniversary of the day of Cecil Sharp's 1889 visit. At his funeral his coffin was borne by six Morris dancers in full regalia.

Macclesfield, Chairman of the County Council at the time, who, in February, 1959, refused to have a road named after him on the new Blackbird Leys estate.

It was on Boxing Day, 1889, that the musician Cecil Sharp (See Cecil Sharp Place), the founding father of the revival of English folk songs and traditional dances, heard William Kimber playing his concertina for the Morris men in Headington Quarry. Afterwards Sharp arranged for William to replay the tunes so that he could write them down. William was invited to London and taught the dances to Mary Neal (1860-1944), the collector of folk dances, and after that there was great enthusiasm for them. Cecil Sharp, in a tribute to Kimber, said that 'he laid the foundations for the revival of Morris dancing'. Kimber trained many Morris men including the Oxford Police in 1923. The Morris dancers continue to delight people today.

John Garne Way off Marston Road was named after the Chief Education Officer of the County Council when he was still alive but the Council has no jurisdiction over the names of roads on private property as this road is. There were once Government Buildings on this site but it now leads to halls of residence of Brookes University.

In 1986 the Highways and Traffic Committee considered that an exception could be made in the case of Don Stuart Place which is in a development off Glanville Road, Cowley. He was one of the founder members of the Cherwell Family Housing Association.

The Highways and Traffic Committee considered whether to make an exception in the case of Nelson Mandela and his wife but in the end did not agree. Since then though Nelson Mandela has been given the Honorary Freedom of the City.

There have been other names such as Gibbs Close (after Councillor Olive Gibbs) which was a private development (See Index) and Williamson Way, Rose Hill, which was out of the City when it was named after the Chairman of the City's Housing Committee at the time, Tony Williamson.

Townsend Square was named after Mary Georgina, Lady Townsend who chaired the Housing Committee. When it was named in 1953 the rule which forbade roads to be named after living people was not rigorously enforced and the City Council wanted to show appreciation of her service. She was Leader of the Council for some years and Mayor in 1935 and

Lady Townsend when Mayor in 1958 in her Parlour.

Roger Bannister finishing the mile in under four minutes on 6th May, 1954. Courtesy Newsquest, *Oxford Mail* and *Times*.

again in 1936 and and 1958 on the death of the incumbents. She was given the Freedom of the City, an honour only bestowed upon a few.

Sir Roger Bannister, CBE, DM (Oxon). FRCP, MRCS, was born in March, 1929. He was Master of Pembroke College, Oxford 1985-1993. A Neurologist and Consultant Physician, he is more usually known as being an outstanding athlete and the first man to run a mile in under four minutes. This was on the Iffley Road running track on 6th May, 1954 when his time was 3 minutes 59.4 seconds.

Sir Roger has been awarded the Freedom of the City of Oxford and holds Honorary Doctorates from a dozen universities at home and abroad. He is involved in many voluntary organisations mainly in the field of sport and medicine.

Bannister Close, near the University Running Ground. Sir Roger Bannister by his street name on 21 January, 2009.

The name Rimmer Close was given to a group of houses off Boult's Lane, Marston by Marston Parish Council and is therefore an exception to Oxford City Council's rule. Born in 1925, Paul was the popular Vicar of Marston from 1959 to 1999. He is an Oxford MA (Jesus College).

The Reverend Paul Rimmer and his wife Joan beside the Rimmer Close street name sign in the Spring of 2009.

Honouring Queens

Just as during the reign of Queen Victoria, many roads in towns all over England were called Queen Street, Queen Victoria Street or Victoria Street, so at the time of the Silver Jubilee of Queen Elizabeth II in 1977 there was a demand to change streets to commemorate her.

The Northway and Marston Residents' Association asked if Redland Road could be renamed Jubilee Road. They were informed by the City Council's Highways Committee that as there was already a Jubilee Terrace in the City (off Marlborough Road in South Oxford), probably named for Queen Victoria's Jubilee, they could not agree to the request. However, the Committee said that they would look sympathetically upon another choice of name. The residents came back with the idea that Redland Road should be called Queen Elizabeth Road. However, the Committee thought that Redland Road was too short a road, containing no front accesses except either garages or service roads, and that the name Elizabeth Place would be more appropriate. This idea was not taken up and Redland Road still exists.

Also, in June, 1977 the Lord Mayor of the time, Councillor Mrs Dora Carr and certain Council officers asked if Queen Street could be renamed Queen Elizabeth Street, also in honour of the Jubilee. The Committee's response was that as Queen Street could be considered appropriate for any Queen it could not agree to renaming it.

Queen Street from Carfax in about 1913.

In December, 1966 a certain Arnold Prosser had written to the *Oxford Times* suggesting that Queen Street should revert to its ancient and more dignified name of Great Bailey. He assumed that Queen Street had got its name 'in some sort of adulation of Queen Victoria' and said that 'today it has little or no significance and is just a name'. (See Street Names in The Early Days).

Today Queen Street can continue to commemorate Queen Charlotte (see Street Names in Early Days), Queen Victoria and Queen Elizabeth II – or even Queen Elizabeth I who visited Oxford on two occasions during her reign.

Osney

Osney Lane is named after Osney (or Oseney) Abbey. It was said to be the finest in England and the envy of all the other monastries at home and abroad. The priory was founded in 1129 by Editha, the wife of the second Robert D'Oyley, for the Augustinian Canons. The name means ousen-eye, an island in the Ouse, a possible early name for the river Thames. It had various spellings including Osanig as early as 1003 and Oseneai in 1130 and 1230.

When the Cathedral Chapter was transferred to Christ Church Henry VIII sold most of Osney Abbey but much of the stone was carted off for the building of Christ Church. Four of its five bells are now in Tom Tower. If the abbey had not been vandalised it could have been a magnificent college of the University at the waterside, changing the face of Oxford.

Osney Lane once ran to the Abbey sited under what is now the cemetery and the railway line. It was sometimes known as Oxmead Walk. Until the 1870s a clear stream ran down the south side of the lane. In the 19thC it was also sometimes known as Kite Lane after the pub of that name.

This drawing by H.W. Brewer (printed in *The Builder* in 1891) is his imaginative reconstruction of what these superb buildings might have looked like. (See Squires). In the distance is the castle, which, unlike the Abbey, still survives. Rewley Abbey, also destroyed, can be seen, with its spire, top left. Osney Mill is in the right foreground.

Osney Town was laid out by the Town Clerk of Oxford, G.P. Hester, in 41 lots in 1851. It was built on a grid plan and some of the houses were occupied by October, 1852. By the mid 1850s most parts had been developed.

Osney Abbey in ruins in 1640 from a drawing by Heskell (Squires p. 109). The ruins were finally destroyed by Charles I in 1644 and used for fortifications in the Civil War.

North Parade and South Parade

Some people are puzzled by the fact that South Parade is north of North Parade. Ruth Fasnacht in *Summertown since 1820* says that we do not know which got its name first. She makes the point, however, that when either was named there would have been no need to consider the other. 'One was in Oxford and the other was in a village in the County.' When Summertown became part of Oxford they kept their names.

The Traders' sign in North Parade in 1977.

Richard Carr developed North Parade in the 1860s whereas South Parade was there earlier but then known as Double Ditch. This was because it was on the line of a boundary between Whorestone Farm and another farm to the south. There was an uncut ridge with ditches on either side. On a map of 1859 it was given three names: South Road, Double Ditch and South Parade. It did not become South Parade officially until as late as 1930.

From the 18th century onwards, Parade became a popular name for a row of shops or a place where people walk about in public. There are eleven roads named The Parade in London alone. Seaside resorts often have a Marine Parade and there is a Grand Parade in Bath and a King's Parade in Cambridge.

Strangely, the traders in North Parade tacked the word 'Avenue' onto Parade, an action which was criticised by an Oxford don who was also the Headmistress of Wychwood School. She lived in the house on the corner of the street. She said that North Parade Avenue only caused ridicule. Such tautology was not for academics. The first English use of 'avenue' was usually a name for a tree-lined drive to a country house. Now, it does not need trees but is usually a broad street and not one suitable for one of the narrowest streets in Oxford.

There is an entertaining and popular myth, first thought up by a German Professor in the 1930s, that North and South Parade had something to do with the Civil War. He suggested that North Parade was the north parading ground for the Royalist troops based in Oxford and that South Parade was the southern parade ground for the Commonwealth troops. But, as Fasnacht explains, 'the idea that the double ditches were Civil War earthworks is firmly ruled out by the archaeologists'. She did admit, though, that this takes the romance out of South Parade'. The Royalist troops in fact paraded in what were then called the New Parks.

Jack Straw's Lane

Over the years there have been various suggestions for the origin of this street name in Headington which has been in existence officially since 1933.

There was once an isolated farmhouse there which was the only habitation in the area and was known as Jack Straw's Castle. It seems to have been a name for a castle or house situated in a remote spot. The lane could also have been called after a man of that name. Jack Straw was at one time as common a name as John Smith. By the 16thC Jack Straw came to signify a man of straw or person of little worth.

Probably the most famous Jack Straw was a leader, with rebel Wat Tyler, in the Peasants' Revolt of 1381. He also comes into one of Chaucer's *Canterbury Tales*. It is just possible that this Jack Straw once stayed at the farmhouse in this lane here in Headington. In that same year of 1381 four priests' orders in Oxford protested about inaccurate reports that they had been responsible for the revolt.

Miss Mary Price, (see index) one time Headmistress of Milham Ford School, who lived with her brother at 'Hillside' in the lane for 52 years, said (in 1971) that when they first went there they tried to find out the reason for the name with no success. The road was then rough and full of potholes and was not officially adopted until 1954.

Jack Straw's Lanes are found in many parts of England once associated with highwaymen. Readers may, therefore prefer the following story:

Jack Straw was a very wealthy and highly respected citizen who farmed on Headington Hill in the days when highwaymen took advantage of the Oxfordshire countryside to hold up travellers and steal from them. It is assumed that this farmhouse was the one which was later called 'Hillside'. Merchants journeying between London and the western ports were easy prey and were frequently attacked and robbed in this area. Many highwaymen were caught but the leader always escaped.

One day, a Mr Jack Straw, who farmed land on Headington Hill, died. In the cellars beneath the farm kitchen were found rolls of silk, gold and silver, spices and other valuable goods which had been stolen from travellers and merchants.

Acland Close

Sir Henry Wentworth Acland (1815-1900)

Acland was Physician to the Radcliffe Infirmary, holding that appointment for 37 years, and also Regius Professsor of Medicine at the University. 'A man of wide culture and deep unobtrusive piety, restless, impetuous and hyperactive, he made a more lasting impact on Oxford than many of his contemporaries' (Martin Murphy).

He was born at Broadclyst, near Exeter, second son of Sir Thomas Acland, Baronet. He went to Harrow School and then to Christ Church, Oxford and was later made a Fellow of All Souls. He was appointed Lee's Professor of Anatomy in 1840.

Science in those days was not looked upon as a serious subject. It was Acland, with his lifelong friend John Ruskin, who over a ten-year period, planned and built the University Museum. Here the sciences could be taught and developed. He thought that there should be a good grounding in the sciences, especially for medical students. When it was being built he made sure that there were plenty of facilities for the workmen.

Acland with his monkey.

Acland also had a large medical practice and it was said of him that no one of any respectability thought of dying without seeing Dr. Acland.   He did a great service to Oxford when, in the cholera epidemic of 1854, it was he who recommended updating the City's sewage and water systems. He gave public lectures in Oxford Town Hall. Acland was instrumental in causing the medical profession and Queen Victoria to cease to oppose the training of women doctors.

After his wife died in 1878 he established the Acland Home (from 1964 the Acland Hospital) in her memory when it transferred from Wellington Square to 25 Banbury Road. He gave £3,000 to mark his retirement. The new building there was designed by Sir Thomas Jackson and opened by the future King Edward VII, then Prince of Wales, in 1897. A new wing and the frontage, designed by R. Fielding Dodd, was built in 1937. The hospital moved to Headington, is owned and run by Nuffield Health and is called the Manor Hospital. The buildings in Banbury Road are now owned by Keble College; planning permission was given to the college in 2010 to redevelop the site incorporating part of the original Jackson buildings.

Acland lived in a house in Broad Street which was demolished for the new Bodleian. He died in the autumn of 1900 and was buried in Holywell Cemetery beside his wife. The funeral route there from Broad Street was lined with those who wished to revere his memory. There is no other memorial to Acland, who did so much for science and the health of Oxford, other than a statue in the Museum and a small close near the Churchill Hospital in Headington.

A view of Broad Street in the latter part of the 19th century. Dr Acland's house is shown behind the horse-drawn waggon, Wadham College is on the right in Parks Road with the University Museum, finished in 1860, in the distance.

Crotch Crescent

William Crotch, (1775-1847) Musical Prodigy

Crotch, who was a composer and described as 'a real musical genius', could play 'God Save the King' at two and a half years old. He played on an organ built by his father. For several years 'little Crotch' or 'Master Crotch', as he was known, exhibited his skills in public, performing in London when he was only four. It was in this same year (1779) that, 'in order to support the attempt to revive and keep up the languishing Music Room in Oxford that Master Crotch, the Musical Prodigy, was engaged to play a concerto on the organ at the regular weekly concerts held there'. (Cox, *Recollections of Oxford*). The Music Room, which was erected in 1742, 'had had a fluctuating state of existence ever since its creation'. (Ibid).

Crotch was born in Norwich, studied in Cambridge in 1786 and then at Oxford in 1788. He liked Oxford and was organist at Christ Church from 1790 to 1807 and St John's in 1787. He became Professor of Music at Oxford in 1797, a post he held until 1807.

The Oxford Music Room the 18thC. Drawing by de la Motte.

The Oxford Music Room, now called the Holywell Music Room, in September, 2009.

He did not remain in Oxford but became first principal at the Royal Acadamy of Music between 1822 and 1832. He composed two oratorios of note and published anthems and lectures on music.

Named in 1937, Crotch Crescent is in Marston and is in the Musicians' group of roads. Although, from time to time, people question whether this name might be changed, because of its connotations, it is good that Oxford is able to commemorate this childhood prodigy who brought such pleasure to lovers of music.

Crotch, as director of the band,
On harpsichord with rapid hand
* Sweeps the full chord: — this youth*
Of late thro' Britain's realms was styl'd
The Wonderous boy — Apollo's child —
* And such he was in truth.*

For when five summers he had told
And scarce his hands a bow could hold
* He Handel's pieces knew;*
The time and harmony would note
Not like a parrot, all by rote,
* But as a master true.*

Attributed to John Skinner (1772-1839).

E. A. Greening Lamborn
1877 - 1950

Edmund Arnold Greening Lamborn, Hon. M.A., gave much to Oxford, not only as a renowned teacher but as a writer about the City on such subjects as historic buildings, archaeology, genealogy and heraldry. He was also a great character.

He was the son of Arnold Lamborn and Susannah Greening and spent his childhood at their home 101 (once 43) Cowley Road. His father, who was an insurance agent, also had his business there. It is not recorded where he had his early schooling but apparently he became a pupil teacher at the age of 15. In 1897 to 1899, starting at the age of 20, he attended Culham College which was then a Diocesan Training College for schoolmasters. It was founded by Samuel Wilberforce, Bishop of Oxford, in 1852. Lamborn's father (who died in 1897) had also been a student there. His first teaching post seems to have been at St Mary Magdalen School near Gloucester Green. He was not a graduate and in his *Who's Who* entry of 1935 Lamborn said that he was educated by 'books, buildings and the companionship of all wild creatures'. However, in 1921 the University of Oxford awarded him an Honorary M.A.

For 36 years he was the Headmaster of East Oxford School in Collins Street where he was affectionately known as 'Ikey'. Because Lamborn was a great hiker the boys called him 'Hikey' but most of them dropped their h's. He became Head in 1908 when he was only 30, and retired in 1944. Because of him the school had an excellent reputation and was given good inspectors' reports, one calling the school 'outstanding'. Part of one of these reports of May, 1927 stated that the school 'had a high standard of effort demanded by thought-compelling teaching' and commented on 'the general keenness, vigour and freedom of the boys, not exclusive of the slower-witted ones'. All the staff were 'inspired, exemplified by the Headmaster with (his) marked intellectual power.....'. H.A.L. Fisher, President of the British Academy, described Lamborn as the 'greatest elementary teacher in the U.K.'

Under 'Recreations' in another *Who's Who* entry he wrote: heraldry, topography, the preservation of old country cottages and the education of education officials'.

His teaching methods were certainly ahead of his time, sometimes described as 'revolutionary'. He believed that teaching was more than putting over facts in exams and winning prizes. He gave boys a chance to teach themselves and encouraged private study. He started a debating society and inspired the boys to enjoy poetry as much as he did himself. In fact, in his book *The English Parish Church* (1929), he said that 'the most precious inheritance of the English is their poetry and their parish'. He also took the boys on walks in the countryside. Despite the fact that he was a strong disciplinarian and could be sarcastic, sometimes calling the boys 'idle villains', he was respected and admired by his pupils.

Above: Pencil sketch of Lamborn by E.Patchey, 1939

Left: E.A. Greening Lamborn with his dog. Said to be the earliest known photograph of him.(Oxfordshire Photographic Archive).

Teachers from all over Europe and from India came to listen to him and, nearer home, the Deputy Head of Magdalen College School sat in on his lessons.

Lamborn wrote numerous books and pamphlets and was a regular contributor to *Notes and Queries*. His works included *The Story of Oxford Architecture in Stone* (1912), *Oxford, a short illustrated historical guide* (OUP 1930), *Armorial Glass in the Oxford Diocese 1250 - 1850* (1949), *Heraldry and the History of Parliament* and *The Parish Church: its architecture and antiquities* (The Clarendon Press 1929).

He did not drive but was often seen in Oxford on his old-fashioned high bicycle and he would ride in from his house at 34 Oxford Road, Littlemore.

He was short of stature and had a neat goatee beard. He wrote in a spidery hand, often in purple ink and sometimes in the margins of books.

After his retirement, he and his great friend Peter Spokes, another local historian, whom he had known since the 1930s, made many trips in Peter's car into Oxfordshire and Berkshire to look at country churches. Here they would note and record the buildings, interiors, stained glass and heraldry. Spokes would take the photographs. They called each other by their surnames, usual in those days. It might have seemed strange that two agnostics spent so much time in churches.

He was very particular about how his name was spelled and it is said that if people wrote to him with anything other than 'Lamborn' he would often send the letter back. It is therefore ironic and sad that the Bursar of Lincoln College, when recommending that a road in Rose Hill be named after him, spelled his name incorrectly. The road is named Lambourn.

It is good that a block of flats in Silkdale Close named Lamborn House is correctly spelled. This is because Mr R. Silk, the developer, was a great admirer of Lamborn. His son Donald was a pupil under Lamborn at East Oxford School. See Silkdale Close.

The Greening Lamborn Trust, which was set up by him in his will, has kindly given a generous grant towards the publication of this book. The Trust, set up in 1951, is a charity for the furtherance of the architecture, topography and heraldry of Oxford and its neighbourhood.

A blue plaque was erected on 34 Oxford Road, Littlemore in September 2010.

Lamborn on the steps of his caravan in August, 1950. (Oxfordshire Photographic Archive)

34 Oxford Road, Littlemore.

The blue plaque erected September 2010.

Tidmarsh Lane

This road, which runs from the junction of New Road and Park End Street into St Thomas's Street, was named after Richard Tidmarsh (1626-c 1708), a tanner by trade, who was recognised as the first pastor of the Oxford Baptists. However, in the Survey of 1772 (Salter) it is shown that early on the lane became corrupted to Titmouse. Squires also confirms this. At the same time it was also called Tidmarsh (Salter's *Council Acts* for 1752-1801). The Ordnance Survey map of 1876 gives it as Tidmarsh although three other maps between 1717 and 1850 give it as Titmouse. See also the Osney Cartulary Vol II map opposite p. 380. In the days when only a small percentage of the population could spell it was not unusual for roads to have different spellings. The name Tidmarsh itself was often spelled Titmouse. By the 20th Century the road had the official name of Titmouse.

However, in July, 1953, as a result of a plea from the Reverend W.W. Bottoms, Minister of New Road Baptist Church, it eventually reverted to its old name officially. Mr Bottoms wrote a letter to Oxford City Council explaining that in this lane, near the bridge over the river, had lived Richard Tidmarsh. He explained that it would be a good time to revive the name in connection with the celebration of the 300th anniversary of the Baptist Church in Oxford and a suitable time to honour the man, a former citizen of Oxford, who had been leader of that church in the City. He had been one of its first members from 1661 until 1691 when he left Oxford. The City Council agreed. 1653 was, in fact, an approximate date because there had been Baptist worshippers in Oxford from at least the 1640s. The lane was connected with the Baptists until the riots of 1717.

There is a memorial plaque on Pacey's bridge (Park End Street) recording the fact that baptisms took place in the river there. There were steps down to the river in those days. Anthony Wood wrote about the baptisms there in December 1659. *The Victoria County History,* volume V (City) 1979. p.417, states: 'The main meeting-house was at Tidmarsh's house in Titmouse (sic) Lane which continued to be used until at least 1715. Tidmarsh used to baptise people in the mill-stream nearby'. In 1672 his house was licensed as a meeting house for Anabaptists. Tidmarsh left for Tiverton in 1691 where he remained as Pastor until his death, the exact date of which is not known. It was probably in 1708 or early 1709.

An item in the *Oxford Mail* of 24th July, 1953 was headed 'Titmouse to become Tidmarsh'. This was not the first time that someone had asked for Titmouse Lane to revert to its proper name. Dr H. E. Salter, the distinguished local historian, had suggested the change as early as 1936 in a letter to Walter Stevens of *The Birmingham Post*, also, coincidentally written on 24 July.

Even some years later, the change back to Tidmarsh was opposed. An Oxford architect who had been writing a critical series of studies of Oxford buildings, street furniture, etc. in the 1960/70 issues of the *Oxford Mail* suggested that Titmouse Lane had been renamed

Tidmarsh 'by the Puritans presumably because of an aversion to rodents'. This indicated that his knowledge of natural history was not good. A titmouse is another name for a blue tit.

A woman writing from Cowley, though, was in support because she thought the name titmouse was 're-pulsive and an insult to the female body'. What problems names can cause.

Even more strange, perhaps was the objection made by Councillor Roger Dudman (See Dudman Way) in 1983 who caused confusion by asserting that the lane had been named after the wrong Richard Tidmarsh.

The memorial plaque on Pacey's Bridge.

He had thought that Tidmarsh could not have been both a Baptist and a tanner. He was put right by the author.

I am indebted to Dr Larry J. Kreitzer, Tutor of New Testament and Tutor for Graduate Studies at Regent's Park College for infor-mation about the Baptists in Oxford.

Spoke in his wheel

ACCOUNTANT Mr Roger Dudman has aban-doned his attempt to get Tidmarsh Lane re-named after getting his figures wrong.

A news item from the Oxford Mail.

Tidmarsh Lane in September, 2010.

Missing Names

Some may wonder why there are no roads named after some famous people who have had strong Oxford connections. They have not, however, been overlooked or forgotten. They could still be commemorated in the future when an opportunity arises.

There are several reasons why they have not yet had a road named after them. It could be that no new roads are being built in the area with which the famous name has a particular connection and those choosing the names prefer to remember people or places connected with a particular locality. When a new road was built which runs from the junction of Charlbury and Belbroughton roads in North Oxford and needed a name there was a chance for Tolkien to be remembered there because he had lived in the next road. Otherwise perhaps Betjeman might have been suitable because of his lines 'Belbroughton Road is bonny'. However, it was just called Charlbury Road as if it were an extension of the existing road. In other cases developers have in the past, or even now, preferred to select names themselves.

In one or two cases the name has sounded too like a name already chosen. In earlier days only the surname was thought necessary and first names were not included. There have recently been many roads named after scientists in the University Science Area or in some of the Science Parks on the outskirts of the City. However, although Heatley and Abraham quite rightly have roads named after them as they were members of Florey's team which gave pencillin to the world as a life-saving medicine, Florey himself is not commemorated. He does, however, have a Queen's college building in St Clement's named after him.

Below is a list of well-known people with local connections who have no Oxford street name at present.

BEERBOHM, Sir Max 1872-1956
Not only a great writer but a well-known caricaturist. The broadcaster, Alastair Cooke described him as 'the greatest parodist that ever lived'. His cartoons are much sought after today. His masterpiece, the fantasy *Zuleika Dobson* (published in 1911) was one of the most famous stories written about Oxford. It tells of a mass suicide on the final day of Eights Week when all the young men of the University hurled themselves into the Isis with cries of ' Zuleika'. At one time Osbert Lancaster's twelve paintings of scenes from this book were on permanent display in the Randolph Hotel.

A caricature of Beerbohm by himself.

BETJEMAN, Sir John 1906 - 1984
Poet Laureate (1972) who loved Oxford and wrote poems about it, including *Summoned by Bells* (1960). He was also a conservationist and admirer of Victorian buildings. His *An Oxford University Chest* was published in 1938.

BUCKLAND, William 1784-1856
Pioneer scientist who had a great influence on the teaching of science in the University. Scholar and Fellow of Corpus Christi college, Professor of Mineralogy (1813) and the first Reader in Geology (1819). He was a popular, though eccentric teacher; his lectures were said to have been a *tour de force*. One-time Canon of Christ Church, he moved to London when appointed Dean of Westminster in 1845. He is buried at Islip and a blue plaque is displayed on the gate-post of the house where he lived nearby.

William Buckland on an expedition
Courtesy of the Fellows and President
of Corpus Christi College.

BURNE -JONES, Sir Edward Coley (1833 -1898)
Member of the Pre-Raphaelite Brotherhood. Examples of his work can be found in the University Museum and the Oxford Union. His stained glass can be seen in several colleges but his windows in Harris Manchester chapel are considered his most outstanding. When an undergraduate at Exeter college he became a friend of William Morris. He designed the Morris tapestry of the *Adoration of the Maji* in Exeter college.

FLOREY, Howard Walter, Baron Florey of Adelaide 18 98 -1968
Nobel Prize winner. Rhodes Scholar, born in Australia. Wayneflete Professor of Physiology. It was in the Sir William Dunn School of Pathology in 1939/40 that he and his colleagues developed and perfected penicillin as a medicine which, in its saving of millions of lives became one of the most important discoveries in the whole history of medicine. (See Heatley Road). He was Provost of Queen's college.

RUSKIN, John 1819-1900
Artist and writer and founder of the Ruskin School of Drawing and Fine Art at Oxford. Ruskin college is named after him. Slade Professor of Fine Arts (1790-1868) and an Honorary Fellow of Corpus Christi college. He was a popular lecturer and also a benefactor of the University. He and his friend Sir Henry Acland (See Acland Close) were the prime movers in the creation of the University museum.

TOLKIEN, John Ronald Reul 1892-1973
Born in South Africa but educated in England. Professor of Ango-Saxon at Oxford and Merton Professor of the English Language. His books *The Hobbit* (1936) illustrated by himself, and *The Lord of the Rings* (1954-5) in three volumes, have become famous throughout the world and have been made into popular films. He has a blue plaque on the house where he lived in Northmoor Road.

J.R.R. Tolkein with his family taken in 1945. (Courtesy of Miss Priscilla Tolkein)

WOOD, Anthony 1632-1695
Otherwise known as Anthony à Wood, he was born in Merton Street (a blue plaque is on his house) and lived all his life in Oxford. Buried in Merton chapel. Oxford's most important diarist who devoted his life to writing about the events in both the City and University (see Bibliography). He was cantankerous and opinionated and tended to quarrel with everyone but his writings are indispensable to Oxford local historians.

Oxford Street Index

A

Abberbury Avenue. After Sir Richard Abberbury, Lord of Iffley Manor from 1385, Chamberlain to Queen Anne of Bohemia, wife of Richard II. He founded Donnington Hospital, Berks, and endowed it with land in Iffley. The Donnington Trust still owns land locally. Street named in 1934.

Abberbury Road. Street named in 1934. See **Abberbury Avenue**

Abbey Place. After Osney Abbey, sited a quarter of a mile to the west, built by Robert d'Oilly in 1129 for Augustine Canons. Street named in 1870

Abbey Road After Rewley Abbey, built 1281, a little to the south of Oseney Abbey. Begun by John Dover, an Oxford builder, named in 1878. Some houses by C C Rolfe in 1886-87.

Abbots Wood (West & East) Slade Park development. From an old field name. Road named in Jan 1977

Abingdon Road After main Saxon track, southwards from Oxford. The name comes from 'Abba's dun' (hill). In 1870's 'an ancient road to Faringdun'. Street named in c1862-5. The road as far as Lake Street was known as The Causey in the 17th century. It is suggested (by John Blair) that St Abba, a 7th century saint, gave her name to Abingdon.

Ablett Close Off East Avenue. After Kellett Ablett, the architect in the City Engineers' Department who designed the Morrell Avenue Estate in the late 1920s. Named in 1994.

Acacia Avenue In the Blackbird Leys tree group, named in March 1997.

Acer Walk Houses in this pedestrian way, a private road, had postal addresses in North Parade Avenue; residents asked for a separate address to reduce postal confusion. Some house names were also changed. Confirmed on 30th September 2003.

Acland Close After Dr Sir Henry Wentworth Acland (1913-1900) Lee's Lecturer in Anatomy in 1845, Physician to the Radcliffe Infirmary in 1847, Aldrichian Professor of Clinical Medicine in 1857, Regius Professor of Medicine - a post he held for 37 years – President of the General Medical Council and Honorary Physician to HRH The Prince of Wales, later Edward VII. He persuaded the GMC and Queen Victoria to accept women as doctors. He probably did more to improve the health of the people of Oxford than anyone before or since. He was largely responsible for establishing the Museum of Oxford with his friend John Ruskin and endowed the Acland Home, named for his late wife Sarah who had died in 1878. It became the Acland Hospital in 1969, and was later moved to Headington where it is now known as the Manor Hospital. When the Aclands lived in Broad Street, in a house later pulled down for the New Bodleian to be built, he and his wife used to invite boy sweeps into their home – the news spread as far as Abingdon and boys flocked to the Aclands' house. Road named in 1991. (See article on Acland)

Acre Close   Slade Hospital site. Named in 1999.

Addison Crescent   After essayist and poet Joseph Addison (1672-1719) fellow of Magdalen (1697-1711) and Secretary of State. Local streets have poets' names. Street named in 1922.

Addison Drive   Street named in 1930s by Wates, the developers of the estate, after Joseph Addison, the essayist. See **Addison Crescent**

Addisons Walk   After Joseph Addison. See Addison Crescent.

Adelaide Street   Possibly after Queen Adelaide, Queen Consort of William IV, the last king of the House of Hanover. She visited Oxford in October 1835. Street named in the 1830s.

Admiral Close   Blackbird Leys. There are no houses on this close, named in 1997.

Alan Bullock Close   After Sir Alan Bullock, the first Master of St Catherine's College and Vice Chancellor of the University 1969-73. He was a writer of some note; his biography of Adolf Hitler was translated into 19 languages.

Albert Street   Jericho. Street named in c1868. See **Victor Street.** Probably named after the Price Consort. There was an Albert Street in St Ebbe's, the north part of which was renamed **Albion Place** and the south part **Butterwyke Place** in October 1980.

Albion Place   After local pub, The Albion. Means 'Britain' . Street named in c1874 with Albion Cottages. Once part of Albert Street (see above).

Aldebarton Drive   Originally proposed by the Highways and Traffic Committee as Aldebarton or Alderbarton. older forms of the name Barton, meaning corn enclosure. Named in 1985.

Alden Crescent   After Leonard Henry Alden, Mayor of Oxford in 1936, of the well known Oxford family of printers and butchers since 17th century. Street named in 1945. See *Snobbery and Street Names*

Aldrich Road,   Cutteslowe. After architect Henry Aldrich (1647-1710), Dean of Christ Church. Although he was called an amateur architect his works included All Saints Church (now Lincoln College Library). The Queens College Library and Peckwater Quad at Christ Church – all well designed buildings that have stood the test of time – are also attributed to him. Street named in 1934. See Wolsey Road for explanations relating to the Cutteslowe Walls.

The last section of the Cutteslowe Walls about to be demolished. Courtesy of Malcolm Graham.

Alec Issigonis Way   Oxford Business Park. After Alexander (Alec) Issigonis CBE FRS (Nov 1906-Oct 1988), designer of cars but chiefly known as the man who made the Mini, launched by the British Motor Corporation as the Morris Mini Minor and Austin Mini, eventually to become known simply as the Mini. Road named in 1995.

Alesworth Grove   After local medieval field name meaning 'Ale's enclosure'. Spelt Allesworth in 1548, Alesworth Furlong Stache in 1605 and Alesworth in c1840. Street officially named in 1949.

Alexandra Road   Street named in 1903. Other roads on this Kingerlee development were named after Kingerlee children, but in 1901, when submitting plans to build the road, Kingerlee had wished it to be called Queen Alexandra Road, after the Consort to Edward VII, but the City, thinking that the road was not a good enough tribute, made him omit the title. In February 1959 the City Council wanted to change the road name so as not to be confused with the one in Botley but residents would not agree, suggesting Alexandra Street, Queen Street or Princess Street.

Alfred Street   Possibly after Prince Alfred (1844-1900), fourth child of Queen Victoria. The nearby University College at one time claimed to be founded by King Alfred, but he is now merely included in college prayers, for his encouragement of learning. Street named in c1899. (Encyclopaedia of

Oxford). Known previously as Bear Lane in 1722, after the Bear Inn, **Vinehall Lane** in 1576 and **Venella Sancti Edwardi** in c1200-10.

Alhambra Lane
Off Circus Street, named in 1985. Newsomes' Alhambra Circus was held in the area in the mid 19th century and was so popular that it was commemorated in the street named **Circus Street.**

Alice Smith Square
After Alice Smith, who founded a charity to help poor children with their apprenticeships. In 1678 she left her land in Littlemore and Iffley to the poor of both parishes.

Allam Street
After Andrew Allam, tutor at St Edmund Hall in 17th Century. Street named in c1881.

Allin Close
Blackbird Leys. After Richard Allin who farmed local Lincoln Farm in 1727. His family still owned the farm in 1830. Street officially named in 1959. (Marriott)

All Saints Road
After local church of All Saints, built in 1910. South side laid out by 1898 and the remainder in 1900s. Street named c1930.

Alma Lane
Houses here had Alma Place addresses and residents had complained of postal confusion. They suggested the name change, for properties between number 11 Alma Place and St Clements Street, confirmed in March 2006.

Alma Place
After Crimean War victory over Russia at Alma in 1854. Street named in 1867. The land for the development here was the first purchase by the Liberal Party's National Freehold Land Society in 1852 – the Conservative Party had formed a Land Society in 1852.

Ambassador Avenue
Oxford Business Park. After a British Leyland car of the 1970s. Named in 1994.

Ambleside Drive
After Ambleside in the Lake District; the first of five adjacent streets named in alphabetical order after lakes. Road named in June 1931 and extended in 1949.

Amory Close
After the Amory family, landowners in the area and descendants of Amoury of Cowley in the late 13th century. The family gave land to St Bartholomew's leper hospital off Cowley Road as well as grants to local religious houses in the reign of Edward I. Street officially named in 1954.

Andromeda Close
In the wildflower series of road names in Blackbird Leys. Street named in 1961.

Anemone Close
In the plant and shrub series of road names in Blackbird Leys. Named in 1997.

Angelica Close
In the plant and shrub series of road names in Blackbird Leys. Named in 1961.

Anne Greenwood Close
A volunteer at the nearby former Iffley House, an Old People's home, who was awarded the Tunstall Award. She died in 1994 – the road was named in the same year, in tribute to "a very special lady" who raised thousands of pounds for the welfare of the residents of the home by holding events of all kinds. She carried on organising these even from her hospital bed.

Andromeda

Annesley Road   After the Rt. Hon. Arthur Annesley, Viscount Valentia, MP for Oxford from 1895 to 1917, High Steward of the City of Oxford. Because of his Irish peerage he was able to sit in the House of Commons, and was made a peer of the United Kingdom in 1917. He was a soldier by profession and was appointed temporary Colonel of Land Forces in January 1900. He served in the Boer War despite having reached his 60th year. He was Commanding Officer of the Queen's Own Oxfordshire Hussars from 1894-1904. His portrait hangs in the Town Hall. He is said to have been the handsomest man in the Commons and to have passed for 40 years old. Awarded the Freedom of the City of Oxford, to the great acclaim of the people of the city. Three nearby streets have similar origins. The name comes from the town of Annesley, which the family owned from about the time of the Norman Conquest. See Valentia Road. Street named in 1935.

Annora Close   After Annora de Braose, a high born individual who, in the 13th century, is said to have chosen a life of contemplation as an anchorite or hermit, living as a recluse in a small cell attached to the church. Walled up in 1232 and unable to leave, with only a window looking into the church and one facing outwards, she may have lived like this for nine years until her death. Henry III sent her firewood and a cloak to keep her warm. Name suggested by Catalyst Housing Group and agreed in 2007.

Apple Tree Close   In the tree series of road names in Blackbird Leys. Named in 1997.

Apsley Road   Probably after a large house called Apsley Paddock (or Paddox) which once stood on the site, renamed Field House by St Edward's School in June 1931 after their purchase from the Clapperton family. The house was possibly named after Sir Allen Apsley, graduate of Trinity College, Royalist supporter, Colonel and Master of the King's Hawks in the Civil War. Apsley Paddox nearby is a private road. Apsley Road named in January 1932.

Argyle Street   After the Scottish town. Four local streets have county town origins. Street named in 1895-6.

Aristotle Lane   After Aristotle's Well, formerly Brumman's Well, now covered over in a shop cellar. In 1661 it was 'frequented in the summer season by our peripatetics' – these were Oxford philosophy students of Aristotle who had popularised the well, and who may have been so called because they would walk around while lecturing. Street named in 1953.

Arlington Drive   Possibly after Henry Bennet, first Earl of Arlington (d. 1685) who entered the service of George, Lord Digby, secretary of state to Charles I, in 1643; the name was chosen by the developer, A C Carter Ltd.

Armstrong Road   After R W Armstrong, Superintendent Physician at Littlemore Hospital 1936-59. The Superindent's house still remains. Named in 1998.

Arnold Road   After Matthew Arnold, (1822-88), poet and Fellow of Oriel College from 1845. He was much influenced by surrounding hills when writing 'The Scholar Gipsy' (1854) and Thysis' (1867). Three local streets have poetical origins. Street named in 1930.

Arthray Road   After F. Arthray Montague, Oxfordshire County Councillor. Montague Road is nearby. Street named in 1939.

Arthur Garrard Close   After Norman Arthur Garrard, died 1973, bursar of St John's 1949- 67. **Garrard Close** was first suggested but thought likely to be confused with **Gerard Place.** Street officially named in February 1973.

Arthur Street
Possibly after first leaseholder or after Prince Arthur (1850-1917), seventh son of Queen Victoria. Street developed between 1869-90, named in about 1886 and shown on a map of 1889. .

Ash Grove
In the tree group of Barton road names. Street named in 1930.

Ashlong Road
After local medieval field, spelt Ash Land Furlong in 1605, Ashlong Furlong in 1613. Street named in 1940.

Ashmole Place
After Elias Ashmole, (1617-92) Oxford astrologer and antiquary. He held several Government appointments and was Windsor Herald in 1660. In 1677 he gave his collection of curiosities to the University, later to form the basis of the Ashmolean Museum, named for him. He also gave his library to the Museum, the oldest public museum in England, founded in 1682 in Broad Street. He was made a Doctor of Physics by the University. Street named in 1967.

Ashurst Way
Rose Hill. Possibly after William Henry Ashurst, High Steward, Justice of the Peace and MP for Oxford, died 1846; but more likely after a Chairman of Littlemore Parish Council.

Ashville Way
Industrial Park. Probably a made up name. Named in the late 1970s

Aspen Square
In the tree series of Blackbird Leys road names. Named in 1997.

Asquith Road
After Herbert Henry, First Earl of Oxford and Asquith (1852-1928) Prime Minister 1908-16. Street named in 1936, a continuation of an existing road, extended in 1946.

Aston Street
After nearby island on the Thames, called Aston's Eyot in c1840. The street was developed between 1884 and about 1900.

Astrop Lane
After Louisa Astrop, a parish councillor and community stalwart in the village for 28 years. She had also worked as a community psychiatric nurse at Littlemore Hospital for about 20 years. Mrs Astrop took a job as an auxiliary nurse at Littlemore Hospital and completed formal nursing training after a doctor told her she would be good at the job. For most of her career, she worked for the Group Homes Association, helping to rehabilitate patients in the com-

munity. She died in December 2005, aged 83. This is a new 21-home development off Railway Lane, and will be run by South Oxfordshire Housing Association. The city council put up a plaque at the development to explain Mrs Astrop's contribution to the community. Named in 2010.

Atkinson Close
After Richard Atkinson, 16th Mayor of Oxford. His memorial dated 1571 is in St Peter-in-the-East Church, now the library of St Edmund Hall. Street named in June 1938.

Atkyns Road
Wood Farm. After a former tenant of the land. Named in 1952.

Atwell Place
After Joseph Atwell, Rector of Exeter College 1733-37. However, a Ralph Attewelle left in his will in 1465 funds to keep the altar lights burning in St Andrew's Church. Street named in 1955

Aubrey Court	The Domesday Book states that from 1066 Aubrey held Iffley from William I (see Woodhouse Way).Named in April 1979.
Augustine Way	On the site of St Augustine's RC School, formerly Blessed Edmund Campion School. Named in 2007.
Avens Way	After the flowering shrub, continuing the street naming scheme in Greater Leys. Named in 1997.
Avenue Lane	After avenue of trees in the area. Street named in c1888
Awger Stone Way	Slade Hospital Site. Probably from a local field name. Named in February 1999.
Azors Court	Iffley. A City Council development, named on 25th April 1979, after Azor, the Saxon Lord of Iffley in the time of Edward the Confessor, later deposed by William the Conqueror who gave the land to the Norman Earl Aubrey.

Azors Court, with Tom Collis, one of the residents, in 1999.

B

Back Lane	Unknown, but presumably self explanatory.
Badger's Walk	Recommended (originally without apostrophe) by developers J A Pye, as there had been badgers living on the site. The apostrophe was added later. Named in 2006.
Bailey Road	After Thomas Bailey, Mayor of Oxford 1436 to 1442. Street named in October 1931
Bainton Road	After St John's College living at Bainton, Yorkshire, acquired in 1703. Street named in 1906
Baker Close	Risinghurst. Possibly after a Risinghurst Parish Councillor. See **Harold White Close.** Named in about 1985.
Bakers Lane	Iffley. The village bakery once stood here. The last baker, Mr Jackman, left in 1933. His ovens were also used by villagers for their Sunday dinners. Also in the lane was a blacksmith and alehouse. A private lane, named in 1930.
Balfour Road	After Henry Balfour, (1863-1939) FRS FSA; Professor of Zoology, President of the Anthropological Section of the British Association 1903-4 and 1929, first President of Oxford Ornithological Society 1924 to about 1939, Curator of the Pitt Rivers Museum from 1891. "Outstanding as an observer, collector, classifier and craftsman" (DNB). Street named in 1959
Balliol Court	Named by the developer in a series after Oxford colleges. Named in 1996.
Baltic Wharf	The site was once owned by a timber merchant, who also owned a wharf of this name on the site now developed by Pembroke College for the Sir Geoffrey Archer Building. Named on 11th August 1998.
Bampton Close	Littlemore. Named for the village shoemaker, Will Bampton.
Banbury Road	Once a rough track to Banbury, named in 1772. Spelt Banbury way or Banneburye Way in 1388. In 1832 north of St Giles Church it was rough and pot-holed with grass down the middle. Apart from Summertown, begun in 1822, isolated houses were built during the 1830s and 40s. First planned development built 1864-84 on the east side, at Norham Gardens. Southern end was called St Giles Road East from 1862-5 (OD). Banbury Road first appeared in directories in 1872.
Banjo Road	Cowley Centre. So called after its shape - see *Evolving Names*. Originally an un-named service road to Cowley Centre, the current name used informally for some time before officially named in April 1965.
Bankside	After the steep inclines of the disused Headington stone quarries. Name suggested by developers, approved by Friends of Quarry and officially named in January 1972.
Bannister Close	After Dr Roger Bannister, neurologist, later Sir Roger, CBE, DM (Oxon), FRCP, MRCS. Born March 1929. Master of Pembroke College, the first man to run a mile in under four minutes, an achievement made on the nearby University running track. This is one of four roads named, against the City's normal practice, in the lifetime of the commemorated, in July 1982. See *"Celebrating Current Celebrities"*

Bardwell Road	After St John's college land at Bardwell, Suffolk, obtained in 1635, when William Laud was President of St John's. Street built in 1890-96 by H W Moore and named in 1893 (V). **Bardwell Court** named in c1950.
Barleycott Lane	Possibly after a local field, spelled Barley Croft in 1814
Barnet Street	After Canon Samuel Barnett of Wadham College, co-founder in 1862 of the University Settlement Movement. Street named 22nd January 1889, together with Hertford and Essex Streets. (Marriott). The road, unfortunately is misspelled with only one 't'.
Barns Hay	Named for the large hay barn that stood in the yard of Cross farm. Named in the 1960s.
Barns Road	Street named by 1939 (Kelly's), formerly Barns Court. Extended northwards in 1961 on completion of the Cowley Centre.
Barracks Lane	After military barracks once here, built in 1874-5 by Captain Hurt. Lane originally called Cowley Marsh Footway or Mud Lane. Until 1959 the headquarters of the Oxfordshire and Buckinghamshire Light Infantry. Street named in c1924 (Kelly's), formerly **The Barracks,** named in c1878
Barrett Street	After T A Barrett, local builder and timber merchant, who obtained an 80 year lease in 1878. (Marriott) Street built in 1879 and named in c1886
Barrington Close	Possibly after Viscount W K Barrington, Student (Fellow) of Christ Church. Street named by 1955.
Bartholomew Road	Land in the neighbourhood formed part of the estate of St Bartholomew Hospital, founded by Henry I and for many years a leper hospital. St Bartholomew's many patronages include nervous and neurological diseases. Street officially named in April 1938. Formerly **Newman Road** but changed to avoid confusion with Newman Road, Littlemore, where residents had complained that the other road was "only a hundred yards away". See also **Bartlemas Road.**
Bartlemas Close	Street named in 1937, despite a complaint from the owner of Southfield Golf Course about the choice of 'Close', as the road had been extended and was now a through road to the course. See also **Bartlemas Road.**
Bartlemas Road	After 14th century St Bartlemas Chapel, still standing near Bartlemas Close, formerly part of St Bartholomew's Hospital. The chapel was used as a pest-house in 1643 by people affected by the plague. In the siege of Oxford in the Civil War the bell was stolen and the lead stripped from the roof to make bullets. The present chapel was rebuilt in 1649. (see *Oxford Archeological and Historical Society report; 1870)* Street named in 1894.
Barton Lane & Road	Street named by 1930. New link road **Barton Lane** officially named in May 1972. See **Barton Village Road**
Barton Village Road	After old hamlet of Barton, meaning 'old corn field'. In 1246 spelt Berton, Aldebarton in 1246-7 and Barton in 1338. Street named in 1939, formerly **Village Road. See Aldebarton Drive.**
Bassett Road	Probably after Thomas Bassett to whose family in 1203 King John gave the Manor of Headington. His support for the King meant he was appointed Governor of Oxford Castle and Sheriff of the County. Street named in c1948.
Bateman Street	After Bateman family who had lived in New Headington since 1855. Name suggested by local residents, street named in 1930 (Kelly's), officially in 1959, when descendants were still living in this street. Formerly **East Street**.
Bath Place	Probably after the city. Named in 1876.

Bath Street	St Clement's. After Oxford Baths, a public facility in the classical style, opened in 1827 (VCH) on the north west corner of the street. Street named in c1862-5 (OD). The baths closed in 1872.
Bayswater Farm Road	See Bayswater Road.
Bayswater Road	After Bayswater Stream which the road crosses, meaning 'the watering place of the bay horse'. In 1676 was Bayard's Watering Hill. The name is older when applied to Bayswater Hill and then means 'Cress Hill'. Street named in 1934 (K). See **Cress Hill Place.**
Bay Tree Close	City Council development in Iffley. There are bay trees still on the site. See also **Azors Court, Woodhouse Close and Wootten Close.** Named 30th April 1979.
Bear Lane	After the Bear Inn. Formerly St Edward's Lane, and Vine Hall Lane in the 17th century (Hearne) The inn was once known as Parne Hall in the 15th century. After a fire in 1421 it was rebuilt and called Le Tabard. It was renamed as the Bear in 1432 after the emblem of the Earl of Warwick, 'a bear and ragged staff'. In the 16th century was a coaching inn. It has now kept its name for six centuries. Lane officially named in 1814.
Bears Hedge	A small development for the City Council designed in 1981. On holidays at around the turn of the 19th and 20th centuries a performing bear was often brought to Iffley to entertain the villagers. During their stay the bear and his master lived rough in a thicket in the vicinity, hence the name.
Beauchamp Lane	After former vicar of Cowley between 1928 and 1939, Rev M H Beauchamp (d1966), who restored the church, schools and buildings of St Francis, St Luke and St James Hall. Street officially renamed in 1955, at the request of the Highways Committee, from Church Street, Cowley, to avoid confusion between the six Church Streets in Oxford at the time. Beauchamp was delighted to give his name. (See *Oxford's Lost Church Streets*)
Beauchamp Place	See Beauchamp Lane.
Beaumont Buildings	Built in 1826. See **Beaumont Street.**
Beaumont Road	Possibly after local quarry used to supply stone for Beaumont Street or after Sir George Beaumont, a Radcliffe trustee. Street named in 1930.
Beaumont Street	After Beaumont Palace once sited on the north west street corner. No traces of the Palace now remain on the site but some stones were found in the garden of "The Avenue", between Woodstock road and Middle Way – these were later transferred to the Carmelite priory on Boars Hill. (see also E A Greening Lamborn's *The Ruins of Beaumont Palace* (with photographs by P S Spokes) in Oxoniensa 1937 Vol II (Notes and News). Beaumont means 'beautiful hill', although the area was flat – there is some dispute as to whether the name is ironic or after a prospect over open countryside. The palace was built in c1130 for Henry I, who called it Beauclerk, after his fondness for learning, and was the birthplace of Richard I and King John. Spelt Beaumont in 1246, Beaumund in 1263-64 and Bellomonde in c 1288. E A Greening Lamborn wrote: "The conqueror's son chose Oxford for his residence and built himself a palace he called 'The King's Hall of Beaumont'. Street laid out in 1828 and built in 1837. In the 13th century, the north of the City was an area of flat arable land called Bellus Mons (Beaumont) but there is no record of a connection with Beaumont Palace, to the south (Salter, *Medieval Oxford*, OAHS 1926).

The ruins of Beaumont Palace, probably in the 18th century

Becket Street

After St Thomas a Becket (1118-70). Many local historians have written about the confusion between St Thomas the Martyr and St Thomas a Becket; The church was originally dedicated to St Nicholas when it was founded by the canons of Oseney in 1141, partly for the use of the parishioners of St George's, who were deprived of access to their own parish church, within the castle precincts, when the empress Maud was besieged there by King Stephen. Dr Ingram in his 'Memorials' wrote "The dedication of this church is not straightforward...there were some who might even claim that it is still dedicated to St Nicholas and not either Thomas". Henry VIII had done his best to blot out the name of Becket. Street named in c1886. See **St Thomas Street.**

Bedford Street

Possibly after local Bedford House built in c 1840 – although Fasnacht suggests it was so named following the fashion to name streets after peers – there have been Dukes of Bedford since 1389. Street named in 1900.

Beech Road
Beech Croft Road

In the tree group of nine streets nearby. Street named in about 1925.

A made up name, often spelled as one word and still with both versions on name plates in the road; the Highways Register from 1896 gives it as Beechcroft but early residents preferred Beech Croft and the City list entry confirms that version. Three parallel streets have similar made up names. Street built in c1890-94 and named by 1897. See Oakthorpe and Thorncliffe Roads; also *Apostrophes and Spaces.*

The Beeches
Beechey Avenue
Beechwood

Name suggested by the developers Wilcon Homes in 1992.

Unknown

Beechwood is a late 18th century house (listed Grade II), belonging to All Souls College, which built flats in the grounds.

Beef Lane

After Beaufo Hall owned by Thomas de Beaufo, later renamed Beef Hall. Hearne wrote that "Mr Wood tells us that this hall was so called from the sign of the ox that was formerly painted either in one of the windows or else over the gate. Others even suggest that it is named after the beef which the scholars ate there" - the name of the owner seems the more likely origin. In 1411 spelled Beefhall. Originally called Kings Streete in c 1620, Beeflane in 1661-66 and later spelled Beef Hall Lane.

Belbroughton Road
After St Johns College living at Belbroughton, Worcs, acquired by the College in 1733. The name appears in one of John Betjeman's poems: 'Belbroughton Road is bonny'. Street named in c1927 (VCH)

Belvedere Road
Unknown

Bennett Crescent
Nuffield Press site, Hollow Way. After JMC Bennett, d1868, headmaster of Cowley College. Named 5th February 1998.

Benouville Close
Brasenose Driftway. Benouville was the first objective achieved in the crucial glider-borne attack in June 1944, when D Company, 2nd Battalion, Oxfordshire and Buckinghamshire Light Infantry successfully took the bridges over the Caen Canal and River Orne, later named Pegasus and Horsa respectively. The attack was led by Major John Howard DSO (1912-1999), who had lived in Oxford before the war and served in the Oxford City Police; in later life he lived at Burcot. Named in 2004.

Benson Place
After George Benson, a local landowner, who gave £1000 in 1639 to St John's College to buy land. Shown on a map of 1889, originally a private road and formally named in 1931. A hutted camp between 1939-45, when known as Benson Place. Housing developed in the 1950s on the site of Wychwood School playing fields.

Benson Road
After Rev Richard Mieux Benson (1824-1915) curate of Cowley and vicar of Cowley St John 1869-86. In 1866 he founded the Cowley Fathers, the first stable religious community of men to be established in the Anglican Communion since the English Reformation. He also built an iron church in what is now Stockmore Street. Street named in 1930.

Bergamot Place
In the plant and shrub series of Blackbird Leys road names. Named in 1997.

Bernwood Road
After a family connected with land in the Headington area. Street named 30th November 1945.

Berry Close
The name Berry is derived from Blackberry Lane, the name of the extension of nearby Roman Way. An Alderman quipped that it was a suitable name, being "berry close to the Works" – which are indeed nearby; perhaps no less jocular than the complaints made by Councillors to the previously suggested name Leyland Close, to acknowledge the proximity of the car factory to this road, that the street name plates would be defaced by adding a 'd' to 'Close'. The road was named in July 1973.

Bertie Place
After the Bertie family, Earls of Abingdon, the family name of Lord Norreys from the 17th to 20th centuries. The family lived at Wytham Abbey. The Bertie arms are in the Lord Mayor's parlour in the Town Hall; they include three battering rams and it is possible that this is a pun on the family name, pronounced 'Bartie' and the word 'battering'. (source – Alderman Michael Maclagan, who became Richmond Herald of Arms). Street named in 1935 . See Norreys Avenue.

Between Towns Road
After local field called 'Betwixt the Towns' in about 1630 and in 1853 spelled Between Towns. The street was cut in 1853. Originally Surmans's Lane, later High Street, Cowley, realigned when the Cowley Centre was built. Street named in March 1930.

Bevington Road	After St John's College living at Wood Bevington, Warks, bought in c1575. The area originally was gravel pits, hence the present dip in the roadway. Isolated houses built here from 1825. The street was called **Jefferys Lane** in the early 1860s, after Stephen Jeffreys' nursery to the north. Street named in c1870 and built in the 1870s mainly by Frederick Codd and William Wilkinson. An application was made to the City Council in June 1969 by the governors of St Anne's College, supported by St Antony's College and the University, to have the road renamed Plumer Road, after the former Principal of St Anne's, the Hon Eleanor Plumer (1885-1967). The City Council did not, however, agree, and opposed any name change. The College arms are the Plumer arms – her father was Field Marshall Viscount Plumer.
Bhandari Close	Mr Bhandari was an Asian community leader in East Oxford, who ran the 'Lace Ups' shop in Cowley Road. He was involved in the Oxford Race Equality Council from its inception, sat on the City Council's Commumity Relations sub-committee and was a campaigner for improvement to the quality of life in East Oxford. He died in 1997 and the road was named after him in October of the same year.
Bickerton Road	After J J Bickerton, former Town Clerk, died 1894. Street named in 1930. (Marriott)
Binsey Lane	After Binsey village, meaning 'Byni's island'. Spelt Beneseye in 1122, Bunesleie in 1141 and Beneseya in 1291. The villages of Osney, Hinksey and Binsey were inhabited islands in the wide River Thames around Oxford. Binsey is one of the places to which one of the places to which St Frideswide is said to have escaped when being pursued by her unwelcome suitor. The healing well still exists next to the church – referred to by Lewis Carroll in Alice in Wonderland" as the "treacle well". Road named in 1907.

Binswood Avenue	Unknown, possibly after a Councillor. Street in existence in 1929.
Birchfield Close	Named after local 13th century field. Street named in 1961
Bishop Kirk Place	After Kenneth Escott Kirk, (1886-1954), Bishop of Oxford 1937-54, honorary fellow of St John's and Trinity Colleges. Built on the site of Bishop Kirk School. See also under Kirk Close.
Blackberry Lane	See Berry Close
Blackbird Leys Road	Means 'way over the black ford', originally related to the Dorchester Roman road to the east as it forded Northfield Brook. Black refers to dark soil found here from burnt Roman and medieval pottery kilns. In 1797 spelt Blackford Lays, 1822 Blacford Leys and Blackber's lane in c1830. Street

Bishop Kirk, with his wife and two of his children, Hilary and Joan, in 1924.

officially named in March 1959. The land was formerly home to Oxford Sewage Farm which contributed to lush vegetation and attracted a large and rare bird population. The rich flora and fauna were commemorated in the Estate street names. Plant and flower named streets are restricted to the south and south east in roughly alphabetical order, with tree names in the east and birds in the west and south west. When the development was first planned there was confusion about how the name should be pronounced – 'Lees' or 'Lays'. It is the former.

Blackfriars Road

After local Blackfriars order. Once here was **Dale Street,** named in 1890-91, now revived in a later development, also **Bridport Street,** named in 1868 (W), **Pike Street,** named in 1874 (S) and **Sadler Street,** named in c1878. Thirteen friars had arrived in Oxford on 15th August 1221 (VCH). See also Preachers Lane. Named in December 1979.

Blackhall Road

After a local medieval house named Blackhall. In 1519 spelt Blakehall and in 1591 Blackhall. There were three Blackhalls of which this is one, first mentioned in 1361, when owned by St John's College. "Blackhall, like Whitehall, was a common name and any large house such as an inn or farmhouse could have been called a hall in the Middle Ages". (*Six Hundred Years of Blackhall,* Edward Pope – unpublished but in local libraries). From at least 1349 until the 19th century it was not only a house and garden, but had 80 acres of arable land and 16 acres of pasture in St Giles and Osney. The property was unique in being a freehold held for many years by private individuals rather than colleges or the University (op cit) - until eventually bought by St Johns College. In 1956 the college leased some of the land there to Queen Elizabeth House which remained there until the lease expired and it moved to Mansfield Road in October 2005. St John's new buildings are now on the site. Street named in c1874.

Blacksmiths Meadow

Blackbird Leys. After a local field. Named in 1993

Blackstock Close

Horspath Driftway. After a local field. Named in 1994.

Blackthorn Close

After the shrub and also a local field spelled **Blackthorn Meer** in the Headington Inclosure Award of 1804. Street named in October 1938.

Bladon Close

After Bladon village near Blenheim Palace. **Blenheim Drive** and **Blandford Avenue** are nearby. The development here is on land once owned by the Dukes of Marlborough. Sir Winston Churchill, born at Blenheim, is buried at Bladon. Bladon is the old name for the River Evenlode. Named in March 1957.

Blandford Avenue

After the Marquis of Blandford, the title conferred on the eldest son of the Duke of Marlborough, who owned local fields in 1834. Street named in 1938, officially in April 1951.

Blay Close

After Richard Blay, Oxford innkeeper and local landowner from 1744. His family sold up in the early 19th century. Street officially named in 1959. (Marriott)

Bleache Place

Means 'pale soil' after a local field spelled Bleache Furlong in 1665. Street named in June 1931.

Blenheim Drive

After Blenheim, the name given to the royal park at Woodstock, granted to the Duke of Marlborough in 1705 – also the name of his palace there. Street named by 1938 (Kelly's). North end of Blenheim Drive, to Woodstock Road, officially named in 1951.

Blomfield Place After Arthur Blomfield (1829-99) who designed nearby St Barnabas Church, started in 1869. He insisted that not a penny was to be thrown away on external decoration. Inside it features colured decoration, in marble, mosaic and painting. (OAHS report, 1871.) Street named in 1968.

Bluebell Court Blackbird Leys. Named in 1993, continuing the plant theme on the estate.

Blue Boar Street The Blue Boar Inn once stood on the site of the Public Library, which now includes the Museum of Oxford. In the 17th century spelt Blewebore House. An original lease is dated 1553, signed by Dean Tresham, Doctor of Divinity at King Henry VIII's college (now Christ Church), once known as New (or Newe) Lane and Little Jury Lane, spelled Tresham's Lane in 1614 and became Blue Boar Street soon afterwards. In 1256, on the site of the Blue Boar Inn, was a tenement owned by 'Moses, son of Simon the Jew'. This was a Jewish area in the 13th century. The blue boar is the crest of the Earls of Oxford created in 1142 by the Empress Matilda. Aubrey de Vere, son of the Aubrey de Vere who was the Great Chamberlain, chose this title and it was continued by Henry II.

Bobby Fryer Close On the site of the former North and South Works of the Rover Plant, named after a trades union activist and senior shop steward at the assembly plant at the Cowley Works. Name suggested by Councillor Hoyle and adopted in 1994.

Bodley Place Cutteslowe. After G.F.Bodley (1827-1907) a descendant of Sir Thomas Bodley. He was the architect of many Cowley Community churches, worked on parts of Magdalen College and Christ Church; a pupil of George Gilbert Scott and friend of Morris, Burne-Jones, Madox Brown and Rosetti. Named in c1934.

Bodley Road Littlemore. After Sir Thomas Bodley (1545-1613), diplomat and scholar, fellow of Magdalen College, began to form the Bodleian Library in 1598, completed in 1603 and endowed by him in 1611. Name suggested by Wates, builder of the Orchard Way Estate of which this road is part. Street named in 1935.

Bonar Road After a field name, Bonar's Place, named in 1952.

Bonn Square Named to commemorate the 25th anniversary of the twinning with the then West German city, agreed on 7 May 1973 and a stone was unveiled in September 1974. In October 1971 the city of Bonn had named part of a street 'Oxford Strasse'. A wooden plaque replaced the stone in 2009 after the square had been redesigned.

STÄDTEPARTNERSCHAFT
BONN–OXFORD

OXFORD–BONN
LINK

Borrowmead Road Named after a local field, Brookes Borrow Lot Meade, recorded on 1605 Corpus map. Named in July 1949.

Boswell Road After William Boswell, Mayor of Oxford in 1622. Named in 1933.

Botley Road The old road to Botley was first a footpath through the river meadows, impassable in floods until a causeway was built in c1530 and later much improved at the expense of John

Claymond (also the benefactor of the Cornmarket). It was narrow and poorly maintained until turnpiked in 1766. Tolls were paid at the turnpike gate near Osney Bridge and the road was made wide and passable, all the way to Eynsham. At this time it became notorious for the activities of highwaymen and footpads and a vigilante committee was formed by Oxford citizens to stem the robberies. Arched stone bridges were built and the road was alternatively known in the 19th century as Seven Bridges Road. the section between the station and the river bridge is shown on a map of 1889 as Osney Road. Spelled Botley Causey in 1750. Botley means 'Botta's island'. Botley Meadow appeared in directories from c1874 .

Boulter Street
After Edmund Boulter, died 1736, who financed Boulter's Almshouses, built in 1780, pulled down in 1885 for Boulter Street to be built on the site in c1886. The foundation was for "six poor, neat and honest men" and a medical attendant - an early type of health centre. Endowments for the almshouses, now known as Cutler-Boulter, are today managed by the City of Oxford Charities.

Boults Close
Named after the farm at the end of Boult's Lane, farmed by the Haynes family, also of Cross Farm.

Boults Lane
See Boults Close.

Boundary Brook Road
After the brook running from Woodlands Road across Cowley Marsh to the Thames, marking the old south west boundary of Cowley. Old stream spelled Broce in 1004. Street named in September 1973.

Bourne Close
Named after Captain Robert C Bourne, MP for Oxford between 1924 and 1938. Street named in 1959.

Bowness Avenue
After the Lake District village, named in June 1931, one of five streets named after places in the Lake District. The area is still known locally as The Lake District. See Ambleside Drive

Bracegirdle Road
After Dr Bracegirdle, Oxford physician, who had erected a mounting stone in c1630 on **Old Road** at the foot of **Shotover Hill.** He placed it there 'out of good intent to ease passengers there to mount their horses'. (Marriott) Street named in 1953.

Bradlands
Marston. After an old field name. Named in the 1960s.

Bradmore Road
After nearby fields, meaning 'broad moor' or waste land, spelled Brademore in 1545-6. There was also a Middle Bradmore Furlong, Nether Broadmore and Bradmore Fields. Street built 1869-74 mostly by Frederick Codd, named in 1872. A Dr Case, who died in 1600, left £100 to St John's College and a 989 year lease on Bradmore, which was purchased for £283 6s 8d.

Brake Hill
Blackbird Leys. Named in 1991, after a local field name.

The Brambles
Off Latimer Road. Named in 2004.

Brambling Way
In the bird series of Blackbird Leys roads. Street named in 1959.

Brampton Road
After Sir W Brampton, five times Mayor of Oxford between 1421 and 1439, whose family was associated with the area. Street named in 1945.

Bramwell Place
On the site of Benfield and Loxley's yard, Bullingdon Road, named in February 1982.

Brasenose Driftway
After local Brasenose Farm and College, which owned land here. A local field was spelled The Open Brasenoze Driftway in 1853. (VCH map, Bullingdon) Street named in 1936, officially in 1946.

Brasenose Lane in April 2009.

Brasenose Lane After the College founded here in 1509. Named after the original door knocker at Brasenose Hall, shaped as a 'brazen nose', first recorded in 1379, it is now safely kept inside the college. Street named in 1890-1. In 1750 it was Exeter College Lane and St Mildreds Lane (Vicus St Mildrede) in 1219. There was once St Mildred's Chapel here, converted into a library in 1656. The lane is said to be haunted and the writer Kenneth Grahame, in a retrospective called "Oxford Through a Boy's Eyes" wrote "I should not much like, even at this day, to pass along Brasenose Lane at midnight".

Brewer Street After a brewhouse, run by a group of brewers who lived here in the 17th century. Originally had been an area of butchers and slaughterers and was therefore known as Sleyng Lane in 1478, Sleyne Lane in 1690, Slaying Lane in 1811, Slaughter Lane in 1840. Became **Brewers Street** and **Lane** in 1772. In 1932 the street name plate at the St Aldate's end read Brewers Street and at the St Ebbe's end, Brewer Street; the City decided on the latter version on 14th January 1932.

Bridewell Square Recorded on a map of 1899. On the site of Bridewell Yard, A Bridewell was a house of correction or gaol.

Briar Way In the plant and shrub series in Blackbird Leys. Street named in 1964.

Bridge Street, Osney After Osney Bridge across the Thames here. Called Hith Brygge in 1465 Osney Bridge in 1766. The bridge collapsed in December 1885, was rebuilt and opened 31st December 1888. The street was developed from 1852.

Brindley Close Waterways. After James Brindley, (1716 –1772) the architect of the Oxford canal and many of its bridges, including Aristotle Bridge (in about 1790). Named in 2003.

Broadfields Littlemore. After a house opposite the 20 acre field belonging to Whites' Farm , Cowley, levelled in 1939 for construction of Cowley airfield.

Broad Street in 2006.

Broadmead Place
After a local field, meaning 'large meadow'. Street officially named in March 1950.

Broad Oak
Originally Road 3, Slade Camp. Named after a field name on the Corpus map of 1605. Named in January 1977.

Broad Street
Originally Canditch, after the ditch here, outside the city walls. Unusually clear and clean for the time, it became known as White Street after the shining whiteness of the stream, later corrupted to Wide Walk and then in the 18th century to Broad street. See *Street Names in the Early Days*.

Broad Walk
An avenue of trees which leads down to the Thames from Christ Church, opposite the Meadow Buildings. The trees were elms, but were felled after Dutch elm disease in 1976 and replaced by plane trees.

Brocklesby Road
After Ted Brocklesby, a Littlemore Parish Councillor for many years. Named in 1996.

Brome Place
Probably after Adam de Brome, died c 1332, founder of Oriel College. He has his own chapel in the University Church of St Mary's, which has had a long association with Oriel College, across the High Street – but also possibly after a lesser known member of the family, John Brome, who was Lord of the Manor of Headington from 1469. Named on 30th November 1945.

Brookfield Crescent
After a local field with brook. Street named on 31st October 1938. Brookfield was the name given to the area, shown on Corpus Map of 1605.

Brooklime Walk
Blackbird Leys. Unknown origin. Named in 1997.

Brookside
Street lies alongside a brook which runs from **Woodlands Road** to Iffley, now culverted underground. Street named in 1936, formerly Brookside Avenue, named in 1930. (Marriott)

Brook Street
After one of two small streams to the east and south. Street named in c1886. (Marriott)

Brook View
Probably after a nearby brook, in Blackbird Leys.

Broughton Close	W H Broughton was a churchwarden in 1884 and Chairman of the School Governors in the 1890s. The family farmed Court Place Farm in the early 20th century Street named in 1970s.
Bryony Close	In the shrub group of Blackbird Leys road names. Named in 1993.
Buckingham Street	Probably after the Dukes of Buckingham, possibly the first Earl, Thomas of Woodstock, the seventh son of Edward III. (Duke of) **Marlborough Road** is nearby. Street named in c1886, shown on a map of 1889.
Buckler Place	Probably after J C Buckler. See **Buckler Road.**
Buckler Road	After Oxford architect and topographical artist John Chessell Buckler (1793-1894) one of the architects of the Littlemore Hospital. His collection of drawings of Oxford is among the most noteworthy. Street named in July 1932.
Bulan Place	Street named in 1930. See **Bulan Road.**
Bulan Road	After a local field spelt Bulandene, later corrupted to Bullingdon Green, used for grazing and for University games and revels. Houses were built in 1928, when in the postal district of Cowley, but by 1930 were reallocated into the Headington district. Street named in 1930. See **Dene Road and Bullingdon Road.**
Bullingdon Road	After the ancient Saxon Hundred of Bullingdon, meaning 'Bula's valley' or 'bull valley'. Spelled Bulesden in 1179-91, Bulindena in 1231, with many variant spellings including Bulandene throughout the 12th and 13th centuries. Street named in c1862-5.
Bullstake Close	After the stakes used to mark out the ford in the stream here. In 1142 spelled Bustache, in c1222 Bulstake and in c1230 Bolestake. Today there is Bullstake Bridge across the original Causey or causeway, also Bullstake Meadow. Street named in 1966.
Bulrush Road	In the wildflower group of Blackbird Leys street names. Named in 1961.
Bulwarks Lane	Formerly **Bullocks Lane** in 1605, 1661-66 and 1787, 'from one Bullock, a scavenger who brought the dung and rubbish of the city there and with the town's permission built himself a house' in 1588. When Bullock was forgotten the lane came to be known as Bulwarks, its present name. In the 17th century and perhaps earlier the Lane extended across what is now New Road into Castle Street. Because of its proximity to the Castle and Mound it is understandable that people thought it should be spelled Bulwarks and not Bullocks. (Spelled Bulwarks Alley or Bullocks Alley in 1772, Bulwark Alley in 1840 and 1852). Present name acquired in 1872.
Burbush Road	After a local field name, in 1605 spelt Burbushe Furlong. Street named in June 1931.
Burchester Avenue	After W de Burchestre, Mayor of Oxford four times between 1311 and 1339. He founded a chantry in All Saints Church in which the souls of Mayors were to be prayed for. Street named on 30th November 1945.
Burdell Avenue	A composite name combining Bursill, the estate developer, (see Bursill Close and Delbush Avenue) and Dell, the owner of Headington End, an imposing Victorian house on the site of what is now Bursill Close. Mr Bursill lived in the house during development of the estate, later changing its name to Headington Hall, a confusing move locally, as mail was regularly wrongly delivered to Headington Hill Hall, (now owned by Oxford Brookes

University) and vice versa. Mr Dell probably also owned the farmland sold to Mr Bursill for what was originally the Sandhill Estate, later Sandhills, and perhaps was also a partner in the scheme. Named in about 1935.

Burgan Close After William Burgan, an important local landowner in the 13th century. Street officially named in 1954.

Burgess Mead After the land between Port Meadow and the easternmost stream of the Thames, originally an ancient meadow called Bishop's Eyot. Recorded on a 1750 map (VCH v4). The road to Burgess Mead from the south was a continual source of contention between the City and the Abbey of Godstow – the City said the Abbey "has narrowed, encroached or neglected it, dug into it and surmounted it" Named in 2000.

Burlington Crescent A composite name from the developer of Sandhills, Frank Bursill (see Bursill Close), taking the first letters of his name and adding the mellifluous suffix, possibly inspired by Burlington Arcade in London. The houses here, fronting the London Road, are larger and of higher quality than those on Sandhills, built, according to sales literature at the time, "in the London style". Named in about 1935.

Burrows Close After Thomas Burrows, whose family lived at Southfield Farm, who gave stone from his local quarry at Quarry Farm Hollow in 1848 for building Headington Quarry Church. Street named in 1936.

Bursill Close After Frank Guy Bursill, who developed the Sandhill Estate, now known as Sandhills. He was an established builder and developer from Leamington Spa and a prominent freemason; on his regular trips to London via Oxford he would drive past the land here and had noticed hoardings advertising it for sale. He was eventually persuaded by his family to view the site, and later bought the land in lots from Mr Dell, who was living at Headington End, later Headington Hall, on the site of what is now Bursill Close. Named in about 1935.

Burton Place Brasenose Driftway. Unknown, but possibly a connection to the Oxford and Bucks Light Infantry. The Regimental Headquarters were once on this site. Named in January 1978.

Bushey Leys Close After a local field name. Street officially named in 1971.

Bushnell Close After Sarah Louisa Bushnell, also known as Louie or "Aunt Lou Lou", whose family lived at 38 Quarry High Street since it was built in 1879. she was the youngest of five children of Isaac, a master mason, and Emily Ann (nee Werring), and lived there until her death in 1987, aged 96. Sarah was a

Sarah Louise Bushnell in the 1960s, when in her 70s.

Quarry washerwoman who took in washing from the colleges, including that of C S Lewis. Her great niece, Councillor Dee Sinclair remembers the huge wash coppers in the small kitchen, boiling the sheets on a Sunday evening ready for Monday wash day. Named in 2002.

Butler Close Named jointly for C.V. Butler, local volunteer Community worker and Oxford's earliest social investigator, a Fellow of St Anne's College, a pioneer of English social work and who could speak four languages. Also after Edwin Butler, wine merchant, owner of the house demolished for the Butler Close development. Named in 1970.

Buttercup Square Blackbird Leys, in the plant and shrub series. Named in 1993.

Butterwort Place In the wildflower series of Blackbird Leys road names. Street named in 1961.

Butterwyke Place St Ebbes. Formerly Albert Street South. Named 10th December 1980.

Butts Road & Lane Marston. Once led to Butts Field, now beyond the A40, and which in WWII was an 'ack-ack' (anti-aircraft) camp. Butts Farm is to the east.

C

Calcot Close	After a local field or landowner. Street named in 1952.
Cambridge Street	As Pembroke College is nearby it is possible that the name was chosen because its namesake college is in that University town.
Cambridge Terrace	Named in c1868. See **Cambridge Street**
Campbell Road	Probably after Sir Colin Campbell, Baron Clyde, (1792-1863) commander in chief of British forces in India during the Indian Mutiny of 1860. Street named in 1935. See **Clive Road.**
Campion Close	In the wildflower group of road names in Blackbird Leys. Named in 1993.
Canal Street	The Oxford-Banbury canal runs nearby, opened in 1790 to bring cheaper goods from the Midlands. Street named in c1870.
Canning Crescent	Charles John Canning, 1st Earl Canning (1812-1862), and his father George (1770-1827) were both graduates of Christ Church and served as Governor-Generals of India. See **Campbell Road** and **Clive Road**. Street named in c1927.
Cannon's Field	After the Cannon family who farmed in Marston in the nineteenth century and married into the Rippington family (See Rippington Drive) Named in the 1990s.
Canterbury Road	Probably after the cathedral city; **Winchester Road** is adjoining. Street built by Frederick Codd between 1871 and 76, and named in c1874.
Capel Close	After a local builder and freemason H Capel, died 1931. Street name adopted by the Council on 31st July 1933.
Cardigan Street.	Possibly after Lieutenant General James Thomas Brudenell, 7th Earl of Cardigan,1797 –1868), alumnus of Christ Church, who commanded the Light Brigade of the British Army and led the disastrous cavalry charge at Balaclava during the Crimean War. Street named by 1852. (Gardners' directory)
Cardinal Close	After Cardinal John Newman, who had strong local associations – see **Newman Road.**
Cardwell Crescent	After Edward Cardwell, (1813-1886) a long serving MP for Oxford between 1853 and 74, Colonial Secretary 1864-66 under Palmerston, in 1874 made Viscount Cardwell. Secretary for War under Gladstone.
Carey Close	After William Carey (1861-1834) vicar of St James', Cowley 1800-15, later Bishop of Exeter and Bishop of St Asaph, the smallest cathedral in Britain, also Headmaster of Westminster School. Street named in July 1935.
Carfax	Means 'four-views' or crossroads, after the French quatre voyes or voies, and is at the junction of four streets in the city centre. In 1483 spelt Carfax, in 1548 Carfoxe and Quartervoys Carfax in 1661-66. The exact origin of the name is obscure and could also be derived from the Latin for four-forked, or where four roads meet. St Martins Church once stood here but only the tower now remains after the church was demolished for road widening. Also removed was the Penniless Bench, against the church walls, where beggars would sit. The tower clock has quarterboys to ring the quarter hours – Carfax is the highest part of the old city. The Carfax Conduit was built here in 1610, bringing spring water from Hinksey Hill, built at the expense

of Otho Nicholson, a graduate of Christ Church and a wealthy London courtier, diplomat and lawyer. It was removed in 1789 to Nuneham Park, now owned by the University. See *Street Names in the Early Days.*

Carlton Road   Cutteslowe. Suggested by the Estate Company. Cardinal Road was preferred by the council (Wolsey Road connects), and so named by Highways Committee in 1934. Officially changed to the present name in January 1948. At one time two name plates were in place, showing Cardinal and Carlton Roads. One of the infamous Cutteslowe Walls was built here in 1934 between the private estate and the Council houses, similarly between Wentworth and Aldrich Roads. The walls were demolished in 1959. See text. See Snobbery and Street Names.

Caroline Street   After the popular Queen Caroline of Brunswick, consort of George IV, tried for adultery and died only two weeks after the coronation. Oxford citizens had sent a petition to London in her support. Street named in c1870.

Carpenter Close   Minchery Farm development. Unknown origin. Named 15th November 1954.

Carter Close   Risinghurst. Possibly after a Risinghurst Parish Councillor. See **Harold White Close.** Named in about 1985.

Cascade Way   Oxford Business Park. Perhaps after the water feature on the Park Named in January 1995.

Castle Mews   St Thomas's. Not far from the castle...

Castle Street   After Oxford Castle, built by Robert d'Oyley between 1067-86. Spelled Castell Streate in 1578 and Castle Street in 1661-66. Realigned in 1969-73 during the de-velopment of the West- gate Centre. In 1750 the part of the street nearest to Carfax was called The Bailey.

Catherine Street   Possibly after Catherine Howard, (1521-1542) 5th wife of Henry VIII. Named in c1874.

Catte Street   The 'street of mouse-catchers', with many references to the street of cats. Spelt Kattestrete in c1210, Cattestreete in 1402 and Cat Street in 1772. Later called Catherine Street, Cat being the diminutive of Catherine, the latter thought more dignified.

The castle in 2010.

There was once a St Catherine's Hall in the street. Reverted to the original name and agreed by the Council in December 1930. The poet Robert Bridges wrote, in his preface to Salter, "If the silly modernist St Catherine Street were done away with and the historic Cat restored, there is I believe no single human being whose affairs would be in any way affected." See *Street Names in the Early Days.*

Catwell Close
Cowley Marsh. Catwell was a small settlement to the north of the site, shown on the Inclosure Map. The City Council had wanted to name the road after a female politician, as it was thought there was a dearth of women so honoured, but the historical connection was nevertheless made in naming the street on 16th July 1990.

Cave Street
Probably after Arthur William Cave, died 1930, Headmaster of Oxford High School 1897-1925 and Freeman in 1925 – but possibly after George, Viscount Cave (1856-1928), lawyer, statesman, Home Secretary, Lord Chancellor – also Chancellor of the University and an Honorary Freeman of Oxford. Street officially renamed in 1955, formerly George Street, St Clements, named in c1878.

Cavell Road
After John C. Cavell (1813-87) who lived at 12 Magdalen Road, Councillor in 1860, Alderman in 1868, Mayor 1865-6, and 1877-8. (Marriott) His shop became Elliston and Cavell, now redeveloped as Debenhams. Street named in 1930.

Cavendish Drive
Unknown, the name was chosen by the developer, A C Carter Ltd.

Cavendish Road
Unknown. Possibly after Charles Cavendish (1620–1643), royalist army officer.   Street named in 1934.

Cecil Sharpe Place
Cecil Sharpe (1859-1924) was responsible for the 20th century revival of folk tunes and traditional (including Morris) dancing. He recorded and published dance history and had first been inspired when he saw Morris dancing at Headington Quarry at Christmas 1899. At that time Morris dancing was almost extinct. He had a BA from Cambridge. Founded the English Folk Dance Society in 1923. See William Kimber Crescent and also *Celebrating Current Celebrities.*

Cedar Road
After the tree, one of nine local streets so named, in 1950.

Celandine Place
Blackbird Leys. Named in 1993, continuing the plant theme on the estate.

Centaury Place
In the Blackbird Leys plant and shrub series, Mowlem development, named in 1993, despite councillors' concerns that the name would be often mis-spelled.

Chadlington Road
After the manor of Chadlington, Oxon, owned by St John's College since 1637. Street named in c1908.

Chaffinch Walk
In the bird series of road names in Blackbird Leys. Named in 1993.

Chain Alley
See **Cheney Lane** for a possible derivation. This was its former name before redevelopment of the way between George Street and Gloucester Green. Named in 1990.

Centaury

Chalfont Road	After the St John's College living at Chalfont St Peter in Buckinghamshire, the living acquired in 1661. Street built by H W Moore 1889-99, named in 1890-1.
Champion Way	After the Rev George James Champion, the popular vicar of Littlemore from 1967.
Chapel Lane	After the Baptist Chapel in the road, opened in 1807 and demolished in 2009.
Chapel Street	On a map of 1889. Possibly after a non-conformist chapel close by.
Charlbury Road	After St John's College living at Charlbury, Oxon. Charlbury vicarage was bought in 1590. Street named in 1904. An extension to the road on the Blackhall Allotments site was named Charlbury Road on 23rd April 1986, after names suggested by Highways and Traffic Committee were considered – these included other St John's College livings and well known Victorian architects.
Charles Street	Probably after the estate builder Percy Charles Howard. See **Percy** and **Howard** Streets. Street named in 1862-5.
Chatham Road	After William Pitt (1708-78), 'Pitt the Elder', 1st Earl of Chatham, Secretary of State in the Seven Years War and later Prime Minister. The street was officially renamed in 1961 as its former name of **Pitt Road** clashed with its namesake in Headington Quarry. In the original proposal for residential development off Abingdon Road, Chatham Crescent was intended to be a close off Wytham Street, but when the roads were developed in 1929-34 this close was omitted. (see text)
Cheney Lane	The word means 'chained lane', a lane with a chained gate across it which is the probable reason for the lane name here. Spelt Cheyney Lane in the 1805 Inclosure Award and Cheney Lane in 1832. Cheney Farm appears on a map of 1899. Formerly Old Road. Street named in directories in 1932. See **Market Street** which also once had this name.
Chequers Place	After the local Chequers Inn, suggested by the Friends of Headington Quarry. Street officially named in 1968. Formerly part of Beaumont Road.
Cherry Close	Blackbird Leys. Named in 1993, continuing the tree and shrub theme on the estate.
Cherwell Drive	After the nearby river Cherwell which has a Celtic origin. 'Cher' is uncertain, 'well' here means stream. In 681 spelt Ceruelle, in 864 Cearwellan and in 1221-6 Cherlewelle. Street officially named in July 1947. See *The Perils of Pronunciation.*
Cherwell Street	See **Dudley Gardens** and **Cherwell Drive**. Named in c1888.
Chester Street	Possibly after a local field spelt Chisterfurlong in c1220 or after the county town of Chester. Street named in 1894.
Chestnut Avenue	One of four roads in Barton named after trees. Street named in 1932.
Chillingworth Cres	After William Chillingworth, born near here in 1602, polemic writer and a Fellow of Trinity College at 26, Mayor of Oxford in 1644. His father was an Oxford trader and left £400 for impoverished tradesmen. Street named in 1952.
Chilswell Road	Near South Hinksey was once a church at a place called Childswell, after Cilla or Cilla's Well, which was nearby. Cilla is a Saxon name in which the C is pronounced Ch, and was a person of rank supposed to have built the

	church, of which no trace now exists. The well was accredited with powers 'to make women that were barren to bring forth children' in the same way as Crowell, in Holywell, cured eye ailments. Street named in 1890-1.
Cholsey Close	After Richard Cholsey, once a tenant of 130 acres here in 1512 and the richest man locally by 1524. Street officially named in 1954.
Cholesbury Grange	Name suggested by Hastoe Housing Society. Street officially named in 1965.
Choswell Spring	Blackbird Leys. Unknown, possibly after a local field. Named in 1997.
Church Lane	A footpath from First Turn to Wolvercote Green, named after St Peter's church, Wolvercote which owned local fields called Lower and Upper Church Croft Furlong and Church Close in1834. Named in 1930.
Church Walk	After the nearby church of SS Phillip and James, built by G.E. Street in 1860-2. Named in c1878. The Church is now the Oxford Centre for Mission Studies.
Church Way	After the Norman church of St Mary, Iffley, built in c1170-80. Named in July 1933 in place of Main Road ,Iffley
Church Cowley Road	After the original village of Cowley, later Church Cowley in the 12th and 13th centuries to distinguish it from Temple Cowley to the east. Spelled Chirche Couele in c 1250, Church Couele in 1316 and Churchcovell in 1307. Street cut between Church Cowley and Iffley Turn in 1853 and named in 1930. Previously Cemetery Road or New Road.
Churchill Drive	Leads to the Churchill Hospital in Headington.
Churchill Place	Charles Churchill was joint owner with St John's College of land in the area, recorded in the Inclosure Award of 1834. Street named in 1939.
Church Hill Road	After St James' church at the top of a steep hill. The road was to be named Churchill Road but this was opposed and officially named in December 1930.
Cinnaminta Road	Named after the beautiful gipsy girl whose family often camped in Cowley and whose name was immortalised in R.D. Blackmore's 'Cripps the Carrier' which describes her in later life… "I saw Cinnaminta – her hair and eyes, and graceful carriage were as grand as ever and her forehead as clear and noble" Street named in 1930.
Circus Street	Named for Newsome's Alhambra Circus of 1861, a short lived but memorable venture run by Mr and Mrs Newsome, who taught riding when not starring in their own circus. Street named in c1870.
Clarks Row	A short path between St Aldate's and Albion Place, named possibly after John Clark, died 1861, who owned land in the city. Street named officially in 1950, formerly **Union Place** from 1872, originally **Clarks Row,** first named in 1867.
Claymond Road	After John Claymond (1468-1537), He was President of Magdalen College 1504-1511 but his friend Bishop Richard Foxe, founder of Corpus Christi College persuaded him to move there as the first President of the College. Claymond could be said to be one of the earliest examples of Gown helping Town, becoming a great benefactor of the City, Corpus, Brasenose and Magdalen; he also built the Corn Market and in 1530 gave money for the upkeep of the poor eastern approach road to Oxford in St Clements Street. Named in c1948. (See Cornmarket Street)
Clays Close	After a local field on Boults Farm, spelled Great and Little Clay Close in c1840.

Clear Water Place	Waterways development. Named in 2005.
Cleaver Square	Blackbird Leys. Unknown origin. Named in 1997.
Clematis Place	After the plant, in a series of roads named alphabetically after wild flowers. See also **Blackbird Leys Road**. Street named in 1961.
Cleveland Drive	After the suggestion of the estate developers or owners. Street named in 1930.
Clifford Place	After Walter Clifford, who lived at Godstow and was a benefactor of the nearby Godstow nunnery. He was married to Margaret and father of Fair Rosamund, mistress of Henry II. Street named in 1939. See **Rosamund Road.**
Clinton Close	After Geoffrey Clinton, once overlord of Iffley in the 12th century. Street officially named in May 1949.
Clive Road	After Robert Clive (1725-74) "Clive of India" who served with distinction in many campaigns between 1748 and 1766, when he returned to England in poor health. He was rancorously attacked by politicians, went through a parliamentary enquiry in 1772-3, became a victim of opium and committed suicide in 1774. (DNB) All **Florence Park** streets are named after British Generals who served in India. Street named in 1930.
Clover Place	After the plant, in a series of roads named alphabetically after wild flowers. See also **Blackbird Leys Road**. Street named in 1961.
Cobden Crescent	After Richard Cobden (1804-65), one of the outstanding Liberal politicians of his day, possibly with a connection to the Oxford Building and Investment Company, which laid out the street and was responsible for much of the development of Grandpont. Named in c1886.
Cold Arbour	Meaning 'shelter from the cold', a place to rest after a long journey. First a hamlet at the junction of **Abingdon Road** and **Weirs Lane** in the early 1800s. Mentioned in 1822-3 and c1840.
Colemans Hill	Off London Road, behind Toot Hill Butts, Headington, a City development, named in the late 1970s.
Coleridge Close	After William Hart Coleridge, vicar of Cowley in 1815 and later Bishop of Barbados and Warden of St Augustine's College, Canterbury. Street named in March 1939.
College Lane	Littlemore. After Merton College which owned land here in 1819.
Collins Street	Possibly after William Collins, Fellow of Magdalen 1741-44, but more likely after Anthony Collins, who augmented the Dawson Charity for the Poor and was a benefactor of St Clements church in 1585. Street named in c1908.
Collinwood Close	After R.G. Collinwood, (1889-1942) Fellow of Pembroke, philosopher and Wayneflete Professor of Metaphysics. **Wayneflete Road** is nearby. Street named in April 1935.
Collinwood Road	See Collinwood Close. Street named in April 1935.
Colterne Close	Means 'colt's corner', named after a local field spelt Colterne Fielde in 1605, Colthorne field in 1710 and Little and Great Colton Hills in c1840. Street named on 1st October 1938.
Coltsfoot Square	Blackbird Leys. Named in 1993, continuing the plant theme on the estate.
Columbine Gardens	Named after the flower, continuing the meadow flower theme chosen for Blackbird Leys. Named in about 1991.
Colwell Drive	After James Colwell who was a shepherd living in Sandhills in the 1861 census. Named in 1994.

Combe Road	After Thomas Combe, superintendent at the Clarendon Press 1838-72. At his own expense built St Barnabas Church and St Luke's Chapel at the Radcliffe Infirmary. A patron of the Pre-Raphaelites, he gave his paintings to the Ashmolean; his widow, Martha, gave Holman Hunt's "The Light of the World" to Keble College. He ran classes for poor boys in Jericho and was a partner in the Bible Press; he bought the derelict mill at Wolvercote, rebuilt most of it and lived at the Mill House. The mill made paper for Bibles and the Oxford University Press became the first known user of Wolvercote paper. Combe was also a benefactor of Wolvercote and was known as "The Patriarch". Street officially re-named in April 1959, formerly Ferry Road after nearby canal ferry and first named in 1890-1.
Comfrey Road	In the plant and shrub series of Blackbird Leys roads. Street named in 1964.
Compass Close	Means 'compost field' after a Cowley field spelled Compass Field in 1773 and Compass in 1841. Street officially named in February 1966 and completed in 1967.
Complin Close	After a field name recorded on an estate map of St John's College. Named in c2000.
Coniston Avenue	After Coniston water in the Lake District. Street named in June 1931. The area is still known locally as The Lake District. See Ambleside Drive
Coolidge Close	After William Augustus Brevoort Coolidge, American Fellow of Magdalen 1875-1926, an authority on the Alps who established a reputation in Switzerland and among Everest mountaineers. Street officially named in 1966 but buildings completed in 1967.
Cooper Place	After an old local family and suggested by the Friends of Headington Quarry. Street officially named in 1965; development completed in 1967.
Cope Close	After the 17th century local Cope family and Sir Anthony Cope, Oxfordshire MP 1614-20. Street named in 1940, formerly Elms Rise.
Coppock Close	After James Coppock who held Methodist meetings at his house in c1820. The Coppock family has been prominent in the Quarry for several centuries – the 1891 census lists seventeen families by that name. Most were in the quarrying and brick industries (Bloxham and Shatford). Street named in 1960 at the suggestion of the Friends of the Quarry.
Copse Lane	After local small wood or spinney. In this area of open ground between Old and New Marston groups of Romany gypsies set up camp each year and would clear the copse and make bean sticks and pegs. Street named in 1935 and officially on 21st October 1938.
Cordrey Green	After Edward Cordrey, well known in the village as the author of 'Bygone Days at Iffley' and who gave the proceeds from its sales to St Mary's Church. Named 30th April 1979.
Coriander Way	Blackbird Leys. Named in 1993, continuing the plant theme on the estate.
Cornmarket Street	Named after the building erected for a corn market in 1536 on the east side of the street, ruined in 1644 in the Civil War so the lead of its roof could be melted down for bullets. (see **Claymond Road**) Originally The Great Streate and Northgate Street in 1445, 1482, 1661-66 and until the gatehouse was demolished in 1781. Many changes have occurred from 1920-73. In 1840 it was still written as Corn Market Street. (Hunt's

Cornmarket in about 1913 or 1914

Cornmarket Street before pedestrianisation, taken in May 1961. Courtesy of Newsquest, Oxford Mail and Times.

Directory) Rubber bricks were used to surface the road so as to reduce noise for a few years until 1955, when they were removed as they were dangerously slippery in wet weather. Woolworths, the first chain store here, opened in 1956-7. Pedestrianised in 1973. Often locally referred to as Cornmarket, the 'street' suffix was added later – University members referred to it as 'The Corn'. See *Street Names in the Early Days*.

Cornwallis Close   Street named in 1961 See **Cornwallis Road.**

Cornwallis Road   In the India group of road names on the Florence Park Estate, After Charles Cornwallis (1738-1805), first Marquis and second Earl Cornwallis, a General in the Seven Years War and also in the American War of Independence, later Governor General of India in 1797. Street named in 1935. See **Outram, Campbell and Lytton** Roads.

Corunna Crescent   Horspath Road Estate, off Kennedy Close. Named after the Corunna Campaign of the Peninsula War, in which the Oxford and Bucks Light Infantry were much involved. See **Kennedy Close** and **Craufurd Road**. Named 17th December 1956.

Cosin Close   On the site of Cowley Road Hospital, the former Workhouse built by order of the Oxford Poor Law Board in 1861 to house 330 inmates. It became a Public Assistance Institution in 1929. During both World Wars it was used as a hospital. With the introduction of the National Health Service it came under management of the United Oxford Hospitals. However, old traditions died hard and elderly patients there were still kept in bed all day when their health deteriorated. It was not until the arrival of Dr Lionel Cosin (1910-1994), who insisted that bedridden patients get up, that the length of time spent in hospital was reduced, from a year down to 35 days. Some were moved to Hurdis House, built in 1958, a half way house, run by the National Corporation for the Care of Old People. Dr Cosin, a surgeon, geriatrician, and pioneer of geriatric medicine was Clinical Director at the United Oxford Hospitals from 1950 to 1976 (Encyclopaedia of Oxford). Road named February 1990.

Costar Close   Littlemore. After Richard Costar, d1840, a major Oxford coach proprietor with stables in Littlemore, occupied land nearby recorded in the Inclosure Award of 1819.

Cotswold Crescent   After the Cotswold Hills. Suggested by the estate developers, A C Carter Ltd.

Cottesmore Road   After John Cottesmore, local landowner in c1418-35. Street named in November 1946 after a suggestion of the Steward of Lincoln College, as it is a name associated with college property in Iffley.

Cotton Grass Road   In the plant and shrub series of Blackbird Leys road names. Named in 1997.

Court Farm Road   After Court Place Farm, one of three local manor houses where courts were held, pulled down in c1895. See also **Court Place Gardens**, Iffley. Court Place was the largest estate in the Manor of Iffley (1899 Ordnance Survey). It had eleven acres of land and a small area of farmland. Sir Alan Gardiner, who lived in Court Place from 1947 to 1963 wrote " It was hardly an exaggeration when a man of taste and discernment recently said that ours was the finest house in Oxford". It is now G II listed. Street named in November 1946.

Courtland Road   After suggestion of the developers/owners. Street built by Benfield and Loxley, named in 1936. In 1931 there was an attempt by the Street Names Sub-Committee to change the name to avoid confusion with Portland Road, Summertown, but residents were not in favour.

Coverley Road   Street named in October 1938. Cowley is a modern corruption of Culverley or Cuvely; Covele is on an early charter of c1180 - although White says that it is named after Sir Roger de Coverley, "the reputed inventor of the well-known dance"

Cowley Place   Off The Plain. See also Cowley Road. Cowley Street once ran from Christ Church to Milham Bridge and a remnant of the Milham Ford end of Cowley Street is now Cowley Place; on a map dated 1899.

Cowley Road   After the village of Cowley, which grew around Cowley church and Beauchamp Lane. Means 'Cufa's wood' or clearing; 'Ley' means a clear tract lying between woodland and a river. Spelled Couelea in 1004, Parva Couele in 1247 and Cohfleye in c1290 with later variant spellings. The street from **Magdalen Bridge** to St Bartholomew's Chapel was originally St Bartholomew's Way in 1605, also part known as Berrye Lane. Cowley Road was always a major route into Oxford, crossing a causeway once called Londonwyke Street.

Cox's Ground After a field name recorded on an estate map of St John's College. Named in c2000

Cranesbill Way In the plant and shrub series of Blackbird Leys road names. Named in 1997.

Cranham Street After the St John's College living at Cranham, Glos; bought in 1827 for £4,500. (VCH) Western end spelled Lower Cranham Street in c1870.

Cranham Terrace See Cranham Street. Street named in c1870.

Cranley Road After Thomas Cranley, Warden of New College 1389-96. Street named in July 1947. See Malford Road. The land here was bought from New College and Magdalen College. Roads are named after prominent members of those colleges.

Cranmer Road After Thomas Cranmer (1489-1556), the martyr burnt at the stake, on 21st March 1556, in **Broad Street** then outside the city walls. He was Bishop of Rochester and London and a supporter of Henry VIII and refused to recognise papal jurisdiction. Another martyr is remembered in **Ridley Road** nearby. Street named in 1934.

Craufurd Road Horspath Road Estate. After Major-General Robert Craufurd (1764-1812), Commander of the Light Division, which included, with the 95th Regiment, the Oxford and Bucks Light Infantry, whose barracks were at Cowley. He fought in the Corunna Campaign of 1808-09, and was killed later in the Peninsula War. He was carried, mortally wounded, off the battlefield by his ADC, Colonel James Shaw-Kennedy. See **Kennedy Close** and **Corunna Crescent**. He was 'a strict disciplinarian, known to his men as 'Black Bob'. Named on 17th December 1956.

Crescent Close Street officially named in 1967, completed in 1968. See **Crescent Road.**

The Crescent Off Rutherway. Named for its road shape.

Crescent Road After the shape of the road. Street named in 1930, and already known as this when taken over by the City in 1929.

Cress Hill Place After the old name for the upper part of Bayswater Hill, meaning a 'hill where cress is grown'. Spelt Karshille in c1225. Street named in 1969, formerly The Butts. See **Bayswater Road.**

Crick Road After the St John's College living Crick (or Creek), Northants. Its rectory was bought in 1613 by William Craven from Oliver Cromwell in order to give it to the College. Street built in 1871-8 and named in c1874.

Cricket Road After the Magdalen Club whose cricket ground was here. Street named in 1898 and shown on a map of 1889. (Marriott)

Cripley Place Street named in 1890-1. See **Cripley Road.**

Cripley Road First part means 'narrow passage, burrow or drain'. Second part means 'island'. Derivation is therefore obscure – certainly the area lies on an island. Spelt Crepeleit in 1135-9, Crepuleyt in 1423, and Cripleys in 1555. Street begun by John Dover, a well known Oxford builder in 1878, named in c1881.

The Croft	After the house of that name in Old Headington. Road named in 1930.
Croft Close	See also **Croft Road**. There was a recommendation from the Highways and Traffic Committee to Council in December 1982 to name this small close, off Croft Road, after Percy Scholes, who compiled the popular 'Everyone's Musical Encyclopaedia' in the 1920s and 30s and 'The Oxford Companion to Music' in 1938. He was made Honorary Professor of Music in 1943. The recommendation was amended in December 1982 to Croft Close and there is no memorial to Scholes, who lived at 41 Davenant Road (now demolished).
Croft Road	In the musicians' group, Marston, after William Croft (c1675-1727) Professor of Music at Oxford. Street named in July1935.
Cromwell Close	After Oliver Cromwell (1599-1658). During the siege of Oxford during the Civil War Marston was held by the Parliamentarians under Cromwell. The treaty was agreed after the siege and signed in the Manor House, Ponds Lane, Marston, owned by Unton Croke, Marston's principal inhabitant. It is said that Cromwell observed the movements of the Royalist troops in Oxford from the church tower. The headquarters of Lord Fairfax, Commander of the Parliamentarian Army were at Marston in 1645. Named in the 1950s.

Cromwell with his troops.

Cromwell Street   Possibly after Oliver Cromwell, although with no clear connection. Street named in c1870.

Cross Street   Probably after the shape of the street as it crosses **Wingfield Road** and **Princes Street,** named in c1870.

Crotch Crescent   In the musicians' group, Marston; after Dr William Crotch (1775-1848) University Professor of Music 1797-1847 and organist at Christ Church 1790-c1807. Regarded as 'the highest musical authority of the age'. Street named in 1937. See text.

Crowberry Road   In the shrub group, Blackbird Leys. Street named in 1964.

Crowell Road   After William Crowell who owned local property in the 15th century, recorded on a Lincoln College conveyance of 1412. Formerly Cruel Lane, supposedly after a local Civil War skirmish but unsubstantiated. Spelled Cwrle Lane in 1512, a field spelt Crowell Close in the early 16th century and Cruel Lane from 1930 until 1939 when changed as a result of a petition from residents to change to one 'of a less gruesome character'. The name may have derived from an old well at the nearby St Bartholomew's Hospital.

Crown Street   After the Crown Stores here, founded in c1876. The old ironmongers were still operating in the street in 1977. Street named in c1878.

Cuckoo Lane   Unknown, but possibly so-named as this was once a quiet rural lane. Once an important route into Oxford but a minor one since 1804. The original lane, from Pullen's Lane to Old High Street is thought to be at least a thousand years old. It is shown on a Corpus Christi map of 1605. It was once called Oxforde Waye, before the days of Headington Road. Anthony Wood wrote about a walk he made along the lane in 1682. A signpost or marker stone erected here in May 2003 is a memorial (by Ruth Harris of Brackley, to her parents - researched by Stephanie Jenkins) Street named in December 1930.

Cuddesdon Way   'The way of the people of Cuddesdon'. Spelt Kudisham Weye and Codenneshammeweye both in c1200. Street officially named in 1960 but completed in 1963.

Cumberland Road   Unknown

Cumberlege Close   After the Revd H.A. Cumberlege, Vicar of Marston between 1899–1904 . There was no vicarage during his time and he walked every day across the fields via Marston Ferry, then said to be called King's Ferry, to visit his parishioners. His daughter recalled being driven over Magdalen Bridge and along country lanes to church in Marston, where the children were taken out before the sermon for biscuits at Miss Gordon's house (see Gordon Close). Named in the 1960s

Cummings Close   Headington Quarry. Mr Cummings was, prior to 1807, the fiddler with the Quarry Morris Men. Recommended by Highways and Traffic Committee 27th January 1983.

Cumnor Rise Road   After the eastern slope of Cumnor Hill. Cumnor means 'Cuma's slope'. Spelled Colmonora in 688, Cumanora in 931 and Comenore in 1086.

Cunliffe Close   After Mrs Cunliffe who in 1929 founded and was Headmistress of Greycotes School. She lived in a large house on the site and added buildings for the school. The school is now relocated nearby to Bardwell Road and is part of Oxford High School. Street named in 1971.

Cutteslowe Close

Cutteslowe was once a hamlet, now an estate. Means 'Cupen's burial ground'. The hamlet was destroyed in the 13th century. Some traces and a mound can still be seen near the Cherwell. Spelt Cuceslaye in 1086 and Cudeslawe in 1122. As recently as 1901 the electoral register (which records only two men as voters) spells it Cutslow; newcomers and strangers often still pronounce the name without the 'e'.

Cyprus Terrace

Possibly after an alternative spelling of the coniferous tree more usually spelled cypress. The houses were built in 1898 but the terrace was not named officially until the 1970s.

D

The Dale	Not known.
Dale Close	There was an old Dale Street in St Ebbe's, demolished for the Westgate Centre redevelopment. Named in December 1979.
Danvers Road	Probably after Sir Robert Danvers, Oxon MP in the 15th century, who was from a local family. The family name is associated with the Iffley property of Lincoln College, which forms part of the land on which this estate is built. Street named in November 1946.
Darlington Link	University Science Area. Named after Cyril Dean Darlington (1903-81), elected Sherardian Professor of Botany at Magdalen College in 1953, Keeper of the Botanic Garden and involved in the acquisition of the Nuneham Courtenay Arboretum. He was heavily involved in the development of teaching of genetics at the University and the establishment of the School of Human Sciences.
Dashwood Road	After High Steward of the University, Sir Henry Dashwood (1816-89) of Kirtlington Park, a magistrate in 1843, High Sheriff in 1867 and Lord Lieutenant in 1883. Street named in c1908.
Daubeny Road	After Sir Charles Daubeny (1795 - 1867), chemist and botanist, pioneer of Natural Science, Professor of Botany at the University from 1834 and of Rural Economy from 1840. He established the first laboratory in Oxford in 1848 and wrote on atomic theory and on volcanoes. He lavished care and money on the physic garden, later the Botanic Garden and lived nearby. He had a collection of monkeys in a cage in the Danby gateway – once they escaped, as far as Iffley Road, after their cage was forced open by "mad" Harry Wilkins of Merton, who had gained access into the locked gardens. Dr Daubeny was so upset he later disposed of his menagerie. Street named in c1908.

Sir Charles Daubeny in 1860

Davenant Road

After Oxford born poet and dramatist Sir William d'Avenant (1606-68), a godson of Shakespeare and Poet Laureate from 1638. His arms are in stained glass in the Old Library of the Town Hall, where there are also other arms relating to literature and the City of Oxford. Street named in c1930.

David Nicholls Close

After Rev Dr David Nicholls, vicar of St Mary's & St Nicholas', Littlemore, Governor of Lawn Upton School. The name recommended by Littlemore Parish Council and agreed in 1996.

Davenant Road in winter.

David Nicholls Close

David Walter Close

After David Walter (1609-79) who lived at Godstow and owned land on which the Templar Road estate is now built. He was a Royalist and High Sheriff of Oxford in 1644 who, during the Civil War, burned down his house in Godstow to prevent the Parliamentarian forces from using it as shelter. His family tomb is in St Peter's Church, Wolvercote where there is also his marble bust on the north wall. Street officially named in 1960.

Dawson Place	Jericho. Possibly after a local builder or the Rev Ambrose Dawson, (1787-1848). Shown on a map of 1899.
Dawson Street	After Thomas Dawson who left land here in 1521 for the benefit of St Clement's church and the local poor. Street named in 1901, formerly Black Horse Yard named in 1890-1 after the local pub, which later became a hotel.
Deadmans Walk	At the edge of playing fields to the south of Merton and Corpus Christi Colleges, once the route of Jewish funeral processions from the Jewry in and around St Aldate's and Carfax, to their burial grounds, then outside the city walls, on the site of the present Botanic Garden.
Deer Walk	Blackbird Leys. Named in 1993, presumably to fit in with, loosely, the flora and fauna theme in the area.
Delbush Avenue	A composite name combining Dell, the former owner of at least some of the the land sold in 1935 to Frank Bursill, the developer of the Sandhill Estate, and Bush, the maiden name of Selina Mary, later Mrs Bursill (d1971) The name was taken by Mr Bursill for his company, The Bush Building Co, and still exists in Bush House, at the entrance to the estate. (see Burdell Avenue, Bursill Close) The building was intended to be a pub, and has extensive cellars, but was never used as such, although for some years housed a dairy and the estate corner shop. The name may originally have been proposed as Dellbush. Named in about 1935. See Bursill Close.
Demesne Furze	After a Barton field name, known in 1804. Named in 1991, on the Heron Homes development near the Churchill Hospital. The name was chosen despite opposition from some Councillors who felt that the name would not be pronounced correctly as 'Demain' but as 'Dem-ez-nee'. (See *Perils of Pronunciation*)
Dene Road	After a local field name spelt Bulandene, later Bullingdon Green. Street named in 1930. See **Bulan Road and Bullingdon Road.**
Denmark Street	Named in reference to the Prussian War in 1862 in Schleswig Holstein, which was under Danish Rule from 1460-1864. Street named in c1870
Dents Close	After the maiden name of Doreen, married to Oliver Haynes, second son of Charles Haynes (see Horseman Close)
Derwent Avenue	After Derwent Water in the Lake District. Street named in June 1931. The area is still known locally as The Lake District. See Ambleside Drive
Desborough Crescent	After the Earl of Desborough, for many years Chairman of the Thames Conservancy. Street named in November 1946.
Devereux Place	After Robert Devereux, High Steward of Oxford 1596-1601. Street named in c1948
Diamond Place	Ruth Fasnacht, the local historian, said that Diamond Street (now Mayfield Road) was 'the only road in Summertown in 1832 which has a generally accepted name and they had to go and change it'. The name was therefore revived for the road into the car park, off Banbury Road. Diamond House was the only building between Banbury Road toll house and St Giles Church from c1760-1820. Diamond House was originally Diamond Hall, a notorious hideout for highwaymen. Street named officially in 1971.
Divinity Road	Possibly after Divinity Walk, which ran from Cheney Lane to Shotover. Road named in 1894, formerly a track also called Divinity Walk, in 1853 spelled

Divinity Footway. Divinity was an important part of the curriculum at Oxford University from the beginning and the first major building erected in Oxford was the 15thC Divinity School. Compulsory divinity ('divvers') was not abolished at Oxford until 1931. It comprised a written paper and a viva (oral exam). However, by the end of the 1890s it had become a 'blasphemous farce' (Brock and Curthoys) with as many as 80 vivas being conducted in one day. It is assumed that Divinity Lane, as it was originally, was part of a walk taken by members of the University from Cowley to Headington.

Dodgson Road
After Charles Lutwidge Dodgson (1832-98) who wrote, under his pseudonym Lewis Carroll, *Alice in Wonderland* (1865), *Alice through the Looking Glass* (1871) and the *Hunting of the Snark* (1872). He wrote these in Oxford when a lecturer in Mathematics at Christ Church. Street named in 1938. See **Gaisford Road** and **Liddell Road**

Don Bosco Close
After the founder in 1859 of the Salesian Order, Don Bosco (1815-88). He promoted industrial schools and apprenticeships "for secular vocations in a religious background" and in later life fostered missionary work. Beatified in 1929 and canonised St Bosco in 1934; Saint's day 31st January. (Cross, 1974)

Donnington Bridge Rd
After local land owned by the hospital at Donnington, Berks, built by Richard Abberbury of Iffley. The hospital land was bought in 1393. The road crossed this land and was named when the new bridge was built over the Thames, replacing an old footbridge, in January 1961, with effect from August 1961. The road was formerly Donnington Lane, named in 1915-6.

Don Stuart Place
After a founder member of the Cherwell Family Housing Association, an exception to the rule that roads should not be named after people during their lifetimes. See *Celebrating Current Celebrities*. Named in 1986.

Dora Carr Close
After Councillor, (Lord Mayor in 1977) Mrs Dora Minnie Carr (1905-91). She was Labour member for Marston and Headington for 21 years between 1958-79 and served for four years for Marston on the County Council. A graduate of St Hugh's College, she trained at the London School of Economics as a social worker. She was an early member of the campaign for Nuclear Disarmament. During WW2 she helped Jewish refugees from Germany and provided temporary homes for child refugees from Franco's Spain. Named in June 1992.

Dorchester Close
Behind Kimberley House, Old Road, Headington. Named in 1994 for its proximity to the Dorchester to Alchester Roman road.

Doris Field Close
Named after a former resident of Jack Straw's Lane who donated land off the Lane to the Jack Straw's Lane Association and Oxford Preservation Trust. Name agreed on 7th January 1993.

Dorothy Hodgkin Road
A private road in the University Science Area. Named for the Nobel Prizewinner in Chemistry, Dorothy Mary Hodgkin, née Crowfoot 1910-1994. She read chemistry at Somerville College from 1928 and became a tutor in Natural Sciences there in 1936. In 1937 she married Thomas Hodgkin (d 1982) and was the first serving Fellow to have a baby. She was elected to the FRS in 1947 and was awarded the Order of Merit in 1965, the first woman to be so honoured since Florence Nightingale. She has had a postage stamp printed in her honour and gained many medals and

honorary degrees. Her publications were on her main work on the X-ray crystallographic analysis of the structure of molecules.

Douglas Downes Close Despite objections from residents ("a bit of a mouthful" and "not exactly redolent of downland") and from the Post office (too easily confused with Downside) the road was named after a graduate of Corpus Christi College, He returned to Oxford from a curacy in Essex and a spell in India, to the chaplancies respectively of University and Worcester colleges. He had a longstanding interest in vagrancy, sometimes inviting tramps he had met in the street for meals in his college rooms. He worked under the Rev John Stansfeld (see Stansfeld Place) at St Ebbe's Church. Named in February 2002.

Dovehouse Close Church Farm Estate, Wolvercote. After a local field spelled the same in 1834, officially named in 1961. See *Apostrophes and Spaces.*

Downside End After a Highways Committee suggestion to distinguish it from Downside Road. Officially named in March 1972 or 73. See Downside Road.

Downside Road Means 'hillside', in reference to Shotover. Named in about 1935.

Doyley Road Possibly after Thomas D'Oylie or D'Oyley (1548-1603) MA Oxford, Magdalen College, a friend of Francis Bacon, author of a Spanish-English dictionary, and a physician. (DNB)

Dragon Lane A short private lane which runs from the Dragon School, Bardwell Road, to Norham Road - the school was founded in 1877, and moved here in 1895. Formerly Lynam's Lane, after the first Headmaster – the name was invented by the boys and became official in 1921. The Junior School is now called Lynams and is in Woodstock Road.

Drove Acre Road After a local large field spelt Drove Acre before 1853, meaning 'droveway', or a route for driven cattle, in this case to one of the larger Cowley meadows. Street named in October 1932.

Druce Way After Dr George Claridge Druce FRS, (1850-1932), Mayor of Oxford 1900-01, Alderman in 1920, councillor and JP. He was the outstanding field botanist of his day, good natured, witty, a traveller, benefactor of the University - a self made man having started out as a chemist's assistant aged 15 who taught himself out of hours. He later set up in business in Oxford in 1879 as a pharmacist, having passed with honours the qualifying exams, without tuition. He had already started a herbarium in 1873 and had produced a series of *Flora of the Counties of the Thames Valley*; his *Flora of Oxfordshire* established his reputation   His arms are displayed in the Lord Mayor's Parlour. Street named in 1967.

Dudgeon Drive After William Dudgeon, a former parish clerk of Littlemore.

Dudley Court Darby and Son, solicitors, had asked the City Council in February 1972 if the flats could be called St George's Court as they had been prevented by covenant from naming it St John's Court after the church once on the site. It was thought more appropriate to commemorate a local Summertown name and Ruth Fasnacht, local historian and author of 'How Summertown Started' suggested the court should be named after Crews Dudley, a developer of Summertown and an Oxford solicitor involved in the speculative development of Summertown in the 1820s. He also served on the council. His son, John Crews Dudley, was Mayor of Oxford in 1852. Named c1972.

Dudley Gardens   Presumably after Crews Dudley, a developer much involved in St Clement's as well as Summertown in the 1820s. See **Middle Way.**

Duke Street   After the peerage. **Earl Street** is nearby. Street named in 1878.

Dunnock Way   In the bird names series in Blackbird Leys. Named in 1993, extended in 1997.

Dunstan Road   After St Dunstan (c924-88), son of a West Saxon nobleman, English ecclesiastical statesman, Archbishop of Canterbury, chief adviser to King Ethelred. Formerly Cemetery Road, Headington, re-named in 1934 to perpetuate the association with the Saxon settlement. See Ethelred Court.

Dynham Place   The Rede family held the bailiwick of Shotover until 1547 when it was sold by Leonard Rede to Thomas Dynham, his son-in-law. Dynham's son in turn sold it, or 'the office of Steward of Shotover and Stowood' as it was then called, to Henry Norreys in 1588. Street named in 1955 .

E

Earl Street	After the peerage. Named in c1878. See **Duke Street**
East Avenue	Denotes the eastern boundary of St Clement's parish and is lined by trees, named in c1874
East Street	When Osney was laid out, in simple grid pattern, **West, East, North and South Streets** were appropriately named, in about 1850.
Eastchurch	The eastern extension of **Church Way**, Iffley. Named in 1936
Eastern Avenue	After the avenue east of **Henley Avenue.**
East Field Close	Horspath Driftway, although with Headington postal addresses. Named in March 1998, probably after a local field name.
Eden Drive	After the River Eden in the Lake District, named in 1934 and continued into the North Way estate when officially named in July 1949. The area is still known locally as The Lake District. See **Ambleside Drive, Bowness, Coniston and Derwent Avenues**
Edgecombe Road	After Sir James Edgecombe, Mayor of Oxford 1484-5, 1492 and 1497. The family name is associated with land in Headington. Named in 1945.
Edgeway Road	After an old way along the edge of the River Cherwell. Formerly Hedgeway Road, on a map of 1897, renamed in December 1938. Formerly in Headington UDC, no records were passed on to the City Council, but an old deed indicates that it might once have been Marlborough Road.
Edith Road	Possibly after Sister Edith, died 1898, assistant superior to the Sisterhood of St Thomas across the Thames. Street named in 1890-1.
Edmund Road	After Edmund of Abingdon whose sacred St Edmund Well was placed near Milham Ford in Cowley Parish. Street named in 1930
Edmund Halley Road	Oxford Science Park. After the astronomer (1656-1742), educated at The Queens College, he laid the foundations of modern astronomy. Savilian Professor of Geometry at the University, Astronomer Royal in 1721. He was electd to the Royal Society at the age of 22. He predicted the return in 1758 of the comet of 1531, 1607 and 1682 that now bears his name. His home still stands in New College Lane and the observatory on its roof was said to be "very convenient and useful to the University".
Edward Abraham Rd.	Science Area, South Parks Road. After Dr Sir Edward Penley Abraham CBE FRS (1913-99). Knighted in 1980, an English biochemist involved in the development of penicillin, on Florey's research team which worked on medical applications. He was specifically concerned with its purification process and the determination of its chemical structure. Funds created by these developments amounted to £30m. His work was recognised when he was appointed as one of the first three "Penicillin Research Fellows" at Lincoln College where he remained a Fellow until his retirement. The research building in South Parks road is also named after him.
Egerton Road	After John Egerton, (1622-1686) second Earl of Bridgwater, High Steward of the City of Oxford in 1663. Street named in July 1935. See **Annesley Road.**
Egrove Close	From Egrove Farmhouse, the old farm which was incorporated into Templeton College and whose lands included the fields on which the Rivermead Hospital was built. Named in 2004.

Elder Way   In the tree and shrub series in Blackbird Leys. Named in 1997.

Eleanor Close   After Queen Eleanor of Aquitaine (c1122-1201) Queen of Henry II. She helped to win the throne and was said to be a charming and lively queen, but was imprisoned by the King for inciting their sons against him. Street officially named in March 1973.

Electric Avenue   Osney Mead. Named, prosaically, after the electricity substation here; informally shown for many years as a painted sign rather than the more usual cast metal plates erected by the Council.

Elizabeth Jennings Way   After the well known Oxford author and poet (1926-2001) educated at the High School for Girls and St Anne's College. She won many awards for her poetry. Named in 2003.

Elizabeth Place   Originally Redland Road (1949) but re-named at the suggestion of the Northway Area Jubilee committee to celebrate the Silver Jubilee of Queen Elizabeth II in May 1978. (See *Honouring Queens*)

Ellesmere Road   After the first Earl of Ellesmere (1800-57) statesman and poet, (DNB) a High Steward of Oxford City. Street named in July 1935. See **Annesley Road**. Many Rose Hill roads are named after High Stewards.

Elms Drive   After the elm trees in the road, now lost to Dutch elm disease

Elms Road   After local trees. Three parallel streets nearby have similar origins. Named in 1912-13.

Elmthorpe Road   Said to be named after local elms. There were once many elms in the area, now all lost to disease. Named in 1909.

Elm Tree Close   Littlemore. A large elm tree once stood nearby.

Elsfield Road   Marston. After the village where the road originally led, meaning 'Elesa's field' spelt Esefelde in 1086, Elshfyld in 1232, Elsfield in 1335, and Eldsfield in 1797. Street named in 1955.

Elsfield Way   Formerly part of North Way. In 1955 this stretch of the A40 between the Banbury Road roundabout and the Cherwell bridge was renamed to avoid confusion.

Elton Close	Sandhills Primary School site. After Miss E Elton, one of the first on the teaching staff of the school when it opened in 1940, along with Miss Bioletti and Miss Candy. See Terrett Avenue. Named 31st January 2002.
Emperor Gardens	Blackbird Leys. Named in 1997.
Erica Close	In the shrub group of Blackbird Leys. Named in 1964.
Essex Street	After the county. **Hereford Street** runs parallel and has a similar origin. Street named on 22nd January 1889.
Ethelred Court	A Saxon name, used here to commemorate the traditional association of the Headington area with King Ethelred's (965-1016) palace. He also had a palace at Islip, where Edward the Confessor was born, and a hunting lodge in the area. Street named in July 1967.
Everard Close	Unknown. Street named in 1955
Ewert Place	After Professor Alfred Ewert (1891-1969), Professor of the Romance languages, former Chairman of the Oxford Delegacy for Local Examinations. The name was suggested by the Delegacy, which was once on this site, and officially adopted in 1970 after his death. *See picture and caption*.

Holding the name plate before installation, left to right: J R Cummings (Delegacy secretary); J Macdonald, Margaret Ewert, (daughter, holding the sign), Professor N Gibbs (Chairman), Elizabeth Ewert (daughter) and J Lankester (University Surveyor); Inset – Professor Ewert. Courtesy of Margaret Ewert.

Ewin Close	Possibly a misspelling of the Ewen family, yeoman farmers in Marston in the 16th century (VCH).
Eyot Place	After the nearby Aston's Eyot, pronounced 'eight', meaning an island in a river. Named in 1984.

F

Faber Close	Minchery Farm development. Unknown origin. Named 15th November 1954.
Fairacres Road	After a house called Fairacres. Street named in 1894.
Fairfax Avenue	After Thomas Fairfax, (1612-71) leader of the Parliamentary army during the Civil War. The name was chosen because of Cowley's association with the Civil War. Fairfax's headquarters were at Marston during the siege in 1646 but moved the following year to Headington. He was anxious that the Royalist army would surrender before the famous seat of learning was destroyed in the fighting. Street named in 1935. See Cromwell Close.
Fairfax Road	After Thomas, Lord Fairfax. See Fairfax Avenue. Nearby is **Rupert Road**, after his opposite number in the Royalist army. Street named in 1935.
Fairlawn End	After Fairlawn House which formerly stood on this site. Officially named in 1966.
Fairlie Road	After suggestion of the developers and owners. Street named in 1937
Fairview	After the local Fairview Inn, with an obvious meaning. Street named in1940.
Falcon Close	In the bird series of Blackbird Leys road names. Named in October 1994.
Fane Road	Possibly after John Fane, died 1924, MP for Oxford for 8 successive Parliaments, or after a Captain Fane, who served on the Bullingdon RDC when these roads were built.
Fanshawe Place.	Horspath Road Estate. After Lt Col (later General) Sir Robert Fanshawe, KCB (1863-1946). A distinguished and much decorated soldier, whose career began in the Boer War of 1899-1902, rising to Lt Col with the 43rd Oxfordshire Light Infantry. He also served in the First World War, becoming KCB in 1917 and appointed CB. He retired to Oxfordshire in 1919, where he became a JP and chaired the Oxfordshire Territorial Association. Named 17th December 1956.

General Sir Robert Fanshawe.

Farm Close	Unknown, but probably after a local farm. Named in 1993.
Farmer Place	After John Farmer (1836-1901) organist at Balliol. Street named in 1939.
Farndon Road	After St John's College living at Farndon, Cheshire, acquired in 1676. Street named in c1878, in evidence by 1886.

Farndon Road in 1997.

Faulkner Street	After a councillor for the south ward in the 1840s and 50s who was active as a radical and a chartist. He wrote political poems and lived at Bishop's Palace. Named in 1983.
Feilden Grove	After Katharine Josephine Dolores Feilden (1864–1954), hospital benefactress who helped to start the Headington Orthopaedic Centre and who built High Wall and Jean Cottage in nearby Pullen's Lane. Officially named in 1972, at the suggestion of the developers.
Fern Hill Road	After a local field spelt Upper Ferne Hill in 1605. Street named in 1931.
Ferry Lane	A free punt ferry once operated nearby, crossing the Thames just above where Donnington Bridge is now. The name was first used as an address at the **Jackdaw Lane** end in 1922
Ferry Lane	New Marston. After the old punt ferry across the Cherwell from Marston to North Oxford. Street named in 1890-1.
Ferry Road,	New Marston. See Ferry Lane. Street named in 1930.
Ferry Hinksey Road	After the punt ferry once operated across the Seacourt Stream in North Hinksey and the south end of the lane, in existence from c1899. The 'ey' suffix means island. In 1821 spelled Hincsy, originally meaning 'Hengest's island'. In its early days it was a footpath, later a lane, then a residential road for the northern part of its length from about 1890. It now links Osney Mead Industrial Estate with the Botley Road.
Ferry Pool Road	After the Ferry Swimming Pool to which it leads. Named in the 1970s.
Fettiplace Road	After the Fettiplace family, who once owned much land locally, and Adam de Fettiplace, Mayor of Oxford 1253-60. Street named in November 1945.
Field Avenue	Named as the main avenue in Blackbird Leys off which the roads are named after field flora and fauna. Street named in 1961.
Fieldfare Road	In the bird series of Blackbird Leys road names. Named in 1997.
Field House Drive	Originally a private road leading to Apsley Paddock, named in 1947, which became part of the estate in 1967 but adopted and named in 1964. When

St Edwards School moved to Apsley Paddock they took the name Field House with them.

Fiennes Road   After William Fiennes, the first Viscount Saye and Sele (1582–1662), of the local family of parliamentarian supporters of Broughton Castle near Banbury, Lord Lieutenant of Oxford in 1642, Privy Councillor, who raised an army to occupy Oxford during the Civil War. His nickname was 'Old Subtlety'. Named in June 1938.

Finch Close   After Letitia Finch who was allocated land near here in the Headington Inclosure Award of 1804. The Finch family lived at the house now known as Ruskin Hall in Old Headington from c1660 to 1863. Named in 1991.

Firs Meadow   Blackbird Leys. Possibly a field name. Named in 1997.

First Turn   The name First Turn was officially recognised by the City Council in 1930. The lower part of the road, nearest the meadow, was known locally as Plough Hill as it was near the pub of that name; also as Whites Hill after a Mr White who lived in the cottage next to First Turn Stores. See *Evolving Names* for how the name arose.

Fisher Row   After Simon le Pecheur who owned property here. Formerly Fishers Row in 1661-6, Fisher Row by 1772 also once known as Weyreham or Wareham Bank. See also **Upper Fisher Row.**

Fisher Row in the 1940s or 50s.

Fitzherbert Close   After a family connection of the Chairman of Donnington Hospital Trustees at the time the street was named in 1969.

Five Mile Drive   Formerly Horsemonger or Horsemanger Lane, later sometimes known as Long Hedge and as Horselow Field Road in 1834. At one time there was no road connecting the Banbury and Woodstock Roads north of St Margaret's Road, except for the very rough Squitchey Lane, until Five Mile Drive. The 'Five Mile Round', or Stingy Drive, was the only exception unless one went beyond the toll gates – and paid the toll. In about 1820 a few senior members of the University collected money to make this a raised walk, suitable for all weathers, starting and ending at St Giles Church, a circular route of approximately five miles. Part of the raised path is still visible between the Wolvercote roundabout and First Turn. See *Evolving Names.*

Flaxfield Road
In the wild flower group in Blackbird Leys. Street named in 1961.

Fletcher Road
Brasenose Driftway. Possibly after Alderman Fletcher (1739-1826), antiquary, bookseller, draper, Freeman of the City, benefactor to the Bodleian Library, three times Mayor of Oxford. Named in January 1978.

Flexney Place
After a local family, from Northmoor and Stanton Harcourt, of landowners and farmers. Ralphe Flaxney was Mayor of Oxford 1551-3, 1562 and 1557. Street named in 1955.

Florence Park Road
After Florence, the sister of the estate builder Cllr F E Moss of N Moss and Sons Ltd, who agreed with the Council Baths and Green Spaces Committee in December 1933 that he would donate the park to the City on condition that it was named after Florence, who had recently died. He wanted a children's corner and that the park would be a place to enjoy flowers rather than to play games. The street was named in October 1933 and the park given to the City on 7 May 1934.

Floyds Row
Between 1812 and 1840 William Floyd owned tenements in this part of St Aldate's. He was probably the son of the cordwainer John Floyd who was one of the City Council's official leather suppliers from 1783-1836.

Folly Bridge
After the two-storey gatehouse built at the old Folly Bridge. Originally Friar Bacon's Study. Roger Bacon (c1214-94) is said to have studied astronomy here. The gatehouse later became uneconomical to maintain and became a folly in the late 17th century. Spelt Folly House and Bridge in 1695. Originally South Bridge in c1225, 1246 and 1699. First recorded as a postal address in 1890-1 The present bridge was built in 1825-7 by Ebenezer Perry. A toll house was built in 1844, and still remains, but by 1855 the bridge was freed from tolls.

Friar Bacon's study, Folly Bridge , in 1829.

Forest Road
After the village of Forest Hill, once named Forest Road. The area was once forested. Earlier spelled Fostel in 1086, Forestel in 1160 and Foresthulle in 1285. Street named in about 1931. (Marriott)

Forget-Me-Not Way   In the plant and shrub series of Blackbird Leys road names. Named in 1998.

Fortnam Close   After a local field. Street named in c1950.

Fox Crescent   Probably after George Fox (1624-91) founder of the Religious Society of Friends, commonly known as the Quakers. Street named in c1924.

Foxglove Close   In the plant and shrub series of Blackbird Leys road names. Named in 1997.

Foxton Close   After a house on the site called Foxton Lodge.

Foxwell Drive   After an old field name spelt Longe Foxwelle in 1605. Street officially named in July 1949.

Franklin Road   Possibly after Jeremy Franklin, Mayor of Oxford in 1728, or Albert H Franklin, resident of the local Headington House in the 1920s, when the street was named.

Frederick Road   Chosen by Messrs Moss and Son Ltd, the estate developers, as it was the first name of a family member of Councillor Moss. Named 3rd April 1933.

Freelands Road   Possibly after a local house called Freelands. Street named in c1924.

Frenchay Road   After the St John's College living at Frenchay, Glos. Named in 1898.

Frewin Court   A narrow lane off Cornmarket, named after Richard Frewin (1681-1761) Doctor of Medicine and Camden Professor of Ancient History, who lived here in the 1760s. The lane leads to the Oxford Union (the University debating society) Formerly Bridewell Lane in the reign of Elizabeth I and previously Bodin's Lane by 1405. The street was possibly built at the end of the 12th century, by the Abbot of Oseney and called Venella Abbatis de Oseneya. Street named in 1890-1. Frewin Hall, with access off New Inn Hall Street, is nearby and was acquired by Brasenose College in 1580.

Friars Entry   After the Carmelite White Friars to whom Edward II gave part of Beaumont Palace built in 1132. The street once led to the palace. Variously recorded as Fryars or Fryers Entry; Hearne, in 1731, called it Friers Entry.

Friars Wharf   After the Black Friars, who had a wharf here in St Ebbe's. The street was made in the mid to late 1840s when the wharf was filled in and houses built over it, later demolished in the redevelopment of St Ebbe's, when the present name was retained. The modern section was officially named in February 1972.

Frideswide Square   Named for St Frideswide, patron saint of Oxford, chosen after a poll of Oxford people. It lies at the junction of Hollybush Row, Hythe Bridge Street, Park End Street and Rewley Road. There are no addresses in the square which is in effect a traffic island with a plethora of traffic lights and signs. (2010) St Frideswide lived in the 8th century. Little is known of her life and the earliest written records date from four centuries later. She was the daughter of a Saxon nobleman who lived in Oxford. It is said that a Mercian king persistently asked her to marry him but she refused and went to hide in woods on the banks for the Thames. This did not deter her suitor who marched on Oxford with an army. He was supposed to have been struck blind before he could find Frideswide, although his sight was later restored. She returned to Oxford and founded a religious house. She was canonised for the many acts of healing she performed in later life. On 19th October each year her life is celebrated in Christ Church Cathedral by the worthies of both town and gown, processing to her tomb during the service. There was a Frideswide Lane in the early 13th century which ran east from St Aldate's to St Frideswide's Priory. It was closed in 1525-6 and became part of Cardinal College, now Christ Church. Named in about 2004.

St Frideswide, patron saint of Oxford; stained glass window in the church of St Thomas the Martyr.

Fry's Hill   Blackbird Leys. Named in 1997.
Furlong Close   After a local field which measured a 'furrow long', spelled Longe Broken Furlonge in 1605 and Broken Furlonge in 1819. Officially named in April 1959.
Fyfield Road   After the St John's College living at Fyfield, Oxon. Street built in c1872-80 and named in c1881. During the plague of 1604 many St John's students were evacuated to Fyfield where they could continue to study in the Great Hall of Fyfield Manor.

G

Gaisford Road	After Thomas Gaisford (1779-1855) Dean of Christ Church in 1831, Regius Professor of Greek, a foremost classical scholar, predecessor to Dean Liddell (See **Liddell Road**) in the 19th century. Two adjoining streets have the same college connection. Street named in 1936.
Galpin Close	On the Initial Laundry site, Leopold Street. After John Galpin (1835-91) Mayor of Oxford in 1873 and 79, developer of land between Randolph Street and Magdalen Road in the 1860s. Named in 1994.
Gardiner Street	After a local family living here from the 1850s and suggested by local residents. Street named in 1959, formerly South Street.
Garford Road	St John's College held the Manor of Garford, Berks, from 1554, bought by Sir Thomas White for £1908 and given to the College in 1557. Street named by 1929.
Garsington Road	After the village, spelled Garshamestred in c1240. Named in c1930.
The Garth	Means 'commons or wastes of pulverised soil', named after a local field. There was a path here, flanked by elm trees, in 1907.
Gathorne Road	After Gathorne G Girdlestone, the surgeon. Formerly Alexandra Road, named in 1927, but renamed to avoid confusion with Alexandra Road, off the Botley Road. A proposal in September 1959 to change to Alice Road, after Alice in Wonderland, was resisted by residents who thought this a childish name. Taunt Road was also suggested, also opposed by residents who mistakenly thought the reference would be to a Labour Party supporter of the time, rather than Henry Taunt, the famous Oxford photographer. See **Henry Taunt Close.** McCoy Road, after another doctor, was also rejected. Road named in 1959. See **Girdlestone Road,** also *Duplicated Names*
Gentian Road	In the flower and herb series of road names in Blackbird Leys. Named in 1961.
George Moore Close	After Rev G Moore (1875-1928), a popular vicar of Cowley. Named in 1974. Many wondered why no road had been named after him already, but the Donnington Oblong Residents Association nearby, noted for its strong views, preferred names associated with flowers, trees and birds, and not people. He was known for some unusually outrageous behaviour and a violent temper, bad language and unorthodox sermons, one of which was based on pub signs. He was nevertheless a hard working, conscientious and dedicated incumbent and served the community devotedly for 53 years.
George Street	Spelled George Lane from at least 1726, after the George Hall and then George Inn, part of which was earlier known as Irishman Street (various spellings) in 1251, 1407 and 1444, because of the abundance of Irish scholars at Oxford, living in the street; later Thames Street in 1661-66. The western end was widened and rebuilt in the 1920s.
George Street Mews	Street named in c1872; same origins as **George Street.** Squires notes that this was once Broken Heyes.
Gerard Place	After Brother Gerard, once Rector of the local Knights Hospitallers Order, given land in the area by Edward II, originally owned by the Knights

Templars. The Preceptory was dissolved and the buildings demolished by Henry VIII Street named in about 1931.

Gibbs Crescent

New Osney. After Councillor Olive Gibbs, former Lord Mayor, a member of Oxfordshire County Council and holder of the Freedom of the City of Oxford, member of an old Oxford family with a close association with the parish of St Thomas. She was born and raised in the area. This private development was named for her during her lifetime, in 1984, at the suggestion of the developers, Cherwell Housing Trust - an unusual accolade to someone still living at the time of the road naming. See *Celebrating Current Celebrities*.

Giles Close

See Giles Road.

Giles Road

Minchery Farm development. Named after a local farmer. Named 15th November 1954.

Gillians Way

After Arthur Gillians, City councillor, d1981, Chairman of the Highways and Traffic Committee, who had worked for City of Oxford Motor Services, whose bus depot is nearby, a former chair of the busmans' branch of the TGWU. The G is pronounced hard, as in Go. Named 16th July 1990.

Gipsy Lane

A favourite haunt for gipsies before being developed for housing, spelled Gipsey Lane in 1832, named in 1930.

Girdlestone Close

Officially named in Feb 1973. See **Girdlestone Road**.

Girdlestone Road

After the renowned surgeon Professor Gathorne G Girdlestone (1881-1950) pioneer of surgery at the nearby Wingfield-Morris Hospital, now the Nuffield Orthopaedic Centre. He is one of few people to have two roads named after him.   Street named in 1953. See also **Gathorne Road** and *Duplicated Names*

Gladstone Road

After William Ernest Gladstone (1809-98) Prime Minister periodically between 1868 and 1894 - a subscriber to Headington Quarry Church in 1848. An undergraduate at Christ Church , he obtained a double first class degree in Classics and Mathematics, and "remained devoted to the University all his life" (Encyclopaedia of Oxford) When a Conservative, in 1847, Gladstone was elected a Burgess, (MP for the University) and, when a Liberal, again in 1853 and 1859. He once said he would like to "kiss every stone in the ancient walls of Oxford". Named at the suggestion of R B McCallum, then Master of Pembroke College, who thought Oxford should honour its famous men and despite a resident's complaint that the choice appeared "politically tinged". (Marriott) The extension to **Elms Road** also took this as a new name.

Glanville Road

Unknown. Street named in c1927.

Glebe Street

After local glebe land that supplemented earnings of St Clements clergy. Street built in c1882 and named in c1886.

Glebelands

After local lands forming part of the Glebe belonging to the clergy living of Cowley. Street named in 1938 despite the developer's preference for the name Merrivale.

Gloucester Green

After Gloucester Hall, a Benedictine house founded nearby in 1283, built on the site of Gloucester College (now Worcester College) connected with Gloucester Abbey. Once a green surrounded by trees in the 16th-18th centuries until 1786 when development removed this rustic charm. Weekly cattle markets were held here between 1601 and 1932. The ground had been levelled to form a square in 1638. In the 17th century it was known as Broken Heys, now part of Walton Street. The City Gaol was built in Gloucester Green in 1789, demolished in 1879 and re-established as the County Gaol at the Castle. The annual Gloucester Fair lasted to 1915. It became a bus station for country buses in 1935. The whole site was redeveloped in 1987 with blocks of flats around a square planted with trees. Markets are still held here. Spelled Gloucester Greene in 1555 and Glocester Greene in 1601.

The cattle market at Gloucester Green in c1900 (Copyright OPA).

Gloucester Lane	A short section of road off Worcester Street (see Gloucester Green)
Gloucester Street	Formerly Pudding Bag Lane, the present street named in c1868. See **Gloucester Green.**
Godfrey Close	After a local brickmaker, as advertised in the 1772 *Jackson's Oxford Journal*. On adjoining land were brickworks in the 18th-20th centuries. Several ponds remain on the land from this use. Named in 2001.
Godstow Road	After Godstow village, named after the Godstow Nunnery (now in ruins) founded in 1133, pulled down in 1539, fortified and then finally burned down in 1645. Meaning – 'place of God', spelled Godstowe in c1150-60, Godestoile in 1427 and Godstowe in 1526. Officially named in July 1930, formerly Williams Lane, High Street and Godstow Road, the latter starting beyond Wolvercote Village Hall and running as far as the toll bridge. Since 1938 the name applies to the stretch from Wolvercote roundabout through Lower Wolvercote, to Godstow.
Golden Road	Presumably after Queen Victoria's jubilee of 1887.
Goodey Close	After a local family, for three generations market gardeners at Long Lane. Named in February 1993.
Goodson Walk	In the musicians group on the Wadham College sports ground development. Richard Goodson (d1718) and his son - also Richard (d1741) - were both Professors of Music and both organists at Christ Church and New College in 1682 and 1718 respectively. Named in June 1979.

Goose Green Close   After the green beside this City Council development in Wolvercote. Name suggested by Councillor Ann Spokes in consultation with local people. The goose became the symbol of Wolvercote when many villagers reared them and grazed them on the common or meadow. Named in June 1991.

Gordon Close   After Rev Richard Gordon, (1894-1977) vicar of Elsfield (where he lived) and Marston from 1849 to 1872. He founded the Church School (now the Church Hall). His daughter Mary Gordon taught at the school – mainly sewing. He continued to support the school until her death in 1918. On her death a local newspaper reported " she kept open house for all, there was a swing and a croquet set for the children in her garden and animals found their way there by instinct". Named in the 1960s.

Gordon Street   After General Charles George Gordon (1833-85) assassinated in Khartoum. Formerly Cross Street in c1874, Strounds Buildings in c1875. Street named in c1886.

Gordon Woodward Way   Gordon Woodward (1918-2002) was Lord Mayor of Oxford in 1980 and City Councillor for 23 years and a Freeman of Oxford. He was a war veteran and survived the sinking of his ship, the Lancastrian, when torpedoed by an Italian warship in the Bay of Biscay in 1940. He escaped down a warp and spent many hours in the water before being picked up, covered in oil, by a cruiser. He was one of a family of nine, living in Jericho. There was not enough room for all in the family's small terraced house and he and his twin brother had to sleep at a neighbour's house. He did not seem to mind and "just accepted it as part of life". He left school at 14 to join City of Oxford Electricity, part of Oxford Corporation, starting as a toolboy, carrying the fitters' tools and ladders on a bicycle. On retirement from the Southern Electricity Board, (as this had become) he devoted time to community work, supported by his wife, Dorothy. The Close is on the site of the hospital, once an isolation hospital – Gordon Woodward had served on the Hospital Committee for many years. Named in 2004.

Lord Mayor Gordon Woodward looks over the shoulders of Archbishop Runcie and Harold Macmillan, Chancellor of the University, as they talk at the Encaenia garden party in 1980. (Courtesy of Newsquest, Oxford Mail and Times).

Gorse Leas	After a local field, meaning 'meadow of gorse'. Named in July 1945.
Goslyn Close	After Oxford MP John Goslyn, in office 1472-8. Street named in 1955.
Gouldland Gardens	After local field spelled Gould Land in 1613. Street named in July 1949.
Grandpont Place	Means 'great bridge', a causeway built with 42 arches over water meadows from Folly Bridge to Hinksey Hill, by Robert d'Oilly in c1085. Spelled Grandpunt in 1180-4, Magno Ponto in 1240-1 and Gramptpond in 1342. The name was applied in the 19th century to the development of New Hinksey. See Abingdon Road.
Grange Road	Minchery Farm Estate. After local farm buildings and Grange converted by John Henry Newman in c1840, demolished in 1951. Named 15th November 1954.
Grants Mews	Unknown. Runs between Rectory Road and Princes Street.
Granville Court	Cheney Lane. At the suggestion of the developers, named in 1973.
The Grates	Uncertain origin, possibly from "greet" or grit, after the fine soil here, or after Thomas Grate who had two adjoining cottages here in 1512. The word Grate was sometimes used for a path protected by posts, such as once existed here, presumably to prevent people on horseback from using it – the origin of the word is as that of a fire grate, the bars preventing the coal from falling out. Once called Church Park; originally a footway, lined with trees and tall hedges now destroyed, from Barns Court to Cowley Church and so named on inclosure award maps. Named July 1935.
Grays Road	After Frank Gray, (1918-38) MP for Oxford in 1922, a popular Liberal politician who was able to draw huge crowds at his meetings. A 1929 article in the Oxford Mail says "Frank Gray was once described as the Peter Pan of politics. He fought four elections, sat in two parliaments and was unseated on petition, all within five years. He was a back-bencher and front-bencher in less than a year". He was also a lawyer, soldier, company director, traveller and explorer, journalist, farmer and landowner. His father Sir Walter Gray, (four times Mayor, knighted in 1903) had led a Conservative revival on the City Council to overturn the Liberal majority, and had become known as "The Father of Oxford Conservatism" Many local streets have MP names - See **Cardwell Crescent, Harcourt Terrace, Stonor Place and Valentia Road.** There is no apostrophe in the road name, indicating perhaps that it commemorates both father and son. Street named in 1930.
Great Clarendon Street	After the nearby University and Clarendon Press, set up in Jericho in 1830. Called 'Great' to distinguish it from **Little Clarendon Street**, which is half its width. Street named in 1890-1. The Clarendon Building was built in c1713 in Broad Street and named after the Earl of Clarendon (1609-1674). The board of Delegates to the Press first met in 1633 although not much printing was done here at that time; the publishing business saw much expansion in the mid 19th century. The Oxford University Press headquarters remain in the Walton Street building although printing work is undertaken elsewhere.
Great Mead	After a local field. Named in 1997.
Grebe Close	In the bird series of Blackbird Leys road names. Named in 1997.
Greenfinch Close	In the bird series of road names in Blackbird Leys. Named in 1993.
Green Hill	Blackbird Leys. Named in March 1993.

Green Place	Uncertain origin – possibly after lush meadow grass here before the street was built.
Green Road	After Headington Quarry village green, now under the Eastern Bypass, nearby. A Roman road was visible across the green until c1880. The Headington roundabout is often called the Green Road roundabout. Street named in c1930.
Green Street	Unknown, possibly after a local person, named in c1886.
Greenridges	Named at the suggestion of the developers, probably after a medieval ridge and furrow field pattern once visible here. Officially named in 1968.
Grenoble Road	Named in honour of the French city, twinned with Oxford in a link formed in 1988, named in a ceremony by the Lord Mayor in May 1989.
Grimbly Place	Harpes Road. Probably after Owen Grimbly who with James Hughes opened business as Grimbly Hughes, the famous firm of high-class grocers, at 56 Cornmarket in 1840. Named in 1997.
Grove Street	Summertown. After a grove in Bates Nursery nearby, probably named in the 1860s.
Grovelands Road	After a local field spelled The Grove in 1805. Named in about 1935.
Grunsell Close	After Grunsell Copse, a corruption of the earlier Grants Hill Copse. Named in 1949.
Guelder Road	After the guelder rose, continuing the plant and shrub theme in Greater Leys. Named in about 1997.
Gurden Place	After an Old Headington family. Named in 1967.
Gurl Close	Barton. Thomas Gurl was a publican at the Fox Inn at Barton, named on the 1881 census. Named in 1985.
Gwyneth Road	Littlemore. After Gwyneth Brocklesby who served, with her husband Ted, on the Parish Council for many years. Named in 1996.

H

Hadow Road

In the musicians' group of roads in Marston, after Sir William Henry Hadow (1859–1937), Doctor of Music at Oxford, composer and music historian, educated at Worcester College, Dean in 1889. His sister Grace (1875-1940) was a pioneer in social work and women's education, Principal of The Society of Home Students (now St Anne's College), and of the Women's and Student Societies 1928-40. She was closely associated with Lady Denman in the foundation of Denman College, at Marcham, owned and run by the WI. Street named in 1938.

Grace Hadow, before 1909.

Haldane Road

In the Blackbird Leys naturalists' group; named after John Burdon Sanderson Haldane FRS (1892-1964), Honorary Fellow of New College, Professor of Genetics and of Biometry, and with many academic honours bestowed on him. Named in 1967 at the suggestion of the Berks, Bucks and Oxon Naturalists Trust.

Halliday Hill

Spelled Hallyday Hill on the Corpus map of 1605, part of Colterne Field. Officially named in July 1949.

The Hamel

Means 'hamlet', or little ham, derived from Old French and a public way between High Street and Osney Abbey, lined with houses mainly inhabited by bookbinders. A nearby bridge was named after them. Spelled Le Hamele in 1407, The Hamel in 1538 and Hammil in 1772. Named in 1878, when spelled the Hammel. The name is not linked to The Ham, which was land given to Osney Abbey by the Countess of Warwick.

Hamel Walk

A new pedestrian way, from The Hamel and Osney Lane into the Lion Brewery residential redevelopment.

Hamilton Road

Probably after Lord Hamilton, the sporting peer. See also nearby Portland and Lonsdale Roads. The developers, Twinings, preferred to name their roads after the peerage. Built and named in 1905.

Hampden Road

After John Hampden (1594-1643) educated at Magdalen College, a parliamentarian who had opposed the King's demands for subsidies and had in 1643 rejected the overtures of King Charles I for peaceful conclusion to the Civil War and urged an immediate attack on Oxford. He fought and was mortally wounded at the battle of Chalgrove Field. Road named in c1938.

Handlo Place

After a family associated with the land or with Headington. Named in c1945.

Harberton Mead	Probably after local Harberton House. As a private road, off Marston Road, Harberton Mead was named in 1944, officially in January 1949.
Harbord Road	Unknown. Probably at the suggestion of the Moorhouse Estate Company, developers of this area, known as Sunrise. Spelled Harboard Road when officially named in January 1932.
Harcourt Terrace	After Sir William George Granville Venables Vernon, Lord Harcourt, MP for Oxford 1868, 1873-4 and 1880. Solicitor-General and Home Secretary in the Gladstone administration in 1880, Chancellor of the Exchequer in 1886. In the MP series of roads in Headington (see Cardwell Crescent, Grays Road, Stonor Place, & Valentia Road) Street named in 1930.
Hardings Close	After a well known Littlemore family.
Harebell Road	In the flower and herb series in Blackbird Leys. Named in 1961.
Harefields	After the house originally on this site, belonging to the White family, in turn named for the hares often seen in the grounds. Street named in March 1970.
Harley Road	After Robert Harley (1661-1724), politican and statesman, created Earl of Oxford in 1711, a moderate Tory who led the party in 1710. He is said to have been a skilful party leader but "an incapable statesman" (DNB). His portrait hangs in Christ Church. Street named in 1923.
Harlow Way:	After Professor Vincent T Harlow,(d1961) Fellow of Balliol and a Commonwealth historian, who lived at Fir Tree House, 14 Oxford Road, Marston. He and his wife had a large English mastiff which was eventually buried in the garden. Many years later the remains caused some anxiety to tree surgeons working here, as the remains were large enough to be thought to be human. Named in the 1980s.
Harold Hicks Place	After the founder of the wholesale fruiterer still operating in Oxford, whose premises were on this site in Percy Street. Named in 1996.
Harold White Close	Risinghurst. After the first chairman of Risinghurst and Sandhills Parish Council, named in about 1985.
Harolde Close	On the Blenheim Nurseries development at Barton. Thomas Harolde of Barton supplied some of the stone for the tower of Merton College.
Harpes Road	No particular meaning or origin. "one of the unimaginative names of the kind thought appropriate to end of the century suburban development" *(Ruth Fasnacht: Summertown since 1820).* See also **Lucerne, Oakthorpe, Thorncliffe** and **Beechcroft Roads.** Named in about 1880
Harpsichord Place	A modern development off Cherwell Street, St Clement's, it is a revival of the old Harpsichord Place, which existed until about 1827, between London Place and the foot of Headington Hill. It was apparently so-called because its plan resembled a harpsichord. The gardens there were mainly added to London Place. Named in July 2002.
Harrow Road	After a local field name, spelt Harrow Ground in c1840. Street named in 1961.
Hart Street	After Horace Hart, printer at Oxford University Press 1883-1915, who had a world-wide reputation in his lifetime. Hart's Rules were the established code for printing houses throughout the world. The Press developed as a major industrial concern largely as a result of his system of management. He was the last printer to have a house on the site. Street officially named in November 1958, formerly Union Street, named in 1868.

The east end of the old Harpsichord Row on the corner of Cherwell Street. Demolished in 1929. (drawing by Shatford).

Hartley Russell Close	Run by the Donnington Trust, which had owned property in Iffley from 1393 when it was granted the Manor (see Abberbury Road). The Close is named after a Patron of the Trust. Built by J Carter Jonas in 1957.
Haslemere Gardens	Previously known informally as Radcliffe Gardens, before officially renamed in 1939. One resident had complained that "even the gas masks have been altered to Radcliffe Gardens" – issued by the Town Hall at the start of the Second World War.
Havelock Road	After Henry Havelock (1759-1857) a British General in India. Street named in 1930. See Clive Road.
Hawkins Street	After George Hawkins, President of the Co-op Union Congress in 1893. Street named in 1900. (Marriott)
Hawksmoor Road	In the architects' group of road names in Cutteslowe. Nicholas Hawksmoor (1661-1736) was employed by Wren and assisted him at St Paul's Cathedral. His own work included parts of Blenheim Palace, The Queen's College and the towers of All Souls, Oxford. Named in about 1932.
Hawkswell Gardens	After Hawkswell Farm, an old house still standing in 1970. Hawks Weir was an old field name. A 14th century map of St Giles parish has field names Hawkswere Furlong and Hawkswere Mede. Developed by Knowles & Son from 1960, named in the early 1960s.
Hawlings Row	Shepherds Hill. After a field name. Named in 2004.
Hawthorn Avenue	In the tree and shrub series in Blackbird Leys.
Hayes Close:	In the musicians' group in Marston, after William Hayes (c.1708–1777), Professor of Music at Oxford 1742 to 1777, and his son Philip Hayes (bap. 1738, d. 1797), Professor from 1777 to 1797. Named 25th June 1979.
Hayfield Road	After William Hayfield who lived in a house named Heyfield's Hutt, on the site of the present Anchor Inn. The street was laid out in 1880 with artisan houses and run by Oxford Industrial and Provident Land & Building Society. The street was named in c1888. Heathfield's Hut Lane is mentioned in a deed of 1644, spelled Heyfield Hutt between 1764 and 1778.

Celebratory dancing in Hayfield Road on the occasion of its centenary in 1985.

Haynes Road	After Raymund Haynes. See **Raymund Road**. Named in the 1950s
Hayward Road	Means a Hayward or an 'officer for fences and enclosures' but origin unknown -probably at the suggestion of the Moorhouse Estate Company, developers of this area, which they called Sunrise. Spelt Haywardeshalfacre in 1388, named 4th January 1932.
Headington Hill	See Headington Lane and Headington road. The part of the road nearest the City from Pullen's Lane was officially renamed Headington Hill in 1970. Beyond the turn to Marston at the foot of the hill the road was "steep and dangerous; its high banks were thickly wooded until the Civil War, when the trees were cut down because they harboured enemies in ambush" - an early defoliation policy. "The old highway to London turned to the right in the middle of the hill" (see Cheney Lane). Further out from the city it becomes Headington Road, then, after Headley way, London Road as it nears the city boundary.
Headington Quarry	Once a separate village. The quarries here have been worked since 1396 but only in the 17th century did a community begin. Spelled Quarry Pittes in 1605, the Quarrys in 1729 and Quarry Field in 1805.
Headington Road	Headington was a royal manor, given by Queen Matilda to one of her Breton followers, Hugh de Pluggenait, in recognition of his faithful service. The road was built through Headington Hill after a campaign led by Dr Tournay, Warden of Wadham. The road was named in 1872 as Headington Hill, but the present name was adopted in 1930. The name means "Hedena's clearing" and the village was known as Hedenandun in 1004, Hedintone in 1086, Hedyngtun in 1330 and Hetynton in 1358. Hedena was probably a Saxon personal name, perhaps related to the name Heoden, or an Old Norse name Heddin. On this road into Oxford was built by the University a fine terrace walk where "on fine summer evenings collegians would resort to taste the refreshing sweet air and look at views of the city" (Wade: Vol II)

Headington, like many Oxfordshire townships, retained its open fields until very late – inclosure did not come until 1804 - directed by the Inclosure Act of 1801.

Headley Way
After a pasture called Heddley, in Headington parish, abutting the road between St Clement's and Marston. The Great Headley Estate is referred to in a report to the Highways Committee on 21st October 1938 and the name was adopted by the Council on 31st October 1938.

Heath Close
Possibly after a local field name. Street named in 1955.

Heather Place
In the musicians' group in Marston, after William Heather (c.1563–1627), Doctor of Music at Oxford and founder of the Heather Professorship of Music. Street named 1st July 1935.

Heatley Road
Oxford Science Park. After Norman Heatley OBE (1911-2004) Honorary Doctor of Medicine (Oxon), who, with Howard Florey and Ernest Chain developed penicillin in Oxford in 1940. It was said (Oxford Times) that his work "changed the course of human health". It is fitting that he should be commemorated in this way because although his colleagues received the Nobel Prize his merit was otherwise hardly recognised. It is now accepted that Fleming received undue praise for finding the penicillin mould; he was unable to isolate it and would have abandoned the research in 1935. It was Florey and Heatley, with Chain, who turned penicillin into the life saving drug. Eric Lax in his work "The Mould in Dr Florey's Coat" (Abacus Time Warner, 2004) says of

Norman Heatley in his laboratory, with penicillin samples. Courtesy of Dr Mercy Heatley.

Heatley that "of all the major contributors to the development of penicillin no one is so little known as Norman George Heatley, yet no one was so indispensable. His manual and mental abilities would be instrumental in solving the most difficult riddle of how to extract penicillin from its multi-substance broth without rendering it impotent". Huntley and Palmers of Reading once gave a hundred round biscuit tins to Heatley for use in the manufacturer of the drug. Heatley has a blue plaque on the house where he lived at 12 Oxford Road, Old Marston.

Hedges Close	After an old Quarry family, one member of which was associated with William Kimber and Cecil Sharpe in the revival of the Headington Morris dancers. Street named in 1967.
Helen Road	After one of the Kingerlee family, long established local builders. Street named in 1907. See Henry Road.
Helleborine Close	In the Blackbird Leys plant and shrub series, although the plant is more usually known as Hellebore or Helleborus Niger (the Christmas Rose) or Helleborus Orientalis (the Lenten Rose). Named in 1993.
Hendred Street	After Hendred House at the end of the street. Officially named in February 1955, formerly George Street, Cowley.
Hengrove Close	Barton Village Road. Named in November 1981.
Henley Avenue	The Oxford to Henley road, originally The Great Wallingford Way, or London Street, later Henley Road, named in 1930. See Iffley Road. In his reminiscences of 1892 Dr Henry Robinson said that in 1838 "the coaches were well horsed and very fast: one used to go by the Iffley Road, 58 miles to London in 5¼ hours".
Henley Road	The road to Henley, where it passes through Littlemore.
Henley Street	Adjoins the Oxford to Henley road. Named in c1881.
Henry Road	After Thomas Henry Kingerlee, or one of his family, whose firm built up the area in the late 19th and early 20th centuries. Street named in 1904. See Helen Road.
Henry Taunt Close	After the famous professional photographer (1842-1922), who took many memorable and historic pictures of Oxford and Oxfordshire and the Thames. He was born in Headington Quarry, had his studio behind 26 High Street in 1856 and was made a Fellow of the Royal Geographical Society in 1893. Widely acclaimed as at "the cutting edge of Victorian location technology" several books have been written about him including one by Bryan Brown in 1973 and two by Malcolm Graham when at the Centre for Oxfordshire Studies, where many of his images are held. Street officially named in 1971. There is a blue plaque on his house at 393 Cowley Road.

Taunt with a lady, on his houseboat c1890. Courtesy of Oxfordshire Photographic Archive.

Herbert Close

At the request of Jesus College, after the family name of the Earls of Pembroke, who were Hereditary Visitors of Jesus College, which had developed much of this area for housing. Street officially named in 1967.

Hernes Close

Street named in c1970. See **Hernes Road**

Hernes Crescent

Formerly Hernes Road North, first named in 1900, renamed officially in 1965 to avoid confusion with **Hernes Road**

Hernes Road

After a local field called Hernes Lake, said to be a corruption of the word Heron. See Heron Place. Built in c1890-4, named in 1894, adopted by the City in 1889.

Heron Place

Off Hernes road, after Heron Lake once here; named in April 1972

Herschel Crescent

After Sir William Herschel, second baronet (1833-1917), eldest of three sons and nine daughters of Sir John Herschel, astronomer and chemist, grandson of Sir William Herschel (1738-1822), discoverer of Uranus and of many stars. He invented the system of identification by fingerprints, having discovered the principles in Bengal while serving there in the Indian Civil Service. He was also a pioneer in colour photography. After settling in Oxford he was awarded a first class degree in theology at the age of 48, and rented (from about 1882) Lawn Upton House, Littlemore. For a few years he was a lecturer in Divinity at Hertford College, engaged in many philanthropic and religious activities and was a member of Oxfordshire County Council from 1895 to 1904.

Hertford Street

After the county. Essex Street runs parallel. Street officially named 22nd January 1889.

High Street

Formerly Eastgate Street – and Bridge Street at the eastern end - it became High Streete in the early 17th century. Many villages had this name (four other High Streets in Oxford have been renamed to avoid confusion) meaning highway and therefore "hardly a name" (Salter). It was a wide street and became a market place. Dr E Tatham (1752-1801) wrote; "High Street is the glory of Oxford. Its famous curve is renowned and some have

High Street on Christmas Day 2009.

called it the finest street in Europe". Many Oxford people refer to it simply as The High. See *Street Names in the Early Days.*

High Cross Way   After a local wayside cross mentioned in 1498, shown on the 1804 Inclosure Award as High Bush Cross, still in place in 1850. It is recorded that Cardinal Wolsey spent £34 8s 5d repairing the road "from the bridge to the High Cross" to benefit the transport of stone for building his Cardinal College (later Christ Church). Named in 1971.

Highfield Avenue   After Highfield Farm, which originally held land here. In the rapid expansion of the 1850s the farm was sold for building. In 1910 a new parish was formed which took the name Highfield. Named in 1907.

Hillsborough Close   Unknown. Street named in 1973.

Hillsborough Road   Unknown. Street named in 1938.

Hill Top Road   Named geographically and self evidently, shown on a proposal drawing of December 1902 for the Southfield Building Estate, for development by the Oxford Industrial and Provident Land & Building Society. Named in 1906. See also Southfield Road.

Hill View Avenue   The view from here is south to Shotover Hill.

Hill View Road   The hills here are Wytham Hill to the west-north-west and Cumnor Hurst to the west-south-west. Named in 1896-7.

Hinshelwood Road   A private road in the University Science Area, named after Sir Cyril Norman Hinshelwood OM FRS (1897-1967) physical chemist and biochemist, graduate and research fellow at Balliol, delegate to Oxford University Press in 1934, worked at the new Physical Chemistry Laboratory provided by Lord Nuffield, president of the Royal Society 1955-60, Nobel prize-winner jointly with Nikolay Semenov in 1956, President of the British Association 1964-65, Honorary Fellow of Balliol, Exeter and St Catherine's Colleges. He was also a linguist and a competent oil painter (DNB)

Hobson Road   After Mrs Louisa Hobson who with her daughter Louisa Maria ran a local school for young ladies. Her husband James H Hobson was a coachman and the family lived in South Lawn, 267 Banbury Road, built in 1872, where Prama House is now. Also named after Mrs Audrey Hobson JP, (1892-1959), née Gotch, well known for her voluntary social work in Oxford, especially in the Red Cross where her rank was Commandant Oxford/2 and Assistant Director of Youth. Street officially named in 1961, formerly Albert Road named in 1890-1; residents, seeing the need for a change to avoid confusion with Albert Terrace, Jericho accepted that this change was "Hobson's Choice". See *Duplicated Names*

Hockmore Street   After one of the two lakes in Cowley: Hock (or great) Mere and Little Mere or More. Spelled Hocce Mere in 1004, Hockemere in 1220 and 1250. An important settlement in 1086; later there had been a Hockmore Farm and Cottages. Street renamed in 1938 at the east end, the west end named officially in 1965.

Hodges Close   After H F Hodges, scorer of the first goal when Oxford City Football Club won the Amateur Cup in 1906. Named in 1993.

Holland Place   Commemorating the twinning link between Oxford and Leiden, Holland – one of the oldest links in England, started in 1946. Named in 1976. See **Leiden Road.**

Hollow Way	The old road here was a track worn deep into the ground by carts carrying timber from Shotover Forest and stone from local quarries, carried on this route to Oxford and to the Thames for shipment downstream. Known as Holeweye in 1240.
Holley Crescent	Named after an old Headington family, first recorded locally in the early 18th century. Thomas Holley (b 1758) farmed Manor Farm in Dunstan Road, once known as Holleys or Hollys Farm. The farm grew to 320 acres in 1807, but had declined to 73 acres when put up for auction by the Lord of the Manor (Revd Thomas Henry Whorwood) at the Angel Hotel in Oxford, on 3 August 1836. The farm failed to find a buyer at that time (Stephanie Jenkins) Street named in 1937 but sometimes spelled Holly Crescent and recorded as such on the City List.
Hollybush Row	After the Hollybush Inn which stood on the site of the Royal Oxford Hotel. The Inn was a guard house and drinking place of Royalist soldiers during the Civil War and became a coaching inn, the headquarters of the coaches to and from Cheltenham and Bath. Spelled Hollybush Row in 1772, previously known as Kingstocke in the 16th century. Distances on milestones on routes west of Oxford are from Hollybush Row and not, as is often thought, from Carfax. Street named in 1862.
Holmes Park	Off Harberton Mead. Name suggested by the estate developers after James Holmes, owner of the land and a history teacher for many years at Oxford High School for Boys, George Street. Named in January 2006.
Holtweer Close	After a local weir spelled Holtisweer in 1509-10, named in 1960.
Holyoake Road	After Holyoake Hall, a local landmark, and a row of houses nearby named Holyoake Terrace, later replaced by the Co-op. A Mr Holyoake was a pillar of the Co-operative movement in the mid 19th century. Formerly Western Road, Headington, named in 1930, renamed in April 1955 to avoid confusion with Western Road, Grandpont.
Holywell Street	After the local 'holy well', now covered over on the north side of St Cross Church. Pronounced as in "holly". The area name was spelt Haliwelle in 1086, Holiwell in 1349, Halywell in 1428 and Holywell by 1772. The well water was thought to be holy or blessed, with healing powers for diseases of the eyes. Usually known simply as Holywell, originally known as Crowell, after the man who found the well, a shoemaker from St Peter in the East, who built a surrounding wall dated 1st May 1661. Dr Rawlinson, principal of St Edmund Hall, built a cover and then a house over the well, with the inscription;

"No man shall hurt this well that's wise,

For this hurts none but cures the eyes".

The cover and house were "demolished in the Civil War and the spring suffocated by the town ditch to which it adjoined". Holywell Cemetery, separate from the Church, is of interest because of the number of well-known people of both Town and Gown buried here. These include Kenneth Grahame, Kenneth Tynan, Sir Henry Acland and his wife Sarah, Walter Pater, Lord Redcliffe Maud and Sir Maurice Bowra. Holywell Music Room, at the west end of the street, is probably the oldest concert hall in the world. Opened in 1748, it had taken some years to raise enough funds. It seats about 250 people and has especially good acoustics. (See **Crotch Crescent**)

Home Close	After a local field name recorded in the Inclosure Award of 1849. The owner, Sir George Dashwood, gave up part of the field for widening what is now Godstow Road. Named in 1940.
Honeysuckle Grove	In the plant and shrub group of road names in Blackbird Leys. Named in March 1993.
Horseman Close	After Helen Horseman, d 1922, mother of Charles Haynes who farmed Boults Farm, and great grandmother of Charles Haynes, Chairman of Marston Parish Council. A devout Catholic, married to Edwin Haynes of Cross Farm, churchwarden of St Nicholas, (Anglican Church) Marston. Named in the 1970s. (See Raymond and Haynes Roads)
Horspath Driftway	After the old driftway, a common way, road, or path, for driving cattle, from Headington to Horspath and a local field name. Spelled the same in 1853.
HorspathRoad	Name for the village and meaning a 'horse path', spelled Horspadan in 1086, Horsepath in 1225 and Nether Horspath in 1338. Street named in 1930.
Horwood Close	Suggested by the estate developers, officially named in 1966 and developed in 1967.
Hosker Close	Built on land left undeveloped for many years after completion of the Sandhill Estate, as this was a former quarry site, possibly considered at the time less suitable for building land. Mrs Bursill had inherited the land from her husband (see Burdell Avenue, Bursill Close and Delbush Avenue) and sold to Percy Bilton Builders. Planning permission was apparently not easily achieved: the origin of the name is uncertain, but Hosker may have been a partner in the development or perhaps a Councillor who had supported the applications. Named in the 1970s
Howard Street	Probably after the estate builder Percy Charles Howard. See **Percy** and **Charles Streets,** or after William Howard, an estate agent connected with the development here, who had a son named Percy. Ruth Fasnacht suggests named after the Lords Howard, in the fashion of the time to name roads after peers. Street named in 1862-5.
Howell Close	Wolvercote Green. Named after the well-known blacksmith of Wolvercote, Howell Saxton, Freeman of Oxford, nicknamed 'Oakie' or 'Oke'. Named in 2009.

Howell Sexton (left) watching his son Ted shoeing a carthorse outside his forge in in about 1919.

Hubble Close	After Miss I D Hubble, head teacher of Barton Village School, on the site of which this development of 54 houses was built. Named in November 2002. The school had in turn been built on the site of a house called The Wick.
Hugh Allen Crescent	In the musicians' group in Marston, after Sir Hugh Percy Allen (1869–1946), Professor of Music at Oxford from 1918 to 1946, "an inspiring influence especially among young people and sought to spread the love of music and teach people to make music". He conducted the Oxford Bach Choir from 1907 to 1920. Street named in 1938.
Humfrey Road	After Laurence Humfrey, President of Magdalen from 1561 to his death in 1588. Street named in 1947. The land on which the estate is built is associated with Magdalen and New College.
Hundred Acres Close	Extended in 2001.
Hunsdon Road	Probably after Henry Carey, Lord Hunsdon, High Steward of Oxford in 1592. Street officially named in 1936, developed in 1939.
Hunter Close	After General Sir Martin Hunter, GCH, GCMG (1757–1846)a British Army officer, and governor of Stirling Castle. His regiment, the 52nd (Oxfordshire) Regiment of Foot, was stationed at Cowley barracks; he fought with them during the American Revolutionary War. Formerly Elliott Close but renamed in 1979 on the petition of residents who had found difficulties in obtaining credit – Elliott Close was also the name of the Homeless Families Unit there.
Hurst Street	After the Hurst family, one of the true yeoman families of England. They held small freeholds in Temple Cowley in the 16th and 17th centuries and by the 19th had styled themselves gentlemen. Street named in 1872.
Hutchcomb Road	After the nearby Hutchcomb Farm, meaning 'Hunds valley' or 'valley of the dogs'. Spelt Hundescumb in 1284 and Hugcombs in 1729. Street named in 1940 when spelled Hutchcomb Road. Formerly Elms Rise.
Hyacinth Walk	In the plant and shrub series of Blackbird Leys road names. Named in 1997.
Hyde Place	After Thomas Hyde, d1875, who lived at The Avenue, next to this Bishop Kirk Place site, from c1836, a wholesale clothier with a large shop and clothing factory in Queen Street, also a churchwarden at Summertown 1850-71. Named in 2000.

Hythe Bridge Street in 1834.

Hythe Bridge Street   So called after the hithe (meaning wharf or landing place) adjoining. Hithe is a Saxon word, (as in Rotherhithe) The first bridge was built in the late 11th century, rebuilt in 1383 and again in 1861. Spelt Hithe in 1233-34, Pontis de Hythe and Brugge de la Hythe in 1286, Hidebrigge in 1262, referred to on a map of 1797 as High Bridge. Formerly Rewley Lane or Ruby Lane. The Oxford to Witney road once passed over this bridge.

I

Iffley Road

The village of Iffley has been spelled more than 84 different ways over the centuries; spelled Gifetelea in 941, Iyftele in 1254 and Yeftley in 1517. The current spelling first appears in the 18th century. The name possibly derives from 'field of gifts or 'plovers' clearing'. Once called Wallingford Way or Londonisshe Way, the Oxford to Henley road via Iffley was turnpiked in 1736.

Iffley Church

Iffley Turn

The road was officially named by the City on 1st December 1930, although it existed long before this date. As with **First Turn, Upper Wolvercote** the name evolved from the horse drawn bus route that ran, every half hour, at the beginning of the 20th century. Grove House, at the Turn, was once owned by Cardinal Newman's mother and later by Mrs Grahame Greene, who built the museum for her dolls' houses in the grounds.

Ilsley Road

After a family associated with the land here, or with the Headington district. Marriott suggests it may be named after the Magdalen College connections with land here and at East Ilsley, Berkshire. Street named 30th November 1945.

Ingle Close

After Alderman Harry Charles Ingle, Mayor in 1943, who was interested in Oxford street naming. Built and named in 1951.

Inott Furze   After a local field name spelled Inott Furlong in the Headington Inclosure Award of 1804, on which this road is built. (See also Town Furze). Street named in 1938.

Isis Close   Rivermead Hospital site. In old deeds the whole length of the river was named the Tam-ese and was possibly known as the Ese, or Ise or Ouse. The name Isis did not appear before the 16th century. Ise literally means 'one river'. Named in 2004.

Islip Place   See **Islip Road.**

Islip Road   After Islip village, meaning 'slippery places' where carts were dragged across the River Ray, possibly derived from 'ac' (water) and 'lyp' (leaping). Spelt Gidslepe in c1050, Letelape in 1086 and Iniccheslape in c1250. Named in 1880, adopted by the City in 1889.

Ivy Close   Hollow Way. Unknown origin. Named in 2004

Ivy Lane   Name suggested by Friends of Old Headington and the hospital architect, as a last resort after Sunnyside Road (after the convalescent home on the Manor House site for the previous fifty years) and Ormerod Roads were rejected, to recognise the ivy covered wall at the junction of New Road and Osler Road. Officially named in 1970.

J

Jack Argent Close
After a former Chairman of the Blackbird Leys Neighbourhood Council. Named in 1993.

Jackdaw Lane
Possibly after a local man, Jack Daw. Street named in 1922 when spelled Jack Daw Lane. (Marriott)

Jackson Road
After the distinguished architect Sir Thomas Graham Jackson RA (1835-1924) Fellow of Wadham, who designed the Examination Schools in 1875, also the spire of St Mary the Virgin, the High School for Boys (George Street) and High School for Girls (Banbury Road) and numerous other buildings in Oxford. He was noted for his kindness, approachability and his considerate treatment of young men; he was said to be uniformly gracious" (Mallett) Named in 1934.

Sir Thomas Jackson (courtesy of the Warden and Fellows of Wadham College).

Jack Straw's Lane
There are several possible origins. See text. The name dates from at least 1932 although was not adopted until 1954.

James Street
After the James family, local landowners. When the original James came to Oxford in 1822 he gave £4000 towards the Examination Schools. Street named in c1862-5.

James Wolfe Road
After General James Wolfe (1727-59) commander of the 43rd, later the Oxford and Bucks Regiment, known for his training reforms but remembered chiefly for his victory over the French in Canada and establishing British rule there, who died at the final battle of Quebec after hearing his attack had been successful. The French army was taken by surprise and the battle lasted only fifteen minutes. He was one of Britain's greatest military heroes, much admired by Nelson, who is remembered each year on Trafalgar Day – in comparison, Wolfe is almost forgotten. Road named on 19th December 1977.

Jasmine Close
In the plant and shrub group of Blackbird Leys road names. Named in c1961.

Jericho Street
After the Jericho Inn which existed here from about about the time of the University Clarendon Press in 1830. The building was earlier known as Jericho House, in isolation from the City as remote as the original biblical Jericho.

Jersey Road   After Sir Victor Albert George Child-Villiers, 7th Earl of Jersey, (1845-1915), Governor and Commander-in-Chief of New South Wales 1891-3, High Steward and Lord Lieutenant of Oxfordshire from 1887 until his death. Rose Hill has several roads named after High Stewards of the University. Street named in c1948.

Jessops Close   After a local field on Boults Farm. Named in the 1970s.

Jeune Street   Probably after Dr Francis Jeune (1806-68) Master of Pembroke 1843-64, Bishop of Peterborough 1864-68. Also possibly after his wife Mrs Margaret Dyne Jeune (d 1892) who wrote under the pseudonym 'Diary of an Oxford Lady' in the local Jackson's Oxford Journal between 1845 and 1862 (edited by MJ Gifford, 1932) But Mr Carl Kingerlee (of the building family) said the street was named after a relative. Street built in 1901 and named in 1903.

Portrait of Margaret Jeune and her children, by Robert Richard Scanlan, 1846.

Joan Lawrence Place   After a popular head teacher (d 1988) for 30 years at the Slade Nursery School, now demolished. She created a happy and healthy environment for children and staff, and had built a long verandah where children could play in all weathers. Named in April 1992.

At the installation of the name plate, 22nd May 1992. left to right – Lady Mayoress Diana Pope, Lord Mayor Councillor Alan Pope, Liz Kearney, former Chair of Governors, Slade School.

John Allen Way

After the founder and chairman of John Allen and Sons (Oxford) Ltd, manufacturers of agricultural equipment. The factory was on the site of the current retail park.

John Buchan Road

Northway Estate. After the writer (1875-1940), first Lord Tweedsmuir. He once lived at Elsfield Manor House and is buried in the village churchyard. The road has a view towards Elsfield. Lady Tweedsmuir, his widow, was asked by the City engineer if she had any objection and wrote back that her family was "very touched" that the City would do him this honour. She also said she hoped the housing would not be ugly and spoil the view. Officially named in March 1949.

John Garne Way

John Garne was a former chief education officer of Oxfordshire County Council; his major achievement was to supervise the amalgamation of the city and county's education services in 1974, when he became the first chief education officer of the combined authority. He died in 2004 and the road was named for him in the same year. See *Celebrating Current Celebrities.*

John Piers Lane   After the Archbishop of York from 1589 to 1595, born in 1538 in a cottage in the lane, opposite the Cross Keys Inn. The cottage carries a plaque in commemoration; the crossed keys are in the coat of arms of the bishopric. Street named in 1940.

John Smith Drive   After the late John Smith MP QC, Leader of the Labour Party. The road name was agreed earlier but allocated in 1994, confirmed in January 1995.

John Snow Place   After a generous local benefactor, who did much for Headington Quarry, including the donation of the village hall and work towards repair of the church, also £200 each to the Wingfield-Morris Hospital and the Radcliffe Infirmary. He lived to 96 and was known in the Quarry as "the second Lord Nuffield". His ambition to meet the first Lord Nuffield was fulfilled on 24th April 1930. Named in March 1970.

John Towle Close   John Towle (1796-1885) was a miller at the nearby Hinksey and Weirs Mills. When he was made Mayor in 1857 he refused to swear the traditional oath to the Vice Chancellor. He organised Chartist meetings in Oxford in the 1840s and had devised a scheme for the drainage of Oxford in the 1860s. Named in 1995.

Jordan Hill Road   A private estate of the University Press, with accommodation for employees who had moved from older housing around the original Press in Jericho. It was said that the name was chosen to signify the move 'from Jericho to Jordan'. Street officially named in 1955.

Jourdain Road   After the Rev F R C Jourdain, founder of the Oxford Ornithological Society, a national authority and a leading figure in British ornithology. He was a former rector of Appleton. Street named in 1967.

Jowett Walk   Formerly part of Love Lane, which continued as far as Wadham and South Parks Road. Named after Professor Benjamin Jowett (1817-93), Master of Balliol 1870-1893, Regius Professor of Greek. There is a much quoted verse about the Master;

> *First come I, my name is Jowett.*
> *Whatever can be known, I know it.*
> *I am the Master of the College;*
> *What I know not is not knowledge.*

Jowett did much for the City, especially to make it healthier; when Vice-Chancellor he was instrumental in the draining of Jericho to free it of disease. He also established Oxford's first theatre. Jowett was in favour of lowering the cost of an Oxford education and strongly advocated reforms. He had a plan for the Indian Civil Service to be opened up to Oxford graduates and successfully lobbied for this. His influence was through contact with his former students, and in lengthy correspondence with Florence Nightingale wrote to her that he would like to govern the world through his pupils. (Richard Symonds; *Oxford and Empire – the last lost cause?*). Margot Asquith said of him that "with women he was like a soft and fluffy owl". Named in 1900.

Jubilee Terrace   After Queen Victoria's golden jubilee of 1887. Street named in c1888.

Junction Road   After the junction between **Temple** and **Crescent Roads**. Street named in 1930.

Juniper Drive   In the plant and shrub series of road names in Blackbird Leys. Named in 1965.

Juxon Street   After William Juxon, (1582-1633). He studied law at St John's College, then took holy orders and in 1609 became vicar of St Giles, Oxford, where he stayed until he became rector of Somerton, Oxfordshire, in 1615. When he held the living of St Giles church, it was "much frequented for his edifying way of preaching". In December 1621 he succeeded his friend, William Laud, as President of St John's College, and in 1626 and 1627 he was Vice-Chancellor of the University of Oxford. Juxon obtained other important positions, including that of chaplain-in-ordinary to Charles I who entrusted Juxon with important secular duties by making him Lord High Treasurer of England as well as First Lord of the Admiralty. At the restoration of King Charles II he became Archbishop of Canterbury. By his will the archbishop was a benefactor to St John's College, where he was buried; he also aided the work of restoring St Paul's Cathedral and rebuilding the great hall at Lambeth Palace.

K

Kames Close

After a local sheep farmer. The original name for nearby Rymers Lane was Kames Sheephouse Lane, and this close leads out of it. Street named in 1932.

Keble Road

After the College, opened here in 1868 – also for John Keble (1792-1866), Fellow of Oriel and Professor of Poetry in 1831, a divine and writer, much revered and loved (DNB). He was one of the main figures in the Oxford Movement, initiated in a sermon he gave in 1833. Many had thought the existing Oxford Colleges were exclusive and unwelcoming to men from poor homes. Keble himself had been in favour of a scheme (considered by the Shirley Committee) to found a college especially for people needing assistance and wishing to be admitted to the Christian Ministry. On Keble's death in 1866 a public appeal was set up in his memory; subscriptions were so many that it was possible to lay the foundation stone in 1868. It was the first new Oxford college since Wadham in 1612. Street named in about 1870.

Keble College in about 1938.

Kelburne Road

After the suggestion of the developers or owners. Street named in1937.

Kempson Crescent

After Charles Oliver Kempson, who served for 27 years as a male attendant at Littlemore hospital, the first President of the Hospital Trade Union and a Littlemore Parish Councillor in the 1920s.

Kendall Crescent

After Rev H E Kendall, Warden of St Edward's School 1924-56. Street named in 1959.

Kenilworth Avenue

After Kenilworth priory, Warwickshire, which owned a virgate here in the 12th century. A virgate is a unit of land measurement prescribed in the Danelaw, equivalent to a quarter of a hide or approximately 30 acres. Street named in 1935.

Kennedy Close   Cowley Barracks Development. After Colonel Sir James Shaw-Kennedy, an officer commissioned in 1805 into the 43rd Regiment, later re-formed with the 53rd Regiment as the Oxford and Bucks Light Infantry. The Regimental Headquarters were once on this site. He fought with the Regiment in the Corunna Campaign of 1808-9 and was ADC to Robert Craufurd 1909-12. See **Corunna Crescent** and **Craufurd Road**. Named in February 1979.

Kennett Road   After a local quarryman in the 15th century, named officially in 1959, formerly New Road, Headington in 1932. See also Norton Close and Piper Street.

Kent Close   Elizabeth Kent was a local landowner in Blackbird Leys in 1819. Street officially named in April 1959.

Kersington Crescent   After William and his son Henry de Kersington who were Lords of the Manor of Cowley in the late 13th and 14th centuries. They gave land to the local St Bartholomew's Hospital in the reign of Edward I. Street named in 1950.

Kestrel Crescent   In the bird series of road names in Blackbird Leys. Named in 1959.

Kiln Lane   After local brick kilns, once common in Headington.

Kineton Road   After Kineton, Worcs. Means 'royal manor' or 'king's town' and was spelled Cyngtun in 969, Quintone in 1086 and Kinctin in 1230. Street shown on a map of 1899, named in 1902.

King Edward Street   Possibly after the 600th anniversary of the accession of Edward I. Oriel College built the new street through its existing property to join High Street and Oriel Square in 1872 and proposed the name at the time. Most houses were built by Frederick Codd in 1873-4 and the street was named in c1872. This street and New Road were the only new roads to be built within the city walls between the Middle Ages and the 1920s.

Conversation in King Edward Street, about 1987.

Kingfisher Green	Named to continue the bird name series in Blackbird Leys, in 1993.
King George's Walk	A pedestrian walk leading to the church of St Michael and All Angels; named in honour of the Coronation of King George V in 1910.
Kings Cross Road	A cross road linking Victoria road to Lonsdale Road, on the Hawkswell Estate, developed by Twining. Fasnacht says it "seems a fanciful name for a connecting road". The connection with the London rail station is probably coincidental and King is probably Edward VII. Named in 1906.
Kingsgate	Oxford Business Park. Named January 1995
Kings Mill Lane	Runs from Marston Road to the River Cherwell, beside Magdalen College Sports Ground.
Kingston Court	Street named in 1973. See **Kingston Road**.
Kingston Road	After St John's College living at Kingston Bagpuize, Oxon given to the college by its founder. The street was pegged out in 1866. The northern end from St Margaret's Road to Hayfield Road was formerly Hut (or Hutt) Road. The southern end was the first built and was then named Kingston Terrace in c1870.. Building on the east side was strictly controlled, with more variety on the west side. The present street was named in 1872. See **Hayfield Road**
King Street	Jericho. There was once a King Street in central Oxford but it no longer exists. Named after William III who reigned 1689-1702. The present houses were built in the 1830s.
Kirby Place	On the site of the former joinery works at 77 Temple Road, named after William Kirby who lived in a cottage on the site in 1856. Named in 1994.
Kirk Close	After Bishop Kenneth Escott Kirk, (1886-1954) chaplain in Flanders 1914 - 19, Regius Professor of Moral and Pastoral Theology and Bishop of Oxford 1937-54. His wife Beatrice had died in 1934 leaving five young children. He died in office in 1954, and the street was named after him in 1955. See Bishop Kirk Close.
Knights Road	Blackbird Leys was in the parish of Sandford on Thames, which had connections with the Knights Templar (see Pegasus Road, Monks Close and Nunnery Close). Named in 1961.

Bishop Kirk with his wife and two of his five children, in 1924.

Knolles Road

After Sir Frances Knollys, educated at the University, MP for Oxford and High Steward of the city. He was cousin to Elizabeth I and a statesman, Treasurer of the Royal Household 1572-96. The elephant in ermine, one of the supporters on the Arms of the City of Oxford, was from the crest and badge of the Knollys family. He and Henry Norreys (whose beaver is the other supporter on the Arms) were the two most powerful men of their day in Oxford. See Norreys Avenue. The developers had suggested the less interesting name of Fredericks Road. Named in October 1931.

The arms of the City of Oxford, with the elephant of the Knollys family as the supporter on the left.

Kybald Street

Means 'stony or jolting street', possibly from 'kibble', meaning cobble. Spelled Kiboldstrate in c1215-25 and Kibold Street in 1374. A house in the street in the 17th century was known as Kybald Twitchin. The present name is a revival and appears in directories from 1927, and was formerly Kybald Place. Previously known as Grove Place, named in c1888.

L

Ladenham Road	After a local medieval field name spelled Loddenham Fields in 1605 and Ladnam in 1819. Officially named in November 1958.
Lake Street	After the Hinksey Lake, dug out for gravel to build the nearby railway embankment in 1850. Street named in 1886.
Lakefield Road	Littlemore. After a local field name spelled Lake Field before 1819, referring to ground that regularly flooded.
Lakeside	The road runs beside a man-made lake left by excavation of clay for the brickworks once nearby; officially named in February 1967. See *Duplicated Names*
Lamarsh Road	After Lamarsh in Essex, a living of St John's College. The road, now a trading estate, was constructed in New Botley for St Johns, on its land, by James Dalziel.
Lambourn Road	Rose Hill (No 3 estate), named after E A Greening Lamborn, antiquary, local historian and author on the history of Oxford. The road was named in 1946. See article *E A Greening Lamborn.*

The blue plaque now on 34 Oxford Road, Littlemore where Lamborn lived.

Lambton Close	Cowley Barracks Site, named after Colonel Lambton who raised the 52nd Regiment in 1755. (See also **Hunter Close** and **James Wolfe Road**). Originally Elliott Close (named in 1979) but renamed in April 1982 after a petition was raised by residents who did not wish to be associated with the Homeless Families Unit there, fearing difficulties in raising credit.
Langley Close	Meaning a long wood or clearing, named for an old field name spelled Langeleta in 1199. A large house named Langley Lodge stood in nearby Pullen's Lane, built in 1895 and now Rye St Anthony School. Close named in 1935.
Lanham Way	Littlemore. After a respected Headmaster of Lawn Upton School between 1938 and 1959.
The Larches	Suggested by the estate developers, named in 1967.
Larkfields	Headington Quarry. Name found on original property deeds and therefore suggested by the developers. Named in 1970.
Lark Hill	Waterways. After the name given to the part of the tramway used for carrying gravel to be used in the construction of the Great Western railway embankment. The original Lark Hill became Chalfont Road when St John's College named it after one of their livings at Chalfont St Peter. Named in 2004.
Larkins Lane	Unknown, possibly after a local person. Officially named in the late 1920s.
Lathbury Road	After the St Johns College living at Lathbury, Bucks. Road named in c1905.
Latimer Grange	See Latimer Road. Named in c1965.

Latimer Road
After the Latimer family of nearby Headington House until about 1846. Edward Latimer (1775-1845) was Lord of the Manor of Headington. The house was built in 1775 for William Jackson, the owner of *Jackson's Oxford Journal*, a well known local newspaper. On Jackson's death in 1793 ownership passed to Mary Jones who in turn left it to her niece, the wife of Edward Latimer, a wine merchant. Road named in c1930.

Lawrence Road
After General Sir Henry Montgomery Lawrence (1806 -1857) British soldier and statesman in India, who died defending Lucknow during the Indian Mutiny. The road was named in 1930, and was later further developed by Hooper & Jones Ltd in 1971.

Leafield Road
Possibly after a field name or after the local village and birthplace of W A J Hooper, chairman of Hooper & Jones Ltd, which had developed the area. Officially named in 1970.

Leander Way
Rivermead Hospital site. After the Leander Club in Henley-on-Thames, open to those who excel in rowing, such as Oxford and Cambridge rowing Blues and cup winners. Named in 2004.

Leckford Place
Named in 1886. See Leckford Road.

Leckford Road
After St John's College living at Leckford, Hants, obtained in 1725, after a donation in 1716 of £2000 from Dr William Brewster, so that the College could buy the advowsons of Tackley and Leckford. Road named in 1874 and completed by 1876.

Ledgers Close
Littlemore. Bessie Ledger came to Littlemore in 1947 and joined the Parish Council in 1952, later serving on Bullingdon and South Oxfordshire District Councils. She represented Littlemore as a County Councillor for 25 years, working in education, child care and social services. In 1976 she retired from the Parish Council to become Parish Clerk and Treasurer, then after four more years went back to being a Councillor, finally retiring in 1993. See *Apostrophes and Spaces.*

Leiden Road
Named to commemorate the city twinning link with Leiden in Holland, the oldest continuous twinning between any English and Dutch towns, commenced in 1947. Officially named in 1975.

The arms of Leiden and Oxford.

Lenthall Road
After William Lenthall (1591-1662), a Royalist politician who served as Speaker of the House of Commons during the Civil war. The second son of William Lenthall of North Leigh in Oxfordshire, he was born at Henley-on-Thames, lived at

Besselsleigh and later left Oxford without taking a degree in 1609. Also after his descendant Miss Jane Lenthall of Lucia House, Iffley. The first part of the road named in 1946, the second in 1948.

Leon Close
After Oxford's twin town of Leon in Nicaragua. The close is on the site of the former College of Further Education in Cowley Road, named 3rd December 1990.

Leopold Street
After Prince Leopold (1853-84), eighth child of Queen Victoria. He laid the foundation stone of St John's Home. The site now includes Helen House, the first children's hospice, and Douglas House, for older children. Named in 1873, formerly Stanton Street.

Lewell Avenue
Unknown. Named in the 1950s.

Lewin Close
Rectory Farm. The estate of Lewin, a royal servant, is recorded in Domesday as including 4½ hides of land in Cowley, including one of the two Cowley mills and two fisheries. (A History of the County of Oxford: Vol 5.) Named 14th January 1982.

Lewis Close
After Clive Staples Lewis (1888-1963) known as CS Lewis to his readers and Jack to his friends, who lived nearby, at The Kilns, Risinghurst. He gained a triple first at Oxford and was a fellow of Magdalen College from 1925-54. A novelist, literary critic and a theologian, he is best known for his *Chronicles of Narnia, The Screwtape Letters* and *The Space Trilogy*. His works have been translated into more than thirty languages. He was a close friend of Tolkien and with him, Hugo Dyson, Charles Williams and others formed The Inklings, a literary group of Christian writers who would meet every week, at first at Magdalen and later at the Eagle and Child in St Giles. (History of the University of Oxford) He died at the Kilns on 22nd November 1963, the same day as the assassination of President JF Kennedy – media coverage of Lewis's death was therefore not great.

Leys Place
After a local field spelled the Leys in 1853. Street named in 1933.

Liddell Road
After Henry George Liddell, Dean of Christ Church, Professor of Moral Philosphy and Vice Chancellor. He was a former headmaster of Westminster School and a noted classical scholar. His daughter was immortalised in *Alice in Wonderland*. **Dodgson** and **Gaisford Roads** are nearby. Road named in c1935.

Lime Walk
After an avenue of limes now all felled. The road was developed gradually during the late 19th century and was named in about 1930.

Lincoln Road
After the city of Lincoln in a series of parallel streets named alphabetically **Lincoln-Monmouth-Northampton-Oswestry**. Oxford was in the diocese of Lincoln from soon after the Norman Conquest until the diocese of Oxford was established in 1542. The arms of Lincoln are on the balcony in the Town Hall. Road named in 1929.

The Link
Marston. A short road linking Mortimer Drive and Salford Road.

The Link
Risinghurst. A short link road between Ridgeway Road and Collinwood Road.

Linkside Avenue
Laid out by Hinkins & Frewin beside the links of the North Oxford Golf Club and named in October 1935. (See *Duplicated Names*)

Linnet Close

One the bird series of roads named in Blackbird Leys, officially named in 1959.

Linton Road

After St John's College living at Linton, Herefordshire, acquired in 1827. Originally a rough lane called Spring Close between the Cherwell and Banbury Road in 1832. The first houses were built here from 1894 – 1910 and the road was named in 1896.

St Andrew's Church, Linton Road.

Little Acreage	After the house originally on the site. Named in the 1960s.
Little Brewery St	After the small St Clement's Brewery, begun in 1826, later Wootten's Brewery and amalgamated with Hall's Brewery in 1896.
Little Bury	Greater Leys. Probably after a local field. Named in 1993.
Little Clarendon St	After the nearby University and Clarendon press set up in Walton Street in 1826. The 'little' prefix is because the street is shorter and half the width

of Great Clarendon Street. Formerly Blackboy Lane and possibly also Workhouse Lane because it once led there. Named in the 1850s, built by Jonathan Barrett , a local builder.

Little Field Littlemore. After a local field name.

Littlegate Street After the medieval stone gateway at the south end of St Ebbe's Street, pulled down in April 1794. Spelled Luttlegate in 1241-64 and Littlegate in the late 16th century, known as Milk Street in medieval times. Near the street name plate at the St Ebbe's Street end, is a plaque stating that in 1244 this was one of the seven medieval gates in the City. It was sometimes known as Little Southgate Street. Named in 1874.

Littlehay Road Means a 'small hay field' after a local medieval field spelled Little Haye on a Corpus map of 1605 and Littlehay Mear in 1840. Formerly West Street, renamed by the Council on 3rd March 1930.

Littlemore Road After Littlemore village, meaning 'small marsh'. Spelled Luthlemorias in c1130, Lutemora in 1177 and Letlemore in 1220. Street named in about 1938.

Lobelia Road Blackbird Leys. In the plant series of road names on the estate. Named in 1961.

Lockheart Crescent After an important tenant associated with the district in the 16th-17th centuries. Officially named in 1954.

Lodge Close After Olive Lodge, a parish worker from 1961-75, who lived at 5 Elsfield Road, one of the first women to be made a Deaconess (at Marston on 1 November 1972). On moving in, some friends carried a tall cupboard into her house; she emerged to find two apprehensive children who said "Miss, we're scared; we've just seen some people going into that house with a coffin..." Remembered for her kindness to many and especially for her cakes given to those returning home after a stay in hospital. Named in the 1970s.

Logic Lane After the University School for logicians nearby. Formerly Horse Mill Lane in 1247, Horsemill in 1298 and Horseman Lane in 1328, renamed Logick Lane after the School in 1661-66, although the name may have applied only to the north end of the lane. Renamed again in 1872. There was once a horse mill there. Ownership was once in doubt but a court order in 1904 awarded in favour of University College. The road is closed to the public.

London Place A terrace of houses facing London Road. Part of the terrace was demolished in 1927 for road widening. The houses here date from between 1820 and 1860, the tallest built in 1883. Street named in c1868.

London Road The road from the city to London, via Bolshipton Farm, was called London Waie in Elizabethan times and by 1762 had become London Road. Improvements under the Turnpike Acts in the 18th century included measurements and marking by milestones; the 53rd stone was at St Clement's. However, the Cowley Road was always the major route, crossing Cowley Marsh as a causeway.

Long Close Possibly after a field name. Wood Farm.

Long Ford Close Grandpont. The first reference to Long Ford is in the Chronicles of Abingdon Abbey in the time of Abbot Faritius between 1100 and 1117, referring to a series of small river fords which once crossed Abingdon Road.

Long Ground Blackbird Leys. After a field name. Named in 1997.

Longlands Road   After an old field name spelled Les Longelondes in 1200. Road named in 1967.

Long Lane   Slade Park development. After a field name. Named in January 1977.

Longwall   Littlemore. Named after a listed old wall nearby.

Long Wall   Wade (1821) describes the lofty wall that ran between a row of elms in Magdalen Grove and the street. It is usually assumed, however, that the street is named after the medieval defensive wall which runs on the city side of the street. Wood (Oxford Topography) refers to the road "going along the walls" or "between the long walls" implying that the name refers to walls on both sides of the road. As the Magdalen high wall is the most conspicuous, this is a more logical explanation. Spelled Long Wall in 1772 and Long Walk in 1797. Now usually popularly known as Long Wall (without the 'Street')

Replacement name plates ready for installation by the City Council, in 2009, with Andrew Burchett, Communal Area and Highways technician, in March 2009.

Longworth Road   Walton Manor. Possibly named after a connection of St John's College with Longworth, Berks. Street named in 1890-1.

Lonsdale Road   Twining development, Summertown. Named after the Earl of Lonsdale (1847-1894). The earldom had been revived in 1807 and the 5th Earl was a boxer and yachtsman, known as "England's Greatest Sporting Gentleman". He was Patron of the National Sporting Club. The oldest belt in Championship Boxing was named after him and first won in 1909. Twining chose other aristocratic names for the roads. See also Portland Road. Named in 1905.

Lovelace Road   After John, Lord Lovelace and family, possibly the same family recorded as Royalist owners of the nearby Water Eaton House, and as landlords in Water Eaton parish. Road named in 1936.

Lovelace Square   See Lovelace Road

Love Lane   It has been suggested that this is named because of 'goings on' along the lane, from Holywell to the Parks.

Lower Fisher Row	Probably after John Le Pecher who had land here in the 13th century. Spelled Fishers Row in 1661-66, Fisherrow in 1772. The area was formerly known as Warham Bank. The Row was named in 1890, formerly Fisher Row. See also **Fisher Row** and **Upper Fisher Row**.
Lucas Place	Homes for elderly people, run by the Oxford Citizens' Housing Association. Named after Mary Keith-Lucas, the Association's Secretary and Housing manager, 1961-64 and her husband Professor Keith-Lucas, in recognition of their services to the Association. Named in 1976.
Lucerne Road	Twining development, Summertown. Probably "a fancy made-up name" *(Fasnacht)* after a popular Swiss holiday destination at the time, but it is not known if Twining ever went there. Named in 1906.
Luther Street	Possibly after Martin Luther (1483-1546)
Lydia Close	After Lydia Roberts, the first Lady Mayoress of Oxford, who died in 1963. Her husband Alderman Evan Roberts was on the Council for 33 years, and was the first to hold the title of Lord Mayor. Named in 1969.
Lye Valley	Overlooking the small valley and stream, Lye Valley. Spelled Lyhills in 1841, named in 1938.
Lyndworth Close	Named in 1939.
Lyndworth Mews	After the developers' suggestion, officially named in February 1972.
Lynn Close	After the suggestion of the developers, N Blake Ltd. Officially named in 1966.
Lytton Road	After General Edward Lytton Bulwer-Lytton, 1st Earl of Lytton (1831 –1891) who served as Viceroy of India during the Great Famine of 1876–80, in which up to 10 million people died. He proclaimed Queen Victoria as Empress of India in Delhi in 1877. He was also a poet writing under the pen name of Owen Meredith. Road named in 1937. See **Clive Road**.

Evan Roberts plants a tree in Lydia Close, on 1st March 1973, with Cllr Fred Kane (far left) and Alderman Henry Nimmo.

M

McCabe Place   Milham Ford School site. After Miss Joan McCabe (b1867) head teacher of Milham Ford School 1917-1931 when it was still at Cowley Place. On her retirement she was awarded the OBE for her work in girls' education. Named in August 2007.

Magdalen Bridge   After Magdalen College nearby, founded in 1458 by Bishop William Wayneflete. The present bridge was built in 1772-82 under the Oxford Improvement Act of 1771 by J Gwyn and widened in 1882. Spelled 'willa bricga' in 1004, known as Pettypont or 'small bridge' in 1285 and c1298 to distinguish it from Grandpont over the Thames. Later East Bridge and then Magdalen Bridge. Spelled Maudlin Bridge in 1661-6 and named in directories in 1890-1. See Grandpont. There is a theory that early undergraduates chose to pronounce the name as 'maudlin', meaning loving, after their beloved college. See *The Perils of Pronunciation.*

Magdalen Bridge and Tower from the Botanic Garden, 2003.

Magdalen Road   After Magdalen College, which had a cricket ground where the road was built in 1832. The cricket ground ceased in 1881 when allotments and recreation grounds were built. Road named in 1932. Many local residents pronounce the road with the "g", as in "magazine".

Magdalen Street   Probably after the church of St Mary Magdalen, which stands between Magdalen Streets East and West. However, possibly after St Mary Magdalen Hall (or Maudlen Hall) on the north side of the church opposite what was the Balliol College ball-court. Earlier spelled Magdalene. Usually pro–nounced as in the College.

Magdalen Street East   See Magdalen Street.

Magpie Lane   An old name revived, after a local inn in existence in 1662, 1772 and 1814.. In about 1220 it was Grope Cunte Lane, Groppe Lane in 1238, Grope Lane in 1483, from a common medieval term for a dark and disreputable pas-sage. In the late 15th century also called Winkin Lane after Wynkin (aka Winken or Winkin) de Wode, who had a printing press in the lane. By 1888 known as Grove Street or Lane chosen as a less disreputable name. The present street name is from 1927. The southern end was still called The Grove on a 1938 map. See *Street Names in the Early Days.*

Magpie Lane in April 2009.

Maidcroft Road   After a local field name, Madecroft Furlong in 1210, Medcroft in 1240 and Maidecroft in 1630. Road named in 1931.

Malford Road   After Richard Malford, warden of New College 1396-1403. See Cranley Road. The land here was bought from New College and Magdalen College, and the roads are named after prominent members of those colleges.

Mallard Close   In the bird series of roads in Blackbird Leys. Named in 1959.

Mallinson Court   After Rev Arnold Mallinson, (1896-1985) vicar of the local St Frideswide's church from 1933 to 1976, noted for his good sermons and keen sense of humour. He had previously been Curate of St Thomas and had served in the Royal Navy in the First World War. He was an expert on coins and became a Fellow of the Royal Numismatic Society in 1923. Street named in 1972.

Maltfield Road   After a local field name spelled Malte Furlong in 1605 on a Corpus Christi map. Officially named in 1949.

Mandelbrote Drive   On the site of the Littlemore Hospital, which opened as a public institution in 1846 and soon started to admit patients from all over southern England. It was able to take in mentally ill patients from the workhouses and to give them more appropriate care.   It was taken into the NHS and in 1982 into the Oxfordshire Health Authority. By 1996 the buildings had become less suitable for modern mental health care; the hospital was moved across the road and the buildings converted and redeveloped into housing, now known as St George's Manor. Bertram Mandelbrote was a consultant psychiatrist and a pioneer of improving methods of helping patients back into the community – many ware enabled to take jobs outside a hospital setting. Named in 1999.

Manor Park   Not known.

Manor Place   Named in 1893. See Manor Road.

Manor Road   After Holywell Manor next to St Cross Church, existing since at least the 13th century, rebuilt by Merton College in 1516; little early architecture remains since modified for Balliol College use in 1930. Street named in 1893.

Mansfield Road   After Mansfield College, founded as a Free Church centre for Oxford in 1886, built in 1887-9, from 1955 had the status of a Permanent Private Hall within the University, made a full college in 1995. Shown on a map of 1888, but the southern end only as a dotted line between Jowett Walk and Holywell.

Manzil Way   An Urdu (or Hindi) word meaning destiny. The name was suggested in 1989 by the Asian Cultural Association whose offices are nearby, and adopted in 1990.

Margaret Road   Possibly after Margaret of Anjou (c1430-82) Queen Consort to Henry VI who in conflict with the Duke of York started the Wars of the Roses in 1455. **York Road** and **Avenue** are nearby. Street named in 1930.

Marigold Close   In the herbs and plant series in Blackbird Leys. Named in 1993.

Marjoram Close   In the herbs and plant series in Blackbird Leys. Named in 1961.

Mark Road   After Captain Mark Ulick Weyland, Chairman of the short-lived Headington Rural District Council. Street named in 1937. See also Weyland Road

Market Street   After the covered market built here in 1774. It has had many names, including Jesus College Lane in 1762 and 1821, named after the College. Originally Cheney lane, with various spellings (Le Cheyne Lane, Cheyne Lane) in 1315, c1330-40, 1384, 1513, and 1618, after the chain fixed across the road to restrict access. Also at one time Mildred's Lane as it led to the west end of that church, and Bedford Street after a family who lived there.

Marlborough Close   Littlemore. After the Duke of Marlborough who owned land in Littlemore in 1819. The nearby Marlborough Head , now converted into flats, was originally a large private house built in 1888, named after the Marlborough, a three masted man-of-war.

Marlborough Road   After the Dukes of Marlborough and laid out in the 1880s. The road follows the line of the first railway into Oxford from Didcot, built in 1842 by the Great Western Railway to Oxford Station, then at the west end of Western Road. The southern end, below Whitehouse Road, was once known as Archer Street. Named in 1884.

Marriott Close   After Sir John Arthur Ransome Marriott, MP for Oxford 1917-22, knighted in 1924. He taught modern history at Oxford and wrote over 40 books on historical and political subjects including *The English in India (1932)* and *The Tragedy of Europe (1941)* Named in the late 1970s.

Marsh Lane   Means 'marshy lane' similar in derivation to the nearby village of Marston. Spelled The Maerche Dyche in 1550, The Common Marshe and Marshe Dich Furlong both in 1605. Street named in 1940.

Marsh Road

After Cowley Marsh which stretched into Florence Park. It ceased to be open space in 1849, when the Enclosure Act was passed. Street named in 1932.

Marshall Road

After F E Marshall, Chairman of the Parish Council when the street was laid out. Named in 1930.

Marston Ferry Road

The first mention of a ferry across the Cherwell is in 1279 in the Hundred Rolls when it was held as a freehold of the Manor by two tithemen of Oxford. The exact position cannot be identified earlier than shown on a map of 1876. The road was once private, known as Marston Ferry Road by 1847, running only a short distance east from Banbury Road before becoming a pathway to the river. This short path was called Northern Meadows on the Inclosure map of 1829 after the farm of that name. Marston Ferry Link Road and bridge were built in 1971 to meet Cherwell Drive, Marston. After consultation with Oxfordshire County Council in April 1971 the City Highways Committee renamed the road Marston Ferry Road for its whole length. The bridge is not the first across the river, as Fairfax flung a temporary bridge from Marston across the Cherwell in May 1646, and quartered his men on the west side facing the northern line of the Parliamentarians in the city.

Marston Road

Marston is from *march*, or marsh, and *tun*, OE, meaning enclosed piece of ground, spelled Mersce in 1050, Mersttune in c1069 and Mershetone in 1402, Mayston in 1529 and Marston by 1531. Road named in 1874.

Marston Street

Presumably after the village. See Marston Road

Mary Price Close

On the site of Milham Ford School, which closed in August 2003. After Miss Mary Price (1902-2002) head teacher at the school 1949-66. As Head, as a member of the Oxford Education Committee and of the National Schools Council she gained a reputation for wisdom and diplomacy and for believing passionately in the importance of providing a good education for girls in public sector schools. She insisted on high standards but was receptive to new ideas (*Times* obituary) She was an author who raised the writing of history to a new literary level and was a keen and accomplished angler. One of her finest achievements was in the merger of Cowley St John and St Edmund Campion schools to form St Augustine's School. After retirement she was awarded the OBE for services to education. Named in August 2007.

Mascall Avenue

Formerly First Avenue, Slade Camp, renamed in 1977 after a local farmer.

Masons Road

Named to perpetuate the stonemasons who worked here in the 15th century. These included William Beckley who lived in the vicinity of what is now Wood Farm. Road named in 1952.

Massey Close

After John Massey, Dean of Christ Church 1686-9. Close named in 1955.

Mather Road

Catherine Mather's endowed school opened at the Chequers Inn in 1805. Her charity was for apprentice boys at Blue Coats School and for the prisoners at Oxford Prison. Mathers Farm nearby was the property of Magdalen college in the early 17th century. Road named in 1946.

Mattock Close

On the site of the former Mattock's Nurseries, established at Windmill Road in 1875. The founder, John Mattock, lived from 1827 to 1913. The Nurseries are among the foremost rose growers in the world, with a reputation for disease resistant varieties and have won many national and international awards. The business moved to Nuneham Courtenay from Headington many years ago. Named in 1983.

Mayfair Road	Named at the suggestion of the estate developers in 1937.
Mayfield Road	After Mayfield House at the east end of the square, now in the grounds of Summerfields School. Road named in about 1897, formerly Diamond Street named after Diamond House built in c1760. Ruth Fasnacht, the local historian, said about the name change "the only road in Summertown with a generally accepted name and they had to change it". See Diamond Place.
Maywood Road	Named at the developers' suggestion in 2007.
Meaden Hill	After a local field named Meaden Hill Furlong in 1613; on a Corpus map of 1605 when it was part of Sutton Field. Officially named in March 1949.
Meadow Lane	After the local Iffley Meadow, known as such in 1762. Lane named in 1927.
Meadow Prospect	After nearby Port Meadow, of which there is a view from this close. The land on which this road was built was formerly known as Robinson's Fields. Road named in 1937.
Medawar Centre	Littlemore Science Park. After Sir Peter Medawar (1915-1987) OM,CH,CBE, medical scientist and zoologist, Nobel Prizewinner for Medicine in 1960. President of the Royal Postgraduate Medical School, Member of the Medical Research Council, Royal Medal of the Royal Society 1959, Fellow of St John's College, Oxford and holder of many honorary degrees in the UK and USA. He worked on graft rejection and it was because of his work on immune intolerance that tissue and organ transplants became more successful. In 1951 he posed the question – why has evolution allowed us to deteriorate as we age?
Medhurst Way	Speedwell First School site. After Marjorie Medhurst, head teacher of the school 1957-75. She promoted the name change to Speedwell School. Named in March 2006.
Mercury Road	Among the plant and herb series of road names in Blackbird Leys. Road named in 1961.
Mere Road	Means 'boundary' and said to have been suggested by H O King, a major landowner in Wolvercote. Port Meadow grassland boundaries were defined using mere stones. Spelled Meer Stone in 1758. There was already a house called Mere House in First Turn, occupied by the Misses Collcutts. The house was later called Fairlawn, and the name was re-used for the block of flats here. Road named in 1939.
Merewood Avenue	A bucolic and rural name, probably inspired by the wooded landscape here before development of the Sandhill Estate and perhaps by a stream once running through it. Named in about 1935.
Merlin Road	In the bird series of road names in Blackbird Leys. Named in 1959.
Merrivale Square	Waterways. After Maria Sophia Merrivale, d1928, Oxford's first woman councillor (1907) – an Independent and later a Conservative councillor for the North Ward. Named in 1996.
Merton Court	Name proposed by the developers, in a series after Oxford colleges. Named in 1996.
Merton Grove	After the College.
Merton Street	After the College founded by Walter de Merton on land bought in 1264. From before 1200 it was St John's Lane after the Merton College chapel which was originally the parish church of St John the Baptist. In 1797 the east end was known as Coach and Horses Lane and the west end King

Street. Later, the eastern end was also Hare Hall Lane, or Nightingale Hall Lane, running from the High Street to Merton College gardens, but this disappeared when the Examination Schools were built. Wood (in the 17th century) says that St John the Baptist Street was corrupted at times to Joneson Street. It was still Merton Lane in 1772. Its medieval cobblestones have been threatened with extinction from time to time but have fortunately survived.

Meyseys Close Horspath Driftway, although with Headington postal addresses. Named in March 1998 after land on the corner of Hollow Way and Horspath Driftway, including this site, recorded on the Inclosure Award for Cowley dated 1853.

Middle Way Parallel to and midway between **Woodstock and Banbury Roads**, known as 'The Furlong called Twene the Ways' in the 14th century. Later Centre Road, with its northern end called Oak Lane after a tree planted at the corner with Squitchey Lane by Crews Dudley (see Dudley Court). The whole lane was known as George Street, Summertown in c1862-5. It was agreed by the City Council in February 1955 to rename it as Twining Street after Councillor (later Alderman) Francis Twining who served on the Council for 50 years and was mayor in 1905. A local boy made good and a member of one of Oxford's oldest families, he developed much of Summertown and gave land to the church and schools. However there was a petition signed by 62 residents of George Street who did not want to live in a street named after a grocer's shop and someone who sold tea. It was renamed Middle Way in the same year. See *Snobbery and Street Names*

Mileway Gardens Heron Homes development, Warneford Hospital site, named in 1992, after one of the many milestones still remaining in Oxford, prescribed by the Turnpike Acts of the 18th century.

Millbank Mill Street. Named in March 1995.

Mill Lane Iffley. After Iffley Mill, first mentioned in 1160. Bought by Lincoln College in 1445, it was powered by the nearby weir. From 1890 to 1908 it was used for milling by the Iffley baker Mr Jackman. It withstood storms and floods for over seven hundred years and had been a favourite subject for artists but was destroyed by a fire in May 1908. Spelled Mill Way in c1840. Lane named in about 1930.

The mill at Iffley in the early 19th century.

Mill Lane   Old Marston. After Marston Mill, now demolished.

Mill Road   Formerly Mill Lane, named after the Wolvercote Mill, a water mill since the 11th century, established as a paper mill by 1660. Dr John Fell, Dean of Christ Church was influential in fitting out the mill and it became famous for its paper, especially for Bibles. The mill was bought by the Clarendon Press in 1870 on the initiative of John Combe (see Combe Road) who had taken on the Mill in 1855 when it had become almost derelict. The mill no longer exists.

Mill Street   After Oxford Castle Mill mentioned in the Domesday Book of 1086, a water mill for corn and a dam for water control to the castle moat, pulled down for road widening in 1930. Street named in c1868-70, mainly developed between 1866-82. The mill was resented by bakers and others after a law passed in 1534 made it compulsory to have all grain milled exclusively there. The mill fell into disrepair and was repaired by the city in 1685.

Oxford Castle Mill in about 1820.

Millers Acre   After a field name of 1300. Named in 1960.

Millway Close   After a local field spelled Short and Long Millway Furlong in 1834. Officially named in 1965, developed in 1967. Thought to be a suitable name as it is situated off Godstow Road, leading to Wolvercote Mill (now demolished).

Milne Place   Northway. After a field name, Milne Furlong, on a 1605 Corpus map. Recommended by the Housing Committee and agreed by Highways Committee in 1949.

Milton Road   After the poet John Milton (1608-74). Street named in 1922. See Shelley Road.

Milvery Way   Littlemore. Originally Smithfield Entry, later named after a combination of the names Miles and Avery – Miles was a Littlemore Parish Councillor and Avery represented Littlemore on the County Council. *(Changing Faces of Littlemore)*

Minchery Road   In the Knights Templar group, Littlemore. Means 'nunnery' after the local Benedictine nunnery built in the 12th century, dissolved in 1528. Some traces remain. Spelled Minsherie in 1661, The Minshery in 1710 and

Littlemore Minchery in 1893. Minchery Farm still exists - called Mynchery in 1935. (Kelly's) Named 15th November 1954.

Minster Road
After the nearby Bartlemas Chapel. Originally shown on a drawing of the Southfield Building estate, owned by the Oxford Industrial and Provident Land & Building Society. Named in December 1902. See Bartlemas Road.

Mistletoe Green
In the Blackbird Leys plant and shrub series, named in 1997.

Moberly Close
A development for St John the Evangelist Trust Association Ltd, named in April 1980.

Mole Place
Blackbird Leys. Named in 1993, presumably to fit in with, loosely, the flora and fauna theme in the area.

Monks Close
Blackbird Leys. After local connections with the Knights Templar. See also Knights Close, Templar Square and Nunnery Close nearby. Street named in 1960.

Monmouth Road
After the town. in the alphabetical series **Lincoln-Monmouth-Northampton-Oswestry**. Road named in 1932.

Montague Road
After F A Montague, Oxfordshire Councillor. Road named in 1940.

Moody Road
After Emma and Jane Moody, two sisters who started up a nursery school in the Iffley Road in 1889, which later moved to Cowley Place and became Milham Ford School. The site is now part of St Hilda's College. Milham Ford School School was bought by the City in 1938 and moved to the site in Harberton Mead in buildings designed by the City Architect, Douglas Murray. The school was closed in 2003. One of three local roads with connections with the school – see **Prichard** and **Peacock Roads**. Named in March 1960. See also *Celebrating Current Celebrities?*

Moorbank
A countryside name as with many others in Blackbird Leys. Street officially named in April 1959.

Moorhen Walk
In the bird series of Blackbird Leys road names. Named in 1997.

Moreton Road
No known origin. There is no St John's College living in any village called Moreton, but as Fasnacht said, "it sounds all right and may be as meaningless as it is harmless" It is usually considered to be the boundary between North Oxford and Summertown. Road named in 1906.

Morrell Avenue
Probably after G H Morrell, Oxford brewer, owner of the nearby Headington Hill Hall, High Sheriff of Oxfordshire in 1885. However, Frederick Parker Morrell was Mayor in 1889 and his arms are displayed in the Lord Mayor's parlour. His son was Philip Morrell, who lived at Garsington and married the celebrated Lady Ottoline Morrell. The Morrell family played an active part in the affairs of both City and University since the foundation of the family firm of solicitors in 1768. The houses in Morrell Avenue, built by the City Council were of "notably high standard, presumably because they were built at a time of generous Exchequer subsidies". (VCH) The avenue of trees remains. Street built 1929-31 and named in 1931.

Morrell Crescent
Littlemore

Morris Crescent
After the poet and artist William Morris (1834-96). He was also an architect and painter, who founded the manufacturing and decorating firm of Morris, Marshall and Faulkner, famous for its wallpaper designs and furniture, of which the Pre-Raphaelites Burne-Jones, Webb, Rossetti and Madox Brown were also members. (DNB) Named in 1922.

A William Morris design: "Strawberry Thief".

Mortimer Drive	After Rev J H Mortimer, vicar of Marston church for 46 years between 1905-51. Famous for playing a hymn each night on the church bells, also for his generosity and absent-mindedness. He would give away his coat to a beggar who would usually sell it, and once gave a lift to a lady into Oxford but forgot about her and came home on the bus. On another occasion he wandered into the church one afternoon to find a lot of people there. When he asked what they were doing there they replied that they were waiting for him to take the service – it was a wedding. He was keen on trains, knew all the timetables and had an engine named after him. Named in the 1950s.
Mortimer Road	Rose Hill. Probably after a High Steward of Oxford, as are many road names on Rose Hill, but there is no record of such.
Mount Place	Links Canal Street with Mount Street, Jericho. See Mount Street
Mount Street	Jericho. Possibly after a stone mounting block once common in the area. (Marriott) Street named in 1881.
Museum Road	After the University Museum erected in 1855-60 nearby in Parks Road. The Pitt Rivers Museum was added in 1885-6. The road has existed at least since 1872, when the north side was Museum Villas and the south side Museum Terrace. By 1877 it was all Museum Road.

N

Napier Road
Possibly after the Napper family, well known farmers and landowners in the parish. Street named in January 1931.

Navigation Way
Waterways. After the Navigation House pub (demolished in the 1960s) once on the canal wharf, north of Aristotle Lane. Named in 2000.

Nelson Street
After Admiral Lord Horatio Nelson (1750-1805). Wellington Street is nearby. The synagogue was rebuilt at the Richmond Road end in 1973. Street named in 1868, formerly New College Street.

Nether Durford Close
Slade Hospital site, after a local field. Named in 1999.

Netherwoods Road
Probably named after the lower (nether) woods, at the foot of which the road is set out.

Nettlebed Mead
Blackbird Leys. Named in 1997.

New College Lane
After New College, to which it leads, founded in 1379 by William of Wykeham, Bishop of Winchester and Chancellor of England in 1386. It is

New College Lane in 1825 (by J C Buckler). MS. Don.a. 3 n.77
Courtesy of Bodeian Library, University of Oxford.

'New' College because it was the first to be purpose built for students; previously colleges had bought and adapted existing houses. Wykeham was bishop of the richest See in England and so had the funds to endow the new buildings. The lane was sometimes called St John's Street 1661-6 (Wood). Un-named in the Middle Ages. In 1648 Vicus Coll Novi ran from Cat Street into Vicus Coll Lincoln. Spelled as now in 1772. New College Street was mentioned in Gardener's Directory of 1852. On maps of 1889 and 1897 the street was that part of the lane between Catherine Street (Formerly Cat Street, now **Catte Street**) to the main entrance of New College. There was no through road from the street to the lane.

New Cross Road   It has been suggested that this is simply a descriptive name for the new road connecting **Pitts Road** and **Gladstone Road.** Named in 1930.

New High Street   Originally High Street, Headington and then, for a while, High Street, New Headington (1930). Then changed to avoid confusion with many other High Streets in Oxford in July 1941.

New Inn Hall Street   Formerly The Street of the Seven Deadly Sins, derived from 'synnes' or 'sinns', meaning poor tenements or cottages, mentioned as early as 1477. This lane was the northern part of the present street; until the 19th century New Inn Hall street continued on into the present St Michael's Street. The medieval New Inn Hall itself was a place of study formerly called Trillocks, used in the Civil War for the melting down of silver plate donated by Colleges to be made into coins, in support of the King against the Parlia-mentarians. It reverted to a place of study after the

The fire at New Inn Hall in October 1776 (by Malchair, courtesy of Magdalen College).

Restoration. On 21st October 1776 a disastrous fire destroyed much of the building. The Hall declined and in 1821 only the Principal's house remained. St Peter's College is now on the site. The Methodist Meeting House was built on the east side of the street in about 1780 and a plaque records that John Wesley preached there on 17th July 1783. See *Street Names in the Early Days.*

Newlin Close
Possibly after a local family in the 17th century who had given a chalice to Iffley Church in 1679. (Marriott) Close named in 1946.

Newman Road
Littlemore. After Cardinal John Henry Newman (1801-90), scholar of Trinity College, Vicar of St Mary's church 1828-1843, when he resigned and was received into the Roman Catholic Church, made Cardinal in 1879 and was beatified on 19th September, 2010. He helped to build Littlemore Church in 1835-6 and built Priory College and School. Formerly New Road.

John Henry Newman

New Road
The 'new' road built beside the castle, one of only two major streets laid in Oxford between 1066 and 1872, the other being King Edward Street. The road was cut through the Castle precincts and part of the base of the mound in 1770-71.

New Road in the early 19th century.

Newton Road
Probably after Sir Isaac Newton (1642-1727), (Marriott) philosopher, mathematician and scientist, a Cambridge man who discovered differential calculus, conceived the idea of universal gravitation and made a reflecting telescope (DNB). Street named in 1890.

Nicholas Avenue Probably after the Norman church of St Nicholas, Marston. Named in the 1950s.

Nicholson Road After Sir Sydney Hugo Nicholson (1865-1947) founder of the Royal School of Church Music; B.Mus.Oxon (1902), organist at Westminster Abbey 1918-1928, Professor of Music at Oxford. In the New Marston musicians' group of road names. Road named in 1948 or '49, extended in 1979

Nightingale Avenue In the bird series in Greater Leys, named in 1993.

Nixon Road Probably after the Oxford benefactor Alderman John Nixon who in 1658 founded a free school at the Guildhall, the site of the present Town Hall. He endowed the school with the salary of a schoolmaster. Admitted a Freeman of the City in 1615. The road existed by 1924.

Norfolk Street Formerly New Street in 1868 and Commercial Road in 1862. Rebuilt, not on the exact line of the original street, in the St Ebbe's redevelopment and named in 1968. Probably named after the pub established in 1874 as the Norfolk Ale and Porter Stores, which closed in 1963.

Norham End See **Norham Gardens**.

Norham Gardens After a local field name meaning 'north meadow', spelled Northam in 1225 and in 1545-6. St John's College bought what was to become the Norham Manor Estate in 1573 from Richard Owen, physician to Henry VIII for £1566. The first wave of development did not begin until 1833, when William Wilkinson (1810-1901) was commissioned to lay out the estate. Most of the houses were designed by him, Frederick Codd, E G Bruton, Charles Buckeridge and John Gibbs. Named in 1870.

Norham Road Built in 1872-80, named in 1870. See **Norham Gardens**.

Normandy Crescent Horspath Road Estate. Commemorating the Normandy landings of 5th June 1944 and the old Cowley airfield from where troops of the Oxfordshire and Buckinghamshire Light Infantry took off in gliders for the assault. Named 17th December 1956.

Norman Smith Road Blackbird Leys. After a former youth leader and employee of Oxford City Council Parks Department. Named in 1994.

Norreys Avenue After Henry, Lord Norreys of Wytham, MP for Oxfordshire in 1571. The family name is Bertie (pronounced Bartie) See Bertie Place. The beaver, one of the supporters on the City Arms, was from his arms. A Bertie shield is in the Lord Mayor's parlour, showing battering (or bartering) rams, a heraldic pun. Lord Norreys and Sir Frances Knollys were two of the richest and most powerful men in Oxfordshire and were with Elizabeth I when she visited Oxford in 1566 and presented the coat of arms to the City. Named in 1893.

Northampton Road After the town. in the alphabetical series **Lincoln-Monmouth-Northampton-Oswestry**. Named in 1932.

Northfield Close Littlemore. After a local field spelled Northfield. A brook and farm are named after it and recorded in 1840.

Northfield Road See Northfield Close. Named in 1930.

Northmoor Place Named c1979. See Northmoor Road.

Northmoor Road After the St John's College living at Northmoor, Oxon, one of the farms given to the College by its founder, Archbishop Chichele; first appearing on a map of 1897 and named in 1898.

North Parade Avenue   To the north of the City, a street and local shopping area developed around old farm buildings from 1833, usually known by residents as North Parade - a resident once said the addition of 'Avenue' "merely excites ridicule". Before the building of SS Philip & James Church this was a cul-de-sac built at the time of the St Giles Inclosure. There is a popular myth that Royalist troops paraded here during the Civil war but there is no evidence of this and there is known to have been a parade and exercise ground in the (New) Parks.

North Place   Possibly after the house of the same name.

North Street   At the northern end of Osney Town square plan. Street named in the 1850s.

North Way   Another name for the A40 Northern Bypass. Next to the Headington roundabout is a row of houses also called North Way. The City suggested changing this to Alden Avenue, after the late mayor, to avoid confusion with the main road but the residents petitioned against the change (see *Snobbery and Street Names*). Named in 1938.

Norton Close   After one of the old Headington quarrymen, whose name is recorded in the accounts of Merton College. See also Kennett Road and Piper Street. Named in c 1967.

Nowell Road   After Dr Thomas Nowell (1730-1801) and his wife Sarah Nowell who were distinguished inhabitants and benefactors of Iffley and who by 1789 had acquired Iffley Manor. He was Regius Professor of Modern History and Public Orator at Oxford, Principal of St Mary's Hall 1764-1801. Sarah Nowell left money for the free education of children; the Nowell scholars in their scarlet cloaks added colour to the village in their time. An annual Nowell dinner was for many years held on her birthday on 1st January. Named at the suggestion of Lincoln College in November 1946.

Nuffield Road   After William Morris, Lord Nuffield, motor manufacturer and great benefactor of Oxford, from whom the City had bought the land for the Wood Farm Estate. He was born in Worcestershire as the pears on his arms allude to – also on the arms of Nuffield College. He was the first of his family not to have been born in or near Oxford since the 16th century. Road named in 1952.

Lord Nuffield in 1939, congratulating the Works Manager on the millionth Morris car (courtesy of Newsquest, Oxford Mail and Times)

Nunnery Close   In the Knights Templar group in Blackbird Leys. Officially named in 1960. See Minchery Road.

Nursery Close   On the site of a former nursery or market garden.

Nuthatch Close   In the bird series of Blackbird Leys road names. Named in 1997.

Nye Bevan Close   After Aneurin Bevan, usually known as Nye Bevan (1897 –1960), the prominent Welsh Labour politician. He was a key figure on the left of the party in the mid-20th century and was the Minister of Health at the time of the formation of the National Health Service. Cowley Road Hospital site. Named February 1990.

O

Oakthorpe Place   See Oakthorpe Road.

Oakthorpe Road   A made up name – it is a type of good quality coal, but it seems unlikely to have been chosen for that reason. See also Beechcroft and Thorncliffe Roads, also probably as whimsically named. The estate originally belonged to the Oxford Industrial and Provident Land and Building Society Ltd, shown on a drawing of 1893, built between 1890-4, and named in 1894.

Oatlands Road   After Oatlands Meadow, a field shown on maps of 1606 and 1848 and known as Bulstake Mede in the Middle Ages. Road named in 1912. See also Bulstake Close.

Observatory Street   After the nearby Radcliffe Observatory built in 1772-75 by H Keene and J Wyatt for the trustees of the estate of the physician John Radcliffe (1652-1714). The upper octagon is a copy of the Tower of the Winds in Athens. It ceased to be used as an observatory in 1935 and was bought from the

The Tower of the Winds – the Observatory.

trustees by Lord Nuffield who gave it to the University for the Nuffield Institute for Medical Research. After the institute moved to the Radcliffe Infirmary in 1976 the building was taken over by Green College in 1979. The college is for graduates only, named after its benefactors Mr & Mrs Cecil Green of Dallas, Texas. Mr Green was the founder of Texas Intruments, born in Lancashire but moved with his parents to Canada when a child. Now known as Green-Templeton College after a merger of the two colleges. See also Wyatt Road.   Street built in the early 19th century, recorded in Hunt's Directory in 1840.

Old Barn Ground   Slade Hospital site, possibly after a local field. Named in 1999.

Old Greyfriars Street   After the Greyfriars' Monastery which once stood on the site. Street officially named in 1969. The 'Old' was added to differentiate it from the original Greyfriars Street. The Grey Friars, or Franciscan Minor Friars, came to Oxford in 1234. Their property ran from the City walls to the Trill Mill Stream. Henry III gave them land there, known as Paradise Gardens. See **Paradise Street**.

Old High Street   Renamed in July 1941, since High Street, Headington, named in 1930, caused confusion with other High Streets.

Old Marston Road   The old route to Old Marston. Road re-named in 1955 to avoid confusion with Marston Road, when the latter was extended to Cherwell Drive. See **Marston Road.**

Old Road   The old coach road from Oxford to London, running from St Clement's, up Cheney Lane, Warneford Lane, Old Road, over Shotover Hill to Wheatley. It had fallen into disrepair by 1775 as a new turnpike road had been built in 1771. There is a highway stone in the present Warneford Lane which reads "Here endeth Oxford Mileway 1667". The flying coach once travelled from Oxford to London in one day in 1669. After that date there are many records of bills for the repair of the highway. The old road was plagued by highwaymen. A short section between Warneford Lane and the old City boundary was called Shotover Old Road in 1824, also London High Way in 1628 and London Way in 1717-8. Old Road first appeared in directories in 1930 and replaced the use of Shotover Road officially in May 1946. The modern road runs from Gypsy Lane to Shotover.

Oliver Road   Probably after Oliver Cromwell, whose sister Robina might have owned property in Cowley. Road named in 1935.

Orchard Court   Built on the site of 113-115 Rose Hill.

Orchard Way   Littlemore. After a large orchard once on this site.

Oriel Square   After the College, which had requested the name, maintaining this was the original name of the square. Formerly Canterbury Square after the Canterbury Gate of Christ Church, but there was no objection to the name change in April 1953; Oriel College is a 14th century foundation, Christ Church is from the 16th.

Oriel Street   After the College, founded in 1324 by Adam de Brome, Rector of St Mary the Virgin, under licence from Edward II. Originally Shidyerdestret in c1220, Sidyerd in 1238 and c1275. Later St Mary Hall Lane in 1772 and 1797. The name derives from La Oriole, the name of a house acquired from the Crown by the College in 1329, sometimes spelled Oryell and from a building with a large projecting window (Pevsner).

Orchard Court. Taken in 1999.

Oriel Square, looking north.

Osberton Road   After Osberton House, then at no 46, set back from the Woodstock Road, pulled down when the road was built through the site. The house had been home to a flourishing boys' school. Osberton Radiators factory was in this road until it was moved to the Morris Radiators site off Woodstock Road in about 1985. Road named in 1908. Charles Ponsonby House (sheltered housing) is in this road.

Osborne Close   After Henry Osborn King, a major landowner in Wolvercote, although spelled incorrectly (see text on Lambourn Road). He was also a musician and hymn writer, and composed the hymn tune 'Wolvercote'. Named in 1940.

Osler Road   After the physician Sir William Osler (1849-1919), born in Ontario, studied at Toronto and Montreal, and appointed to many Chairs in North America. FRCP in 1884, FRS in 1898, Regius Professor of Medicine at Oxford 1904-19. He was the best known physician of his time and was a great teacher. One of his charms was the interest he took in obscure workers in any field of medicine. The road was formerly Manor Road, which was named in 1930 at the request of John Mattock, the rose grower, after the 17th century Manor Farm, but officially renamed in November 1958 despite objections from Mr Mattock.

Osney Lane   Spelled Osanig in 1003, Oseneia in 1130 and Osneia in 1230, but also with many other spellings. The City revived an early version in naming Oseney Court, on Botley Road. The name derives from ousen-eye, an island in the river; Ouse is a possible early name for the Thames. See text on *Osney*.

Osney Mead   Name suggested by the estate developers and adopted in February 1966. The mead was formerly a meadow at the end of Ferry Hinksey Road, first developed as an industrial estate in 1961.

Oswestry Road   After the town, in the alphabetical series **Lincoln-Monmouth-Northampton-Oswestry.** Named in 1934.

Ouseley Close   In the musicians' group of Marston road names, after Sir Frederick Arthur Gore Ouseley, second baronet (1825–1889), Professor of Music at Oxford from 1855 to 1889. He was a gifted composer, musician and pianist and was said to have "made music more respectable in Oxford". He was known to have escaped to a friend's house because "imploring remonstrants chivvied him in the streets, but he kept conscientiously to the line he had drawn, with the result that in a few years time the Oxford doctorate came to be estimated as it never had been before" (Tuckwell). In 1979 residents petitioned the Council to have the trees in this road felled because they oozed a sticky substance, but the Council refused. Named in 1936.

Sir Frederick Ouseley in about 1856.
(From Tuckwell)

Outram Road	In the India series of colonial military figures, after General Sir James tram, first baronet, 1803-1863) who fought in the Indian Rebellion of 1857 . (See also **Cornwallis, Campbell** and **Lytton roads**.) Named in 1935.
The Oval, Rose Hill	After its street plan. Named in 1946.
Overbrook Gardens	Not known.
Overdale Close	Off Barton Village Road. Name suggested by the Housing Committee in October 1948 because of "the topographical features of the land... as "it is at the top of the dell or ravine" in this case that of the Bayswater Stream. Named in November 1948.
Overmead Green	Blackbird Leys. Means 'above a meadow', after a local field name spelled Le Overmede in c1240. Its old spelling was used by the Education Committee for one of its junior schools on the estate. Officially named in 1960.
Owens Way	Temple Cowley school site. Named after Henry Robert Owens, the first Head of School, appointed in 1932 and remained there until about 1947.
Oxeye Court	In the plant group of road names in Blackbird Leys, after the ox-eye daisy, abundant in hayfields and pastures, sometimes known as the dog daisy. Named in 1997.

The oxe-eye daisy.

Oxford Road	Cowley. The city name is supposed to derive from the 'oxen ford', probably under or close to the present Folly Bridge; however it is also possible that the name comes from "ousen ford" meaning a ford across a river. The earliest form of the name appears in the Anglo Saxon Chronicle of 912 as Oxnaforda. St Frideswide gives Oxenford and Domesday has Oxeneford. There were many variations in medieval times. Formerly Pile Road spelled Pyell Furlong in 1345, and Pile in 1752, it ran from Marsh Road to Temple Cowley. Also formerly Temple Cowley Street from Temple Cowley to Hollow Way. The stretch between the City boundary and Hollow Way was in the early 20th century known both as Pile Road and Cowley Road; in March 1930 the City agreed to name this entire length Cowley Road.
Oxford Road	Old Marston. (For the derivation of Oxford, see Oxford Road, Cowley.) The old road from Oxford to Marston now applies to the stretch between Old Marston village and Old Marston Road.
Oxford Road	Rose Hill. Part of the old Henley to Oxford road, the present stretch running from Ashurst Way to Littlemore. (For the derivation of Oxford, see Oxford Road, Cowley.)
Oxpens Road	After a local farm that once penned oxen, but the name may originally have come from a field name. In the 1870s the Rev W H Smithe of St Thomas' Church recalled "a cowman employed at the Ox-Pens Farm was frequently at evensong and often fell asleep from weariness as his working day lasted from 4am until 6pm" (Squires) Even in the 1920s the fields to the south were known as the Ox Pens. The road did not exist before the 1850s and earlier was known as Nuns' Walk. Road named in 1932 when called The Oxpens Bypass.

P

The Paddox

A large house called Apsley Paddock (or Paddox) once stood on the site, in 1869 directories given as Apsley Lodge. It was the home of Charles Robertson who paid for the building of the Roman Catholic Church, the family's private chapel to which the public were admitted. Between 1922-25 it was owned by the Clapperton family. Renamed Field House in 1931 by St Edward's School, which had bought it in 1925. Apsley Paddox nearby is a private road. Named in about 1969.

Paddox Close

See The Paddox. Named when it was thought there would be a connection between this road and The Paddox. In the event there is no through road here. This can still cause confusion. The close is off Squitchey Lane

Paget Road

Horspath Road Estate. Possibly after Francis Paget (1851-1911), Dean of Christ Church in 1892 and Bishop of Oxford in 1901. Named 17th December 1956.

Palmer Road

After a Headington curate, Mr Palmer, who had supported the Quarry villagers in a dispute with landowners at the time of the Inclosure award. Road named in 1953 when spelled Palmers Road.

Paradise Square

Built 1838-47 and called a 'desert waste' in 1851. However, some attractive domestic buildings replaced the waste land. St Ebbe's rectory was built in the square in 1852, designed by G E Street, and a school in 1858. In 1971 the eastern side of the square was pulled down for the Westgate multi-storey car park, built 1973-4. The earliest reference to the land is on a map of c1605; in 1661-66 it was an orchard. Paradise is a Persian word for garden. An Edwardian guide book states that the gardens "were the fashionable resort of all the Oxford toasts and beaux". The Paradise

Paradise Square.

Gardens replaced the orchard of the Greyfriars. Market gardening was especially developed after the Civil War. Thomas Wrench (d 1714) of Paradise Gardens was called 'the best kitchen gardener in England'. The Tagg family took over from him and were paying their workmen as much as £700 in 1725, a large amount in those days (VCH). See Paradise Street.

Paradise Street   After the medieval fruit garden in the grounds of the Penitentiary Friars, a haven in the poor surroundings of the medieval parish. In 1710 the traveller Zacharias von Uffenback wrote about a visit to the Paradise Garden near a waterside inn, "with countless little retreats... where the Fellows drink in the summer". Also "The garden is chiefly dedicated to cookery, though it has fine fruit trees and yews. Never have I seen such a mass...of these last together". Spelled Paradise and Paradise Garden in 1890-1 and c1874. Formerly West-Gate Street (Wood)

Park Close   After the adjoining Cutteslowe Park as suggested by the developer. Officially named in 1969.

Park End Place   Named in 1961. Off Park End Street.

Park End Street   The street was laid out in 1772, under an Act of Parliament of 1771, together with New Road, as a new western approach to Oxford. With many garage premises it was known between the World Wars as 'The Street of Wheels'. Some of the coal delivered to the nearby canal wharf came from Park End Colliery in the Forest of Dean, now known as Parkend. The company was formed by Edward Prothero in 1820 and it was soon advertising that coal would be available in Oxford from 1821. By 1831 Prothero owned 32 pits in the Forest of Dean and employed between 400 and 500 men. The company continued to trade until March 1892 when it was taken over by another firm. (Parkend Local History Society)

Parker Street   Possibly after J H Parker (1833-1912) celebrated author of *Early History of Oxford 727-1100*. Street named in 1900. (Marriott)

Parks Road   After the University Parks. Spelled Newe Parkes in 1642, when used as troop practice grounds during the Civil War. In the 19th century it was known as Park Street and also Park Road; Parks Road, in the plural, became the correct name as there were both old and new parks here in the 16th century, possibly earlier. From the 17th century the Parks was a place for games and "the cry for new parks" was a cry for a football match between colleges, in those days a "rude and unlawful game" not so regulated as later college matches. On a map of 1817 (published by R Pearson) it was the 'way to the Parks'.

Park Town   Originally named Park Town, Park Crescent and Clarendon Villas. Park Town was the first part of North Oxford to be developed. Until 1849 it was known as St Giles Field and was then owned by New College. In 1853 two architects, E G Bruton and Samuel Lipscombe Seckham, submitted drawings and the latter was chosen. Earlier plans were for a workhouse and even a railway terminus. In 1858 it became the property of the Park Town Estate Company (dissolved in 1861). Seckham designed Italianate Villas nearer to Banbury Road, then the Crescent (around a central garden) and the Terrace on the eastern part of the site. The separate parts of the estate became known as Park Town in June 1938.

Park Way	Marston, unknown,
Parry Close	Most likely after Sir Charles Hubert Hastings Parry (1848–1918), knighted in 1898, Professor of Music at Oxford from 1900 to 1908. He wrote the music for William Blake's "Jerusalem" and many settings for Aristophanes' plays, including "The Frogs" and "The Birds". On the Wadham College Sports Ground development, in the Musicians' Group in Marston. Named in June 1979.
Parsons Place	After John Parsons, Alderman of Oxford, founder of Parsons' Almshouses, now in St Clement's (Wade) and probably lived at 93 High Street (Gardiner's Directory 1852) near where the almshouses were first established. Named in 1932.
Partridge Walk	In the bird series of Blackbird Leys road names. Named in June 1995.
Pattison Place	After Mark Pattison (1813-84) Rector of Lincoln College, which owned land here. He was an author and journalist with a high reputation as a tutor and was ordained in 1841. A leader in University reform and said to be an inspiring lecturer (DNB). Street named in c1948.
Pauling Road	Wood Farm. After Robert Pauling, mercer, lessee of Mather's Farm in the 1680s. Many cottagers moved out of the city at this time for cheaper living costs. Named in 1953.
Peacock Road	Possibly after a teacher or governor associated with Milham Ford School - see Prichard and Moody Roads. Named in November 1960. See also *Celebrating Current Celebrities.*
Peartree Close	In the tree series of Blackbird Leys road names. Named in 1997.
Peat Moors	The road adjoins the area of land shown on the Headington Inclosure award of 1804 as Peat Moor. There was also a Peat Moor Poor's allotment of 5 acres given in another Inclosure award of 1802, then worth £3 10s. (VCH Bullingdon). Named in 1940.
Peel Place	Probably after Sir Robert Peel (1788-1850) MP for Oxford University in 1817, Prime Minister 1834 and 1841-45. He formed the party known from 1831 as the Conservatives and was the founder of the modern police force (known at the time as Peelers). Wellington said of him "I have never known a man in whose truth and justice I had more confidence". (See **Chatham Road, Fox** and **Canning Crescents**) As an undergraduate at Christ Church he was noted for his hard work Named in 1929.
Pegasus Grange	Retirement complex. Named in 1993. See **Pegasus Road**.
Pegasus Road	Pegasus is a mythical figure, half horse and half man; It is said to have come from an alleged misdrawing of two Knights (Templar) on one horse, and appears on the arms of the medieval order of the Knights Templar, who had connections in the area. Also after the famous University football team that played on the ground here and once won the Amateur Cup. Road named in 1961.
Pembroke Square	Named in 1969.
Pembroke Street	After the nearby College. Known as Pennyfarthing Street from about 1349 to about 1772 (Salter). The original name for the College, before it was founded and renamed by James I in 1624, was Broadgates Hall. The college owes its name to William Herbert, 3rd Earl of Pembroke, then Chancellor of the University. See **Penny Farthing Place.**

Pennycress Road   In the herb and field plants series of roads off Field Avenue in Blackbird Leys. Named in 1961.

Penny Farthing Place   After the medieval street and city bailiff William Pennyferthing (Wood) recorded in 1238. Spelled Pyneferthyyng in 1363, Penie Faerthing Streate in 1578 and Penyfarthing Street in 1772. The present street is not on the line of the original, which is now Pembroke Street; the name was revived when the Westgate Centre was developed between 1969-73 and the modern pub kept alive the old name for a while. See *Street Names in the Early Days.*

Pennywell Drive   After a wood at Elsfield, probably at a spring known as Penniwell in 1703, where votive offerings were made. Named Pennywell Close in 1960 and renamed Drive when extended in 1969. The new road took in Marriott Close which was then discontinued and the name reused for a new road nearby.

Penson's Gardens   Recorded in Gardners' Directory of 1852, with an apostrophe. The Penson family were market gardeners in the area. See *Duplicated Names*

Peppercorn Avenue   Formerly Fifth Avenue, Slade Camp, renamed after a local landowner, in January 1977.

Percy Street   Probably after the estate builder Percy Charles Howard. See **Charles** and **Howard** Streets. Street named in 1862-5.

Peregrine Road   In the bird series in Blackbird Leys. Named in 1959.

Periwinkle Place   In the herb and plant series in Blackbird Leys. Named in 1961.

Perrin Street   After Canon Howard Nasmith Perrin who built the local mission church, after which the street was formerly named Church Street, New Headington in 1930. The present name was suggested by the Vicar, the Rev C E C Markby, in 1955. There had been some disagreement about the nature of the services held in Old Headington from about 1901; the Bishop appointed Perrin to Highfield (All Saints) to build a new Parish Church responsible to the Bishop, on the understanding that the services reflected those of the Church of England. Services at St Andrew's, Old Headington had apparently become "more Roman than Rome". He was married there in 1920. See *Oxford's Lost Church Streets.* Named in 1955.

Peterley Road   After a local field spelled Broad Peterly in 1778, Broad and Little Peterley in c1840. Road named in 1961.

Peters Way   Littlemore. Unknown origin.

Pether Road   Richard Pether and his brother Frederick William held Bartlemas Farm and by 1851 Richard was also renting Wood Farm from Magdalen College. In 1876 Richard's daughter Emily Ann married Frederick Morris at Holy Trinity Church, Headington Quarry and they moved to Worcester where their first son William Richard was born on 10th October 1877 – this William Morris eventually became Lord Nuffield. His father returned to Oxford in about 1881 and was bailiff at Wood farm until about 1891. Named in 1967.

Phelps Place   St Clement's. Unknown, but possibly after a supporter of a parish charity. Named in 1940.

Phipps Road   After the Rev James George Phipps, Lord of the Manor of Cowley in the 18th century. His son, William Phipps, the last lord of Temple Cowley Manor, left it to Pembroke College, where he had been a scholar. He was Rector of Elvethorn, Hants. Road named in January 1931.

Pickett Avenue   Formerly 2nd Avenue, Slade Camp. Named in January 1977, after a local field.

Pike Terrace There had been a Pike Street in the area at least before 1889, now extinct. The name was revived by Highways and Traffic Committee in 1986 for this street of 14 dwellings, off Faulkner Street.

Pimpernel Close In the herb and field plants series in Blackbird Leys. Named in 1961.

Pine Close In the shrub and tree series of Blackbird Leys road names. Named in 1964.

Piper Street After a 15th century local quarryman. Formerly Cross Street, New Headington in 1930, officially renamed in 1958.

Pipit Close In the bird series of Blackbird Leys road names. Named in 1997.

Pipkin Way Alderman Pipkin was Mayor of Oxford 1934-5. The family has long associations, including as builders, in the area. The Donnington Oblong residents, on being consulted, said the name "lacked originality" and would have preferred "flowers, trees or birds". Road named in May 1974.

Pipley Furlong Saunders Dairy site. Named after a local field in 2001

Pitts Road Headington Quarry. After the Headington Quarry pits that existed here from 1396. They were known as Quarry Pittes in 1605, when stone was quarried here for many of the Oxford colleges. There was a Pitt Road elsewhere in the City but this was renamed Chatham Road in 1961 to avoid confusion with this road. Named in 1930. See *Duplicated Names*

Pixey Place Wolvercote. After a local meadow, Pixey Mead, meaning Pic's island, possibly from the Latin *pisces,* meaning fish - spelled Perchesia in 1171-3 and therefore possibly a reference to fishing activity; also recorded as Pekeseye in c1182 and Pixey in 1774. Road named in 1937.

The Plain Means an 'open space among houses', built in 1830. St Clement's Church and many of the houses around it had already been pulled down by 1777 and the churchyard gradually became disused. As traffic increased, particularly on the Iffley Road, a toll house was built here in 1810 and remained until 1874. The Victoria Fountain was installed on 25th May 1899 to commemorate it, restored in 2009. A Boer War memorial was also built in the Plain in 1903, but was removed in the 1950s despite its site being chosen so that it "would always be prominent before the citizens".

Plantation Road After the plantations once here – the site of Tagg's Garden but also possibly

Plantation Road, looking west, 1998.

	of Mr Yates' orchard and garden. Once known as Cabbage Hill. Developed in the 1830s, before the St John's development of Norham Manor, but by then the houses were beyond repair and were replaced by seven new cottages. The name is on a map of 1850.
Plater Drive	After Father Charles Plater who founded the Catholic Social Guild in 1909. It had a Catholic workers' college at nearby 1 Walton Well Road; this later moved to Headington where it was renamed Plater College. Named in 1996.
Plough Close	After the nearby pub on Wolvercote Green, once popular with bargees from the canal, and still very busy in summer nowadays. For more on The Plough, see *Growing Up in Wolvercote* by Michael Stockford (privately published).
Plover Drive	In the bird series of Blackbird Leys road names. Named in 1997.
Pochard Place	In the tree series of Blackbird Leys road names. Named in 1997.
Polstead Road	After the St John's College living at Polstead, Suffolk, acquired in 1830 for £5,500 (VCH). The street was built by H W Moore in 1891-92.
Pond Close	After a pond on this site dating back to at least 1878. Named in March 1997.
Ponds Lane	Named after the ponds which used to surround the church at Marston, and the streams which ran along the sides of this lane.
Pony Road	Horspath Trading Estate. Pony is a slang term for £25 and therefore thought appropriate for a trading estate with a horse connection. Named in 1961 at the suggestion of Councillor Ann Spokes.
Portland Road	On the Twining Estate, where Lonsdale and Hamilton roads are named after peers. Lords Lonsdale and Hamilton were known as sporting peers but there is no sporting connection with the third Duke of Portland (William Henry Cavendish Bentinck, 1738-1809), who had been Chancellor of Oxford University 1792-1809, Home Secretary in 1794-1801 and Prime Minister 1807-9. There is no connection with Summertown but Twining chose the names for his development because "the peerage was a much used source at this time" (Fasnacht). Road named in 1905.
Pottery Piece	Blackbird Leys. Named in 1997.
Poulton Place	In the naturalists' series of Blackbird Leys road names, after Sir Edward Bagnall Poulton (1856-1943) Hope Professor of Zoology 1893-1933, a foremost exponent of protective colouring of insects, founder of the Oxon Natural History Society, lecturer and tutor at Keble and Fellow of Jesus College. He was a great supporter of Darwin's principles of evolution, President of the British Association, FRS, knighted in 1935. He married Emily Palmer, daughter of George Palmer MP of Huntley & Palmers of Reading; they lived at 56 Banbury Road and because it was bought by his father-in-law it was said that he "married the biscuit and got the tin". Named in 1967.
Pound Field Close	After a local field in Barton. Named in March 1971.
Pound Way	After a local field name, thought suitable for Cowley Centre where there are banks. Named in 1962.
Poxon Place	Littlemore
Preachers Lane	An historic name, revived in 1961; the old name for Speedwell Street which runs into the present lane. It was formerly Gas Street, after the gasworks

there, but a proposed name change to Gaslight Street was not liked by Highways Committee. Preachers' Bridge and Preachers' Gate (near Albion Place) were a continuation of Gas Street and Speedwell Street. The common name of the Dominican Order was the Blackfriars or Preaching Friars. Ingram (Vol III) suggests that it was known as Water Lane at one time, also that there was "still a preachers' pool near the gasworks." A road sign in place here for some years after the change back to Preachers' Lane was "Preachers' Lane, formerly Gas Street" but is now removed - the slang word 'gas' describes talk that goes on for too long.

Prestwich Place
On the site of the former City Council Depot, after Joseph Prestwich, Professor of Geology, who was influential in improving the poor drainage in New Botley in the 1880s. Named in July 1993.

Informative plaque in Prestwich Place.

Prichard Road
Harberton Mead. After Alderman Mrs Mabel Prichard, Governor of Milham Ford School, formerly nearby, closed in 2003. She was University member of the City Council and Chairman of the Children's Committee. The name was suggested by the school "as a mark of appreciation for her long and outstanding work in the interests of the school." Another school in Oxford is now named after Mabel Prichard. Road named in November 1960. See *Celebrating Current Celebrities.*

Primrose Place
In the plant and shrub series of road names in Blackbird Leys. Named in 1993.

Princes Street
In the St Clement's Benefactors group, named probably after Edward Prince who bequeathed £500 in 1651, to be lent to five poor Freemen without charge for five years. There was once a Prince's Well in St Ebbe's now demolished. Street known by 1862.

Priors Forge
After a close in Cutteslowe of 15 acres, spelled Priors Piece in 1545, later Priors Forge. Named in 1959.

Priory Road
After the priory built in c1840 by John Henry Newman. See **Newman Road**. Named 15th November 1954.

Prunus Close
In the tree and shrub series of roads in Blackbird Leys. Named in 1964.

Pulker Close
After the Pulker family, well known in the area. In the 15th century Walter Pulker had been a major sheep farmer. In 1518 John Pulker leased from Oseney Abbey the Cowley demesne and rectory. A later Pulker was the Hospitallers' Tenant in Littlemore. William Pulker of the same family founded the Oxonian Press in 1925 and in 1972, when 80, said his family had lived in the area since Domesday and that his ancestors came with Julius Caesar from Rome. *Pulcher* is Latin for beautiful. Formerly Westbury Close, in 1961 it was officially renamed at the suggestion of the developers, G Wimpey & Co.

Pullen's Field
Constructed to serve the new development at 'High Wall', Pullen's Lane, named at the suggestion of the Pullen's Lane Association in February 1972. See **Pullen's Lane**.

Pullen's Lane

After Dr Josiah Pullen, (1631-1714) vicar of St Peter in the East, who had planted a tree in 1711 to commemorate his favourite walk from Magdalen, of which he was Vice-Principal, to Headington Hill. At the time there was an uninterrupted view of Oxford from the hill, as the trees had been felled in the Civil War in case they gave cover to the enemy. Pullen's Tree later became a well known landmark for travellers and could be seen from Wadham College in the 19th century. Spelled Pullen's Tree in 1797 and Joe Pullen's Tree in 1805. Its stump was immortalised in the Reform Act since it marked the boundary of the Parliamentary borough. Road named in 1930.

Joe Pullen's tree.

Purcell Road

Probably after the composer Henry Purcell (1659-95).one of the most distinguished composers to be commemorated in the Marston group of musicians. He, however, had no connection with Oxford but his younger brother Daniel Purcell (1660-1717) had been organist at Magdalen College before moving to London. He copied the style of his brother "but displayed no originality" (DNB) Road named in 1935, extended in 1979.

Purland Close

Unknown. Named in 1968.

Pusey Lane

See Pusey Street.

Pusey Place

Known as Alfred Place until 1948. See Pusey Street.

Pusey Street

Named for Dr Edward Bouverie Pusey (1800-82). The name comes originally from the Berkshire village. He was a leader of the Oxford Movement (a religious movement founded in Oxford in 1833) followers of which opposed liberalism in the church and wanted a return to the pure church of the Early Fathers without interference from the State. (Encyclopaedia of Oxford) The Rev W Tuckwell (*Reminiscences of Oxford*, 1900) described Pusey as a "veiled prophet, always a recluse, and after his wife's death in 1839 invisible except when preaching". Pusey became more influential after Newman left the Church of England and the names 'Puseyite' and 'Tractarian' began to replace 'Newmanite'. Tuckwell also wrote that "no sermons attracted undergraduates as his did". He was a Fellow of Oriel from 1822 and ordained in 1828. Pusey House, founded in 1884, on the corner of St Giles, is named after him. The Library, of which Dr Pusey's books and pamphlets make up the greater part, forms the centre of the original building at 61 St Giles. Buildings were added in 1912 and 1914, including a chapel. The buildings have been shared since 1982 with St Cross College. Formerly Alfred Street, renamed in August 1925, although shown as the older name on a map of 1938.

Q

Quarry High Street   The main road in Headington Quarry, officially named in February 1942, formerly High Street, Headington Quarry, named in 1930. Headington Quarry was recorded as Quarry Pittes on the 1605 Corpus Map, and later became known as The Quarry and Quarry Coppice. The stone from here had become popular in the 17th century as "it cuts very soft and easy" (Plot 1667). However, the reputation of the stone declined in the late 18th century, as it became susceptible to atmospheric conditions and would crumble and weather badly. Its use declined as demand increased for higher quality Clipsham and Portland Stone and the quarries became worked out.

Quarry Hollow   After the many excavations left by quarrymen since the 14th century. Renamed in 1959, formerly St Mary's Road, named in 1930.

Quarry Road   Named in 1930. See Quarry High Street. Quarry became a separate parish (from Headington) in 1850

Quarry School Place   After the local village school. Named in February 1955, until when it had been known as School Place, Headington Quarry – this was to avoid confusion with School Place in Grandpont.

Quartermain Close   After Mrs Quartermain's school, probably the first in Cowley. In 1815 it had 12 children. Road named in 1973.

Queen's Lane   After The Queen's College, by which the lane runs, founded in 1340 by Robert de Eglesfield, named after Queen Philippa, wife of Edward III – he was the King's Clerk and Chaplain to the Queen. He had bought up old tenements and cottages on the site but the college was not built until the 18th century. The college statute provided for a Provost, Fellow, Chaplains and 'poor boys'. The road had no name in the Middle Ages. Part of it was once called Edmund Hall Lane, after the Hall, now a college. Named in 1881.

Queen Street, looking west, in August 1907 (Courtesy of Newsquest, Oxford Mail and Times).

Queen Street

After the popular Queen Charlotte, wife of George III, who both visited Oxford in 1785. Formerly the Great Bailey, or Bayly, or Great Baylly (Wood 1661-2). Salter says it was first called the Bailey in about 1260, and that this term included the castle itself. In 1653 it was known as the New Butcherue, or Butchers' Row, after the City built stalls for the butchers there. Spelled as now in 1817 and 1821-2. See *Street Names in the Early Days* and *Honouring Queens.*

R

Rackham Place   Waterways. After the old name for St Margaret's Road. Named in 2003.

Radcliffe Place   Marston. Presumably after Dr John Radcliffe.

Radcliffe Road   After Dr John Radcliffe (1652-1714). See Radcliffe Square. Named in the 1920s.

Radcliffe Square   After the Radcliffe Camera (1737-49), first known as the Physic Library, enclosed by the square, the western side of which was originally Radcliffe Street. John Radcliffe (1652-1714) was physician to William III and later to Queen Anne. He left most of a considerable fortune to Oxford University, including £40,000, then an enormous sum, for the building of the Library which bears his name, built between 1737 and 1749. He also left money for the Radcliffe Infirmary and for the Asylum, once called the Radcliffe Asylum, now the Warneford Hospital, at the end of Cheney Lane. He made the original designs for the Radcliffe Observatory but

Dr John Radcliffe

after his death the work was completed by James Wyatt with a grant from the Radcliffe Estate. The John Radcliffe Hospital in Headington is also named after him.

Reinstating cobbles in Radcliffe Square, in 2006.

Radford Close	After Rev John Radford, d1851, Rector of Lincoln College, which might have owned land here. Close named in 1948.
Rahere Road	After Rahere, d1144, a famous jester, also the founder and first Prior of St Bartholomew's Hospital, Smithfield, London. Adjacent is **Bartholomew Road** named after the leper hospital once sited in Cowley Road. Road named in 1938. see Bartholomew Road.
Railway Lane	After the branch line that once ran to Littlemore, Horspath and Wheatley.
Rampion Close	In the plant and herb series in Blackbird Leys. Named in 1961.
Ramsay Road	After Sir William Ramsay (1852-1916) Scottish chemist who discovered the gasses helium and argon. Road named in 1930.
Randolph Street	Most likely after the Randolph family who were here in Cowley in the 14th century. Street named by 1870.
Rawlinson Road	After Bishop Richard Rawlinson DCL (1690-1755), who joined St John's, his father's college, in 1708. An antiquary, who, because of his indefatigable habit of collecting material, became an important benefactor to future historians. He was elected FRS at 32 and consecrated bishop in 1728. He was a nonjuring bishop and therefore lost his see, having not taken an oath to William and Mary because he had already sworn to King James. Buried in St Giles after "living the life of the scholar with notable frugality", he left his collections and manuscripts to the Bodleian Library. Road named in 1890-1.

Rawlinson Road in 1998.

Rawson Close	Upper Wolvercote. After Catherine (or Katherine) Rawson who, in her will of 1705, left money to the church for the purchase of land to be settled on trustees. The land bought (with the help of another bequest from David Walter - see also David Walter Close) was nine acres of meadow in Wolvercote known as Poor's Plot. She also left a pound a year for an annual sermon, with ten shillings for the clerk, to be given on her birthday, 16th October. The title deed for Poors Plot was signed by many distinguished

Oxford City and County people on 18th June 1706. The plot belonged to the trust until 2009. Rental income was to help the poor of Wolvercote to buy coal and goods each Christmas. Now known as the Rawson Trust, money is granted to the local school as a bursary for children to pay for school outings. The annual sermon has now lapsed.

Raymund Road After Raymund Haynes (1886-1961), who lived and farmed at Cross Farm, Old Marston for many years, a Councillor for Bullingdon RDC with a special interest in housing after WW2 when these roads were built and housing allocated in the 1950s. He was also a County Councillor for a short time. He served in the Home Guard during the War and was said to have persuaded inebriated locals on the way home from the pub that regulations required them to wear a red light on the back of their trousers. Named in the 1950s. See Haynes Road.

Rectory Road After the nearby St Clement's Rectory built in 1861. The name was suggested by St Clement's Parochial Church Council and by residents as its former name Pembroke Street caused confusion with its St Aldate's namesake. The present road was named in 1959.

Rede Close After Katherine Rede who owned land here at the beginning of the 16th century. Named in 1953.

Redland Road Possibly after a local field name, in reference to the soil colour. Road named in 1950. See *Changing Names*.

Red Lion Square After the local pub, first recorded as a street name in 1842, when George Collins was the publican, one of many pubs serving the nearby cattle market at Gloucester Green. The present building replaced the earlier pub in 1904. After refurbishment in the 1980s it was Oxford's largest pub. In 1990 it was refurbished again and became the Brewhouse, later the Fuggle & Firkin, it is now the Red Lion again..

Redmoor Close After a local field name, in reference to the soil colour. Spelled Redmoore in 1605 and Redmoor in 1849. Named 15th November 1954.

Redwood Close Named after the tree, continuing the namimg theme in this part of Greater Leys, in 1993.

Reedmace Close Greater Leys. In the plant and shrub series, after a type of bulrush with poker-like heads; named in 1993 despite councillors' concerns that the plant is little known and recognised.

Regent Street Probably after the first Prince Regent, later George IV (1811-20). In existence since at least 1884.

Reliance Way Named in August 2003. Named after the Reliance bus manufactured from 1928 by AEC of Southall, west London, used for many years and in large numbers by the Oxford Bus Company, which had a large depot and garage on this site until redeveloped.

Remy Place Robert de Remy was the Norman Lord of the Manor of Iffley in the reign of Henry II and probably built Iffley Church in about 1172-82. The family claimed descent from St Remy (437-533) the French apostle. This was a joint development by The Alice Smith Charity and the Oxford Citizens Housing Association, named in about 1976; the first flats here were occupied in March 1974.

Renaissance Park Barton. Unknown.

Rest Harrow	After an agricultural term for easily worked ground. Named in 1961.
Rewley Road	After local land owned by Richard, King of the Romans, brother of Henry III, the name meaning 'royal place'. In 1281 Rewley Abbey was founded by Edmund, Earl of Abingdon and was built to the north of the present road. Spelled Loco Regali in 1284-5, Rewley in 1289 and Regal Loco in 1290. There was a Rewley (or Ruley) Lane in 1538. Wood, in the 17th century, writes of "a hollow way from....the Abbey". Named in 1874.
Richards Lane	Recorded on the Inclosure Map of 1829 (Fasnacht) Possibly after Robert Richards, recorded here in the 1851 census as living in a nearby cottage, "a haggler, a poor sort of pedlar who was prepared to haggle over his wares" (op cit) Named by 1889, "the most minor road in Summertown" (Fasnacht, op cit)
Richards Way	Risinghurst. After the (lady) inaugurator of the League of Friends of the Radcliffe Infirmary, named in about 1985.
Richmond Road	Possibly after Worcester College land at Richmond, Surrey. Formerly Worcester Terrace. Named in 1899.
Rickyard Close	Named in 1997. On the Rewley Road development. An old deed cites a grant of Nicholas de Holcomb to Sir Henry Grapnel, conveying some land in Rickyard Close, Oxford – however, no location is mentioned.
Riddell Place	After James Ian Campbell Riddell (d1973) former City Engineer with Oxford City Council. He was churchwarden at St Peter's Church, Wolvercote and lived nearby in Sunderland Avenue. The accent is on the second syllable. Named in December 1976
Ridgefield Road	After an old field name, means an area under ridge and furrow cultivation. Spelled Ridge Field and Furlong in 1778, Old Ridges in 1778 and Ridge Field in 1853. Street named in October 1932.
Ridgemont Close	Built on the former Highways depot in Woodstock Road. Named after the type of facing brick, an unusual shade of grey known as Ridgemont Grey; the name suggested by the estate developers. Named in January 1972.
Ridgeway Road	After the straight ridge once a Roman road running from Alchester to Dorchester, alongside the present street to the west. A section is still visible in the grounds of Bayswater School. The road named in October 1931, soon after it was cut.
The Ridings	Possibly after a track popular for horse riding
Ridley Road	Brasenose Estate. After Nicholas Ridley (1500-55) one of the Martyrs sent to Oxford with Bishop Latimer, tried for heresy, excommunicated, declared a heretic and burned alive at the stake in Broad Street on 16th October 1555. He had been Bishop of Rochester and London, became Cranmer's Chaplain in 1537and had begun to reject many Roman doctrines. Road named in 1934.
Rimmer Close	After Rev Paul Rimmer, MA Oxon (Jesus College), b1925, a popular Vicar of Marston from 1959 to 1990. On the site of Boults Farm yard. See *Celebrating Current Celebrities.* Named in the 1990s.
Ringwood Road	Unknown. Named in about 1935.
Rippington Drive	Possibly after the Rippington family, who farmed or owned much of the parish of Marston in the nineteenth century. Named in the 1950s.
Rivermead Park	Developed in 2004.

Rivermead Road	Named in 1946, because of proximity to the river and meadows.
Riverside Road	After a tributary of the Thames and the Seacourt Stream to the west. Road named in 1924.
Roberts Close	Not known.
Robin Place	In the bird series of Blackbird Leys road names. Named in 1997.
Robinson Close	A private road in the University Science Area, named after Robert Robinson (1886-1975) Wayneflete Professor at Magdalen College until 1955, when he retired and became an Honorary Fellow of the College. He was awarded the Nobel Prize for Chemistry in 1947 "for his investigations on plant products of biological importance". Named in 1994.
Rock Edge	After a disused quarry still showing a ragged rock face and cliff edge. Named originally as Rock Hedge, but reverted to the present name in April 1935.
Roger Bacon Lane	After the great scholar, scientist and Franciscan Friar (c1215-c1292) who studied and worked in Oxford for 45 years. A footpath between Pennyfarthing Place and Turn Again Lane, beside St Ebbe's Church. The vicar suggested the name as Bacon lived, died and is buried nearby – a plaque marks the spot. Another suggestion was for "Penny Lane", but this was thought to evoke 'spending a penny' (as opposed to any connection with The Beatles), with which unfortunately the lane inevitably remains connected. A tower known as 'Friar Bacon's study' once stood at Folly Bridge. Named in 1976. See **Folly Bridge.**
Roger Dudman Way	After Roger Alan Dudman, City Councillor for West Oxford 1962-68 and 1971-90. He was Lord Mayor in 1985 and being a widower he invited his friend, the well known Oxford character Olive Gibbs, also a West Oxford Councillor (see Gibbs Crescent) to be his Lady Mayoress. He died in 1995. Road named in 2001.
Rogers Street	After Alderman Harold Sydney Rogers, a distinguished local resident and architect, Mayor in 1937, whose house at 269 Banbury Road backed onto this street. Renamed in 1955 from Church Street, Summertown, named in 1890-1. See *Oxford's Lost Church Streets.*
Rolfe Place	In the New Marston musicians' group, named after James Rolfe, d1972, of Keble, founder and conductor of the Oxford String Players and conductor of the Oxford Youth Orchestra. He was organist at St Andrew's Church, Linton Road, from 1928 to 1965, before moving to Spelsbury. Named in April 1973.

Harold Sidney Rogers as Mayor of Oxford, 1937.

Roman Way

A settlement existed at Cowley as far back as the first century AD and remnants of Roman pottery kilns were found on the corner of Rose Hill and St Luke's Road. Pottery was sold to travellers on the Roman road which then ran from Dorchester (Dorset) to Alcester. Early maps show Roman Way as the eastern boundary of the parish of Cowley.

Roosevelt Drive

After Franklin Delano Roosevelt (1882 –1945), the thirty-second President of the United States, a central figure of the 20th century during a time of worldwide economic crisis and world war. Elected to four terms in office, he served from 1933 to 1945 and is the only U.S. president to have served more than two terms – a third term is no longer permitted. On the Churchill Hospital site, occupied by US troops in WWII. Named in 1992.

Rosamund Road

After Fair Rosamund, d1176, mistress to Henry II and thought to be mother of two of his children. She was educated and buried at Godstow Nunnery. This was to be called Godstow Avenue when it was under construction, but fortunately the name was changed to avoid confusion with Godstow Road. Named in October 1934.

Rosamund Road being built in the 1930s.

Rose Hill

After a house called Rose Hill, built here in c1820 by Dr Ireland, an eccentric medical practitioner, the last man in the neighbourhood to wear a pigtail and ruffles at Mass. The road name was established by 1835 and officially named by the Council in January 1930. The once extensive views from Rose Hill over the spires and towers of Oxford were known to Matthew Arnold. A pottery kiln was found near the road in 1935, thought to date from the 2nd century. In 1871, *Jackson's Oxford Journal* commented that it was hoped the new Rose Hill road would give "some slight relief to Oxford's unemployed". The housing estate here was named after the house and road in 1930.

Rose Lane

After the roses associated with the Botanic Garden set out next door in 1621. Spelled Rose Lane in 1772, Trinitie Lane in the early 17th century and Trinity Lane in 1661-6.

Rose Place	Unknown. Named in about 1868.
Rotha Field Road	After a local field name. Named in April 1955.
The Roundway	After the street plan.
Routh Road	After Martin Joseph Routh, Doctor of Divinity (1755-1854) the longest serving President of Magdalen College, who died in his 100th year, so old that he was said to have spoken to James II. He had a chair made for him from a giant oak which grew in Magdalen Meadows gateway. The name was suggested by the Bursar and accepted in 1947. (VCH)
Rowan Grove	In the tree series of Blackbird Leys road names. Named in June 1995.
Rowland Close	After an old Wolvercote family. Richard Rowland, a farmer, bought the meadow in 1834. Named Rowland's Meadow in 1884 when bought by Wolvercote Mill. The close is on the site of a riding school run by Dennis Organ. Named in 1967.
Rowney Place	Thomas Rowney practised as an attorney at law in the days of Antony Wood – they were said to be close friends. Thomas's son 'young Tom Rowney' was High Steward in 1691. Both had been MPs for Oxford, the father from 1695 to 1705 and the son from 1706 to 1754. Young Thomas, at nearly all his own expense, built the Town Hall in 1692 (replaced by the present Town Hall in 1894). He also built and lived in the house which became the Judges' Lodgings in St Giles. He gave five acres of land on which the Radcliffe Infirmary was built (where a ward was named after him). He died "on the hunting-field" in November 1759 and was much missed. One tribute to him was "to the friendless he was a father". (Oxfordshire: Lord Lieutenants, High Sheriffs and Members of Parliament – Davenport – Clarendon Press)
Rupert Road	After Prince Rupert, Royalist commander during the Civil War 1642-6. His opposite number occurs in nearby Fairfax Road. Named in 1935.
The Rushes	Waterways development.
Russell Street	Possibly after an early leaseholder. Street named in 1868. (Marriott)
Rutherway	A late 14th century name for the northward continuation of Walton Street which lay to the west of the modern Kingston Road. This modern road in the Waterways development was named in 1996.

Martin Joseph Routh, by Karl Hartmann. By kind permission of the President and Fellows of Magdalen College.

Ryder Close   Waterways. After H A Ryder, the first general manager of Osberton Radiators, a business he had helped to set up on this site in 1919. Named in 2003.

Rylands   After John Ryland, a baker in Oxford in the 1660s, who owned land in Marston. Named in 2006.

Rymer's Lane   Formerly Kame's Sheephouse Lane in 1605. Named for a local farmer called Ryman whose farm was on the site of John Allen's Works, now a retail park. The name evolved gradually into Rymer — Reg Smith, knowledgeable about Cowley, said on Radio Oxford in 1975 that the man's name was Rhyme, later corrupted to Rhymers Lane. Named in 1930.

S

Sadler Walk

There was a Sadler Street in St Ebbe's from at least 1899 but lost in the redevelopment of the area, and this close named after it, (as was Dale Close for Dale Street, and Trinity Street.) The original Sadler Street was possibly named after Michael Sadler (1753-78) a balloonist who made his first ascent on 4th October 1784 in a hydrogen-filled balloon. There is a plaque commemorating this in St Edmund Hall Library and in Deadman's Walk, Christ Church Meadow. However the original street might also have been named for Alderman Charles James Sadler, three times Mayor, in 1849, 1854 and 1860 and a powerful man in the City; his obituary referred to him as "the father of the Corporation; no man ever held so many public appointments". In 'Early Recollections of Oxford by a Freeman (Stephen Quelch) he is described as "a fine old gentleman with a noble presence. An excellent speaker full of life and animation and a great leader of the Liberal Party". Also "he exerted much influence over the Freemen and citizens generally". He was the Liberal Party agent and "when the electors would not listen to anyone else they would listen to King Charlie, as he was called". Because of the fashion for naming streets after Mayors it is more likely that this one was named after the Alderman and not the balloonist. Named Sadler Green in 1979, later changed to Sadler Walk.

Sage Walk

In the Blackbird Leys plant and shrub series. Named in 1993.

St Aldate's

Originally Great Jury Lane in c1215-25, Fish Street in 1369, South-Gate Street in 1661-6, but this may have applied only to the section from Brewer Street to Carfax. From South Gate to Folly Bridge it was Grandpont. (Salter) In 1772 it was again Fish Street and in 1878 known as St Old's or commonly St Owl's. The church of St Old or Ald is possibly a corruption of Old Gate, itself another form of Aldgate, as in the London gateway. (Oxford Architectural and Historical Society report, 1897) There was a saint called Aldad or similar, although the Normans had a St Aldate. Part of a Saxon wattle causeway was discovered under the street in 1971. See *Street Names in the Early Days.*

St Aldate's from Folly Bridge in 1811.

St Andrew's Lane
Formerly Church Lane, Headington in 1930, renamed after the village church in 1955 to avoid confusion with many other Church Streets and Lanes in Oxford. See *Oxford Lost Church Streets.*

St Andrew's Road
After the local Saxon church, mentioned in 1004. Formerly Church Street, Old Headington in 1930, renamed in July 1955. See *Oxford's Lost Church Streets.*

St Anne's Road
After St Anne's School, Headington, which used to operate at no 8 in the road in the 1930s. Road named in 1930.

St Barnabas Street
After the church, designed by Arthur Blomfield, built by Thomas Combe at his own expense, in 1869. (See Blomfield Place and Combe Road) Combe said the church was the warmest in Oxford because it was the driest; although the site was low-lying the foundations were of twenty inches of concrete, "harder than stone and better than wood". (Oxford Architectural and Historical Society report, 1897) Street named in 1874.

St Bernard's Road
After St Bernard's College founded prior to St John the Baptist College, on the same site, as a Cistercian Order. Formerly St John's Road but renamed in October 1961 at the request of the Fire, Ambulance and Police services, supported by St John's College, to avoid confusion with St John Street, although the change had been requested by residents as early as 1946. St Bernard's Road was suggested by St John's College. The road was laid out in 1829 after the St Giles Inclosure of that year. Earlier in the 1800s it was known as Horse and Jockey Road or Lane after the local pub. (*Jackson's Oxford Journal*, 1829) This name came from horse races on the nearby Port Meadow. It is said the road is on the route of the march out of Oxford by Charles I and his troops (Hutten's Oxford Topography) See *Duplicated Names*

St Christopher's Place
Named for, and built on land behind St Christopher's School. Named in 1995, extended in 2001.

St Clement's Street
After the church of St Clement's which originally stood on The Plain, known in 1122, when granted by Henry I to the monks of St Frideswide. The church was pulled down for road widening in 1829. The St Clement's area became developed in the 17th century, earlier called Bolshipton, after the Bolles family who owned a cattle shed here in the 13th century. Formerly High street, St Clement's, renamed in 1862 to avoid confusion with many other High Streets in Oxford parishes. The roads to London via Henley and High Wycombe went from the suburb of St Clement's in 1821 when St Clement's Church at the Plain had "a little whitened tower, adorned with pinnacles (and) contributes a pleasing object on either entering or quitting Oxford by the London roads" (Ingram, Vol II) the Reverend M Tuckwell however, in his *Reminiscences of Oxford (1900)* wrote "St Clement's, sordid by day, by night oil lighted, stretched from Magdalen Bridge to Harpsichord Row at the foot of Headington Hill..."

St Cross Road
Holywell. After the church in existence from about 1100, the chapel of ease to St Peter in the East. The original name is from the dedication to the Holy Cross but it became Holy Well before the reign of Edward I. St Cross Cemetery, where many well-known people are buried (including Henry Acland, Kenneth Grahame, Walter Pater and Kenneth Tynan) is south of the

churchyard. The church closed in 2009 to become a library for the rare books of Balliol College. Balliol has been a tenant of the Manor since 1930. Named in 1898.

St Ebbe's Street
After the local church. Formerly Little Bailey in the early 17th century and St Ebbe's Lane in 1772. The present church is on the site of one dedicated in about 1005; St Aebba or Abba was a 7th century saint, daughter of the King of Northumberland, who became a nun and later an Abbess. She died in about 683. The church is late 12th century but is much restored. A beautiful Norman door disappeared during the restoration. See *Street Names in the Early Days.*

St Ebbe's Street in the early 20th century.

St Edward's Avenue
A private road next to St Edward's School buildings and playing fields. The school was founded by the Reverend Thomas Chamberlain in 1863, when it was in New Inn Hall Street, where a plaque commemorates its foundation. The school was moved here in 1873, into buildings designed by William Wilkinson.

St George's Place
Connects George Street with Gloucester Street. Named in 1936.

St Giles
After the local church dedicated to St Giles, who was born in Athens in the 7th century, patron saint of lepers and beggars. There are many similarly dedicated churches built outside medieval cities, where "lepers sometimes lived in a hospital nearby". (Wade) There was a church here in 1066 but it was not dedicated to St Giles until 1120. The widest street in Oxford, with refuges and lamp standards down the middle and trees lining the sides, there was once a pond where the war memorial now stands. St Giles' is well known for the annual Fair in September, held in its present form since the 1830s, before when it was for children only. Wade (in 1882) describes it as a street which "appears to be a favourite with the genteeler classes of inhabitants"

St Giles' Fair in 2004.

St Helen's Passage   A narrow lane running from New College Lane, with several turns, into Bath Place and the Turf Tavern. Also called Hell Passage, possibly because there was a gaming house there, or be-cause it was a dark passage against the city walls.

The blue plaque for Jane Burden who lived in St Helen's Passage.

St John Street   After St John's College which owns land here. The street was laid out in 1825-35 in the same scheme as Beaumont Street and runs from there to Wellington Square. The terraced houses are now Grade II listed. See *Duplicated Names.*

St Leonard's Road   Unknown. There is no church here by this name. Formerly Southern Road, the site of Jacob's Nursery. Named originally in 1934 and renamed together with Southern Road when a new road was built to connect the two in 1958.

St Luke's Road   After the church built here in 1937-8 by H S Rogers. The church and its site were the gift of Lord Nuffield; the building was awarded a Bronze Medal by the RIBA for its "outstanding merit as a building". Its bells were electrically operated. The church is now deconsecrated and the building houses the Oxfordshire County Archives. Named in 1939.

St Margaret's Road   After the local church built here in the decorated gothic revival style in 1883-93 to the design of H G W Drinkwater. It was earlier a chapel of ease of SS Philip & James but became an independent parish in 1896. In the 17th century the road was called Gallows Baulk after the place of execution here at the time. Later named Greenditch, then Rackham's Lane and finally

	the present name, after the church, in 1884, when developed for housing to the design of Wilkinson & Moore. See *Apostrophes and Spaces*.
St Martin's Road	The remaining part of the original St Martin's Church is at Carfax and it is uncertain why this road was so named in 1948.
St Mary's Close	Unknown.
St Mary's Passage	Runs beside the Church of St Mary the Virgin.
St Mary's Road	After the local church of St Mary and St John, designed by Martin Mowbray in 1875-83 in early decorated style, intended to have a spire but this was never built. Road named in 1874, formerly German Street and later John Street.
St Michael's Street	After the church of St Michael at the Northgate, on the other side of Cornmarket, on the corner of Ship Street. The church is commonly known as St Michael at the Northgate and is now the City Church with the City Rector as its priest. Its Saxon tower is probably the oldest building in Oxford. Recorded in the Domesday Book of 1086, it has stained glass from 1290, certainly the oldest in Oxford. Various chapels and the north transept were added in the 13th and 14th centuries. It was severely restored by GE Street in 1853-4, not without opposition at the time. See *History of the Church and Parish* by Canon RR Martin, vicar, in 1927. Formerly Wood (or Wode) Street in 1405, Bocardo Lane in 1548 later part of New Inn Hall Street, renamed after 1899. The nearby North Gate, built in about 727, was known as Bocardo, a prison for debtors and scholars who had committed petty offences. These prisoners would let down hats and bags on cords, shouting to passers-by "pray remember the Bocardo birds". The Martyrs, burned at the stake nearby, were held at the Bocardo. It was pulled down in 1771. For picture see page 11.
St Nicholas Road	After the Littlemore church of St Mary and St Nicholas, built by H J Underwood and planned by Cardinal John Henry Newman. In 1842 Newman left St Mary's in Oxford for its smaller sister church in Littlemore where he converted stables into a 'college' and started a small chapel on land belonging to Oriel College, on land consecrated in 1836, extended in 1848. Named 15th November 1954.
St Omer Road	After the founder of the Order of Knights Templar which owned the nearby preceptory in Temple Road. Street named in about 1931.
St Peter's Road	Wolvercote. The road runs southwards from opposite St Peter's Church to the Council estate. The church was originally a chapel of ease to St Peter's in the East until the 14th century. All that remains now of the early church is the 14th century tower – the remainder was rebuilt to the designs of C Buckeridge in 1859. Named in 1937.
St Thomas' Street	After the local church in nearby Becket Street, drastically restored in 1846-7 by J P Harrison. The Canons of Osney Abbey had built a chapel here in 1441. There was also a church dedicated here to St Nicholas and until 1220 it was St George's. Now known as St Thomas the Martyr, after Thomas á Becket. Originally St Thomas Street, then High Street, St Thomas in 1862, renamed in 1954 or 55. See **Becket Street.**
Salegate Lane	Off Hollow Way. Named after the annual hay sales held at a gate on the edge of Bullingdon Green. Spelled Sare Yate in the 16th century, Saleyt in

1512, and Sale Gate Lane in 1853. (Cowley maps & St Fridewide's cartulary – a collection of records) The hay came from common pasture land on the Green. The Templars had a sheepfold there in the 13th century and Charles I reviewed his troops there in the Civil War.

Salesian Gardens   On the site of the Salesian College and its gardens. Next to the Roman Catholic church of St Francis of Assisi. Named in August 1993.

Salford Road   Marston. Unknown origin. The name was chosen by the developer, A C Carter Ltd. The word Salford possibly comes from 'Salt Ford' which is probably a crossing across a stream, perhaps on a trade route for salt.

Salisbury Crescent   Probably after Robert Cecil, 3rd Marquis of Salisbury, who had been Chancellor of the University. Named in 1934.

Salter Close   After Rev H E Salter (1863-1951) of the nearby Isis House, Grandpont, the most knowledgeable historian of Oxford since Anthony Wood and a prolific writer. He was an authority on the history of Oxford Street names and wrote the first book on the subject *The Historic Names of the Streets and Lanes of Oxford (intra mures)* OUP 1921. Also possibly after Sir (James) Arthur Salter, (1881-1975) MA; Hon.DCL; Gladstone Professor of Political Theory and Institutions at Oxford, Fellow of All Souls, later Lord Salter, MP for the University from 1937-50. Named in 1975.

Samphire Road   In the wildflower group of road names in Blackbird Leys, named in 1961.

Sanders Road   Oxford Science Park. Dr A Gordon Sanders was a member of the team of Oxford scientists including Florey, Chain and Heatley, who successfully developed penicillin in 1941-42 for the treatment of infectious diseases. Until then penicillin was seen as a scientific curiosity with no practical use. When his three colleagues went to the USA during the War to oversee the mass production of peni-cillin, Sanders remained behind to continue development work and is attributed with having refined the apparatus for ex-tracting a more stable form of the drug. Eric Lax in his book *The Mould in Dr Florey's Coat* (Abacus Time Warner, 2004) writes that "Sanders' capabili-ties for invention and impro-visation were almost the equal of Heatley's" and that he included in his plant "a bronze letter box and a couple of aquarium pumps". For the next two years it would be the largest penicillin plant in Britain. His name is commemorated on a plaque at the Radcliffe Infirmary where the first successful tests of penicillin took place, and also,

Gordon Sanders tending to the penicillin extraction plant he designed (Courtesy of Dr Mercy Heatley).

with his colleagues' names, on a plinth at the Botanic Garden. The Business Development Officer at the Oxford Science Park and the tenant companies preferred not to use first names for the roads here. Named in 1994.

Sandfield Road Possibly after a house once here called Sandfield Cottage, shown on a map of 1899 – although there was also a local field spelled Sand Furlong in 1805. The road already existed in 1930 when its continuation was officially named.

Sandy Lane Named in 1957. See **Sandy Lane West**.

Sandy Lane West After the local soil type here. A very old road, the western end of which was spelled Sandy Waye in 1246. The old name was perpetuated when the Blackbird Leys Estate was built.

Saunders Road A cul de sac adjoining the old bus garage in Cowley Road, named after Jason Saunders, the first Chairman of the Oxford & District Tramway Company and Mayor of Oxford in 1875. Named in January 1978.

Savile Road After Sir Henry Savile, (1549-1622) Warden of Merton in 1585. He had been Provost of Eton and Greek tutor to Elizabeth I. There had not been many outstanding mathematicians in Oxford from medieval times until 1619, when Sir Henry founded the professorships that bear his name, in geometry and in astronomy. Christopher Wren was elected Savilian Professor of Astronomy in 1661 and Edmund Halley to Savilian Professor of Geometry in 1704. *(Mechanicks in the Universitie; Alastair Howatson).* He was also a benefactor to the Bodleian Library. Road named in about 1897. Part of Love Lane on a map of 1897.

Sawpit Road Blackbird Leys. After a local sawpit where tree trunks were cut into boards and beams. Officially named in April 1959.

Saxifrage Square In the plant and shrub series of Blackbird Leys road names. Named in 1997.

Saxon Way An old route connecting Marston and Headington in the reign of Ethelred (968-1016). Headington was then the seat of the Royal Palace said to have stood on part of this route. Named in 1949.

School Court Jericho. Housing built on the site of the former St Barnabas School. Named on 26th February 1979.

School Place After the nearby St John's School, replaced by the present New Hinksey School in 1892.

Scott Road After the architect Sir George Gilbert Scott (1811-78) who won the competition to build the Martyrs Memorial in 1840 at the age of 29. He also worked on the restoration and improvement of many important college buildings. His son Sir George Gilbert Scott Jr designed St John's College Quadrangle and his grandson Sir Giles Gilbert Scott designed Liverpool Cathedral, the Bodleian Library extension and many other important college buildings. Road named in 1933.

Scrutton Close After Miss J M Scrutton JP, once Secretary of the Oxford Citizens Housing Association; this is one of their developments. Named in 1967.

Seacourt Road After the medieval village of Seacourt, about a mile to the north beside the old Wytham Road. Means "Seofeca's home". The stream was named for the village. Named in 1940, formerly Seacourt Slope.

Sefton Road Unknown. Once a private road. Named in 1930.

Sermon Close	Risinghurst. Possibly after a Risinghurst Parish Councillor. See **Harold White Close**. Named in about 1985.
Shaftesbury Road	After Anthony Ashley Cooper, MP, known as Lord Ashley and later 7th Earl of Shaftesbury (1801-85), who gained a first class degree at Christ Church in 1822; he was a philanthropist involved in much social reform legislation, including better housing for the poor, President of the Board of Health between 1848 and 54. Named in 1971.
Sheepway Court	A private development off Woodhouse Way, Iffley, built on allotments. Named after an old field name Sheepway Furlong at the south end of Tree Lane. Sheepway was the old name for Tree Lane and marked the beginning of an old track from Iffley via Rose Hill and St James Church, Cowley, ending at Shotover where Iffley farmers had grazing rights. Named in 1981.
Sheldon Place	Not known.
Sheldon Way	After Gilbert Sheldon (1599-1667) who commissioned the Sheldonian Theatre when Chancellor of the University in 1669. He was Archbishop of Canterbury 1663-77, attended Charles I at Oxford and was imprisoned in the city in 1648, later an important adviser to Charles II.
Shelford Place	Suggested by the architect Anthony Del Nevo, with no derivation but thought by him a "pleasant name not already taken". The developers had suggested Shotover Close, but the Council thought this would be confused with their residential home at Shotover View. Named in 1964.
Shelley Close	See **Shelley Road**. Named in 1946.
Shelley Road	In a poet series of residential streets (see Morris Crescent and Milton Road). After the poet Percy Bysshe Shelley (1792-1822) who often walked on Shotover Hill in his Oxford undergraduate days. Named in 1922.
Shepherds Hill	After a local field name. Named in 1993.
Sherard Road	A private road in the University Science Area, named after William Sherard (1659-1728) the botanist and founder of the Sherardian Professorship of Botany, a Fellow of St John's College from 1677-1703.
Sheriff's Drive	On the site of a large house called Church Croft. Named to commemorate the drive traditionally made annually by the Sheriff of Oxford on Wolvercote Common and Port Meadow, generally followed by breakfast at a local pub. The apostrophe is sometimes placed wrongly, but correctly placed shows that the drive is for one Sheriff only. Named in 1981. See *Apostrophes and Spaces.*
Sherrington Road	A private road in the University Science Area, named after Sir Charles Scott Sherrington (1857-1952), Wayneflete Professor of Physiology and Fellow of Magdalen College from 1913 until his retirement in 1936. He dedicated his life to the study of the nervous system, but was also interested in bacteriology, the metabolism of the body in cancer, histology and the formation of scar tissue. In 1932 he was awarded, jointly with Lord Edgar Adrian, the Nobel Prize in Physiology for their fundamental studies on the nervous system.
Sherwood Place	After William Edward Sherwood, twice Mayor of Oxford, 1913-14 and 1914-15. He was a councillor representing the University. Named in November 2004.

Ship Street
After a local inn, known as The Ship Alehouse in 1773. There have been many names, including Somenor's Lane in 1385 after the tenant of the Blue Anchor Inn. (Salter) Also once known as Lawrence Hall Lane after the Hall once at the east end of the Street. It was St Michael's Lane in 1679 after the church. By 1762 it had become Ship Lane from the sign of the Ship alehouse (Salter) and was still Ship Lane in 1838. There was once a sheep market in the street and the pub might have been known as the Sheep Inn in earlier days. It had livery stables in the time of coach travel and ceased to exist as

Ship Street in 1821, looking west towards Corn-market. MS Don. a. 2 n. 46. Courtesy of Bodleian Library, University of Oxford.

an inn by the 1870s. The first common room of the society of Home Students (now St. Anne's College) was in Ship Street and this is the reason the college magazine is called *The Ship.*

Shirelake Close
Corner of Thames Street and Folly Bridge. Shirelake Ditch was the name of the branch of the river which once ran across the site of the development. This tributary stream once formed the boundary between Oxfordshire and Berkshire. There was an earlier suggestion to name the road Isaac Grubb Close after a former member of the City Council who refused to take the oath to the University but Shirelake won the day.

Shoe Lane
After the Sewys family, well known here in the 12th and 13th centuries, mentioned in a will of 1353. Spelled Venella Sewy in 1279-80, Sewyslane in 1405 and Shooe Lane in 1578. The lane was described in 1378 as "a receptacle of malefactors, felons and all refuse". A Mr Sprunt, who lived in Sewyslane in 1405 was fined for "the dirt and ashes he throws out and filthy water by which the way is greatly deteriorated" Officially named in 1890.

Shorte Close
Slade Hospital site. Named in 1999.

Sibthorp Road
A private road in the University Science Area, named after John Sibthorp FRS (1758-1796) MA; born in Oxford, graduate of Lincoln College in 1780, Radcliffe Travelling Fellow of University College, Sheradian Professor of Botany, later endowed the chair of Rural Economy at the University. He did much work on the flora and fauna of many countries on the continent and published many books on the subject. (DNB)

Sidney Street
Possibly after Sir Philip Sidney (1554-86), soldier, statesman and poet, educated at Christ Church. Named in 1874.

Sidgwick Close
A private road in the University Science Area, named after Nevil Sidgwick (1893-1952), a graduate of Christ Church, Fellow of Lincoln College from 1901-1948. A chemist of renown, who carried out important work on atomic bonding during the 1920s.

Silkdale Close

Named in 1967 by Robert Silk (d 1992) who ran his grocery shop in Cowley Road, from which he sold tea and other goods. In 1939 at the start of the Second World War, he brought relatives out of London to Oxford to escape the bombing and bought houses for them in Cowley. When the relatives returned to London after the war he acquired a taste for

91 year old Robert Silk (in about 1992) standing by the close he named, with his son Joseph and housekeeper Angela Spencer. Courtesy of Mrs Hilary Silk

property development and bought up gardens and land in Cowley. He founded Robert Silk and Partners and developed many roads in Risinghurst. He made it clear that Silkdale Close was named after the tea he sold and not after himself or the company.

Silver Road

Formerly Donnington Road, named in 1881. Renamed in about 1960 to accompany the nearby Golden Road and to avoid confusion with Donnington Bridge Road.

Singletree

After a house of the same name, once on this site.

Skene Close

After Felicia Skene (1821-99), described on the blue plaque on her house in St Michael's Street as "Prison Reformer and Friend of the Poor" She was the first official prison visitor in England and would call twice weekly at

Oxford Prison to visit men in the condemned cells and meet released prisoners at the gate. She trained nurses for the Crimean War and was commended by Dr Acland for her work in the cholera outbreak in St Thomas' parish. She was a best selling novelist with some of her books based on personal experiences. Named in February 1992.

Skylark Place

In the bird series of road names in Blackbird Leys, originally named Kestrel Place in 1961 but renamed as suggested by residents to avoid confusion with Kestrel Crescent.

The Slade

An old name for the road from Headington to Cowley and shown as such on the old Award Maps. Possibly after an old field name meaning 'valley' but with no written record of whether this is the derivation of the name in this case; White suggests the name probably came from the word 'slide' because is was "extremely slippery in the old days at the dip near Moor Cottages". Slade Park was a wartime development of temporary housing built in nine avenues, demolished in 1961 and redeveloped from 1974. Spelled Northslade in 1246, The Slade in 1805 and '72. Formerly Barrack Road in 1930, the old name was revived in May1931.

Slade Close
Named in 1955. See The Slade.

Slaymaker Close
Risinghurst. Possibly after a Risinghurst Parish Councillor. See **Harold White Close.** Named in about 1985.

Snowdon Mede
After a local field name meaning "snowy hill meadow", spelled Snowdon in 1297 and Snowdon Mede in 1545-6. Named in 1961.

Sorrell Road
In the plant and herb series of Blackbird Leys road names. Named in 1961.

South Bridge Row
St Aldate's. See **Trill Mill Court.** A City Council development, named in July 1980 after the old name for the south end of St Aldate's.

Southcroft
After a local field name, Succrofte, on the 1605 Corpus Christi College map, named in the 1990s.

Southdale Road
Probably a made up name. Named in 1934.

Southfield Park
After Southfield Farm. See Southfield Road. Named in 1822.

Southfield Road
Runs beside Southfield Park. Named after Southfield Farm and a medieval field name spelled Southfelde in 1512. Laid out, with Bartlemas Road and Divinity Road, by the Oxford Industrial and Provident Land & Building Society in 1891 and shown on a map of 1897.

Southmoor Place
See Southmoor Road

Southmoor Road
Walton Manor. After the St John's College living acquired in c1590 at Southmoor, then Berks, now Oxon. Road named in 1884. Apparently once called Cabbage Hill.

Southmoor Road in 1998.

South Parade   Originally Double Ditch, then Prospect Road, after its fine views of the City, and Union Street in 1832. A German professor once suggested it had been named after South Parade the southern patrolling limits of the Parliamentarian guard during the Civil War but there is no evidence of this. As Fasnacht explains *(Summertown since 1820)* "North Parade was built in about 1855 and was so called from the start. When the roads were named there would have been no need for one to have considered the existence of the other – one was in Oxford and the other in a small village out in the country". The first house was built here (now no 23) in 1824. See text.

South Parks Road   Runs southwards from Parks Road, named after the University Parks. Road named in March 1871 and appears in directories from 1874. In 1889 it was South Park Road. See Parks Road.

South Street   The southern street in the Osney Island grid pattern of streets. Named in the 1850s.

Southern By-Pass Road   Runs from Botley to Hinksey Hill roughly on the line of a medieval track between the two Hinkseys. Named in the 1930s.

Sparrow Way   In the bird series of Blackbird Leys road names. Named in 1997.

Sparsey Place   Possibly meaning "sparrow island". There is a small island in the River Cherwell to the North, in the district of Water Eaton, and the road may be named after this. Spelled Spareweseyam in c1130-50 and Spareweseye in 1183-5. Named in 1960.

Speedwell Street   Originally Mill Lane in 1427 and 1639, as it led to the mill of the Black Friars, also known as the Preaching Friars; Butterwyke Lane in 1427 after one of the University bedels (the Oxford University spelling of beadle, an officer of the University) who owned a house on the south side of the lane in 1660. The modern street now covers a new extension from Speedwell Street to Thames Street, named in 1969. See Preachers Lane.

Spencer Crescent   Possibly after John Spencer-Churchill, 10th Duke of Marlborough, (1897-1972), High Steward between 1937-72. Other Rose Hill roads are named after High Stewards.

Spindleberry Close   In the plant and herb series Blackbird Leys. Named in 1960.

Spinney Field   Blackbird Leys. Possibly after a local field. Named in 1997.

Spooner Close   After Dr William Archibald Spooner (1844-1930), who was a member of the Committee of Management of the Warneford Hospital from 1903 and its chairman from 1906 to 1923. Ordained in 1872, he was a Poor Law Guardian and Warden of New College 1903-24, a lecturer on ancient history and philosophy but supported the promotion of natural science studies in the University. He had poor eyesight because of his albinoism. He is popularly remembered for his slips of the tongue which became known as spoonerisms, as in, for example, "This pie is occupewed, may I sew you to another sheet?" Most spoonerisms are now known to be apocryphal however. His daughter Rosemary, who lived in Oxford from 1930-1969 also played a prominent part in the organisation of Oxford hospitals. She told one of the authors that the question of spoonerisms was never mentioned in the family and that once she suffered a slip of the tongue and blurted out: "Oh, I nearly said one of those things!" Named in 1999.

Spring Lane   Littlemore. After a spring called Chawdwell in 1512, to the south, running into Northfield Brook. The lane was originally Chowleswell Lane in 1605, also known as Long Lane. Named in 1959.

Springfield Road   After a local field with a spring. Named in the 1940s.

Spruce Gardens   In the tree series of Blackbird Leys road names. Named in 1997.

The Square   Cowley Centre. The name given by the Cowley Centre Committee for their shopping precinct, sometimes known as the Main Square. Named in 1961.

Squitchey Lane   Known in 1832 as Green Way and in 1859 as Victoria Road, the street appeared on maps of 1896 and 1897 as Squitchey Lane. By 1906 it had been decided that Green Lane would be a more respectable name but the change proved unpopular and eventually Squitchey Lane became the official name when adopted in 1937. Because of its often muddy state it was often thought that the name was a corruption of 'squelchy', but the name derives from the piece of land on the lane's south west side which, because of the squitch and couch grass growing there was known as late as 1929 as Couchy or Squitchey piece.

Stable Close   Named in 1997, probably after a field name on the site.

The Stables   Unknown.

Stainer Place   After Sir John Stainer (1840-1901) composer and organist, Professor of Music 1889-99, founder of the Oxford Philharmonic Society. The Rev M Tuckwell (*Reminiscences of Oxford*) quoted the rhyme: "St Pauls had a loss, In Dr T Goss. I'm sure it's a gainer, In Dr J Stainer". Also "If Sir Frederick Ouseley made music respectable in the University, then Sir John Stainer made it beloved" One of his most famous works is the oratorio 'the Crucifixion' and legend has it that he composed this in the garden of Wood House, Iffley (see **Woodhouse Way**). He also wrote 40 anthems and 150 hymn tunes. Named in 1936.

A cartoon of Sir John Stainer by 'Spy' in Vanity Fair.

Stainfield Road   North Way. After an old field name, Stain Furlong (1613 Brasenose Terrier). Named in 1949.

Stanley Close   See Stanley Road. . Named in the 1940s.

Stanley Road   After Arthur Penrhyn Stanley (1815-81) Dean of Westminster Cathedral, 1864-1881 Regius Professor of Ecclesiastical History at Oxford in 1856 and canon of Christ Church, until 1863. Westminster Close is nearby. In

1961, because of confusion with Stanway Road, Headington, it was suggested this be changed to Livingstone Road, as it was then thought that the road had been named after Sir Henry Morton Stanley, the explorer who found Dr David Livingstone in Africa in 1871 - but the residents resisted this with a petition of 49 signatures. Named in 1938.

Dean Stanley

Stansfeld Place   After Rev John Stansfeld, Rector of St Ebbe's from 1912-26 and founder of the Stansfeld Field Family Centre in Quarry Road. He worked for 30 years as a civil servant in the Customs and Excise, but in his spare time took a BA at Oxford in 1889 and later qualified as a doctor of medicine in London. William Temple said in tribute: "one of the greatest men and truest Christian whom I have known." He founded the Oxford Medical Mission in Bermondsey. At over 70 years old he travelled to

Stanfeld's plaque

East Africa and became Principal of a mission school – and attempted to learn to drive when he was 80. He liked to build swimming baths. He died at Spelsbury in 1939 where he had been a parson for the last ten years of his life. A blue plaque now commemorates him on the Old Rectory in St Ebbe's.

Stansfield Close	Unknown. Named in 1967
Stanville Road	After a local field spelled Stanville Field in 1823.
Stanway Road	Means "stony way" possibly named after the Roman road to the west. Named in April 1935. See **Ridgeway Road.**
Stapleton Road	After Sir Thomas Stapleton, MP for Oxford 1759-61. Road named in 1930.
Starwort Path	In the wildflower group of Blackbird Leys road names. Named in 1961.
Staunton Road	Possibly after Edmund Staunton, President of Corpus Christi College 1648-60. Named in December 1930. The name may be connected with Staunton Hall, a tenement in the High Street, long since demolished.
Staverton Road	Unknown. There is no record of Staverton being a St John's College living. Named in 1899.
Steep Rise	After the steep gradient of the road here. Named in 1948.
Stephen Road	Unknown. Named in 1930.
Stewart Street	New Hinksey. Unknown origin. Named in c1886.
Stile Road	After a field path stile in North Place, used by Quarry people as a route to church before the Quarry church was built in 1849. Named in 1940.
Stockleys Road	Means "stock or tree trunk", after a field name spelled Stock Leaes in 1605 and Stock Leys in c1840. Named in 1955.

Stockmore Street	Originally Hockmore Street in 1874, renamed to stop confusion with its Cowley namesake.
Stoke Place	After Stoke House nearby, now part of Ruskin College. The house was acquired from a reverend gentleman Mr Taylor whose wife, one Jane Mould, was born at Stoke Damerel, Plymouth, where they were married. Named in 1930.
Stone Meadow	After a field name. Named in about 2000.
Stone Quarry Lane	Self-build development, named 25th April 1979, on the site of an ancient quarry from the Middle Ages, from which the stone probably came to build the 12th century church. On the Inclosure map of 1830 it was shown as the 'stone pit'.
Stone Street	After Rev William Stone, Principal of New Inn Hall, now St Peter's College, d1685, benefactor of Stones Almshouses built in 1700 in Caroline Street on the site of Tyler's Close. The almshouses were for the poor and sick, as is explained by an inscription on the building. Parsons' and Mary Duncan's Almshouses were built in 1816 and 1964 respectively. Named in 1932.
Stonor Place	After Thomas Stonor, MP for Oxford 1832-5. Four nearby streets have similar MP origins. (see **Cardwell Crescent, Harcourt Terrace, Grays Road, and Valentia Road**). Named in 1930.
Stowford Road	Barton. Named 30th November 1945 after a family connected with land in Headington.
Stowood Close	Barton. Stowood was part of the Royal Forest and lies on either side of the old London-Worcester road, now a country road connecting Stanton St John and Islip. It never had a church and, until the Crown sold Shotover, was closely linked with Shotover and Headington, Stowood came to be treated as a separate parish and so remained until 1932. Named in 1976.
Stratfield Road	Unknown, probably a name contrived by the Oxford Industrial and Provident Land and Building Society, which had also named **Beechcroft, Oakthorpe** and **Thorncliffe Roads**. Named in 1893.
Stratford Street	Unknown. Named in 1916.
Strawberry Path	In the plant and herb series in Blackbird Leys. Named in 1961. The Housing Committee had told the Street Names Sub-Committee that this would be a path with no homes built along it, but then developed the street without notifying the change when it was too late to change to a more suitable name.
The Stream Edge	St Thomas Street. Named in 2004.
Stubbs Avenue	Formerly Third Avenue, Slade Camp. Renamed in January 1977. A 'stub' is brushwood or stumps of trees and shrubs. There is a reference to an 'elderstubs' coppice in this area in state papers of 1628. By 1642-3 the word was spelled 'stubbs'. Stubbs was also a well known local family name from the 1500s.
Sturges Close	Joseph Sturges was a shepherd at Barton Farm, recorded in the 1881 census. Named in 1985.
Summerfield	New Hinksey. Recorded on a map of 1897.
Summerfield Road	After Summer Fields School, opened in 1864. In 1832 the road was an access lane to fields. Also after the house in which Miss Gertrude McClaren, a classical scholar, started the school (the name of which was changed

from Summerfield to plural and two words in 1863). Two of Miss McClaren's sons-in-law became in turn headmasters of the school, which remained in the family until 1939. Named in 1899.

Summerhill Road After a house once in the road. Named in 1929.

Sunderland Avenue After the family name of the Duke of Marlborough, who owned the land here. The Duke sent his approval to Councillor Capel, the builder of the development here, on 19th January 1938. Until then the residents of the houses built by Capel called it 'Northern By-Pass, Banbury Road end'. The name applies to two service roads, one on each side of the Northern By-Pass. Named in February 1938..

Sundew Close In the wildflower series in Blackbird Leys. Named in 1961.

Sunningwell Road After Sunningwell village, then Berks, now Oxon, meaning "valley, hill and stream of Sunna's people", spelled Sunningwellan in 811, Sunnugauuille in 821 and Soningeuel in 1086. Named in about 1880.

Sunnyside After Sunnyside Mansions once on this site. It was formerly a private road leading to the Osler Hospital. Named in 1967.

Sutton Road After a local field spelled Sutton Field and Furlong in 1605 (Corpus map) and Sutton in c1840. Named in July 1940.

Swallow Close In the bird series of Blackbird Leys road names. Named in 1997.

Swan Street Osney. After the medieval swannery kept locally by the City. In 1578 it had to provide a fat swan annually to the city. Named in c1886.

Sweet Green Close Sandhills Primary School site. After a field name, to the east of the site. Named 31st January 2002.

Swift Close In the bird series of road names in Blackbird Leys. Named in 1993.

Swinbourne Road Littlemore. A combination of the names or Mr Colbourne, the builder of the houses here, and Swindon, his birthplace. Formerly Laundry Field.

Swinburne Road Presumably after the poet A C Swinburne (1837-1909). Named in 1922. See Arnold and Addison Roads

T

Tackley Place	After St John's College living at Tackley, Oxon. In 1716 Dr William Brewer had left the College some £2000 to acquire the advowson; when the money had accumulated the college made the purchase with two others for £590 in 1725. (VCH University) Street named in 1878.
Taggs Gate	After a local field name. Named in March 1971
Talbot Road	After John Gilbert Talbot, MP for Oxford University from 1878-99. Talbot is the family name of the Earls of Shrewsbury. Talbot's parliamentary business "was always directed to some public object, never for any desire for egotistical display". He had the rare quality of "giving all his powers and attention with a single-minded disregard for himself or his notoriety" (Lock) The Moorhouse Estate Company named their development "Sunrise Estate". Named in January 1932.
Tarragon Drive	In the plant and shrub series of Blackbird Leys road names. Named in 1993.
Taverner Place	In the musicians' group of New Marston road names, after John Taverner, an eminent musician, made Master of the Charities by Wolsey at what was then Cardinal College (now Christ Church) in about 1525, organist at the college 1526-30. He was the last of the pre-Reformation composers, and wrote masses, motets and songs. Named 4th March 1934.
Tawney Street	After Richard Tawney, Mayor of Oxford in 1748, '64, '78 and '90. The Tawneys were a prominent Oxford family; Charles Tawney had given a site in New Headington, on the London Road, for Headington School, later rebuilt in 1894. Several generations of the family were Mayors from the mid 18th century. A later Richard Tawney was the architect of the imposing Canal House (1828) now part of St Peter's College. Miss Lily Tawney (Vice Chairman of the Housing Committee at the time the name was chosen) was the first woman Mayor of Oxford, elected in 1933. Named in October 1930.
Teal Close	In the bird series of Blackbird Leys road names. Named in 1997.
Templar Road	After the Knights Templar who once owned land in Cutteslowe. Named in April 1934.

Temple Road	Cowley. Formerly Temple Street, renamed in March 1930. After the Knights Templar, given land near here by Queen Matilda in 1139. Temple Couele in c1200. There were two Cowleys; during the Middle Ages the men of Temple Cowley were mostly tenants of the Templars, later the Hospitallers. Although this is where most of the men lived, it was the smaller settlement and was called little Cowley in the mid 13th century. (see Cowley Road)
Temple Street	After the medieval Temple Mill once situated just south of Magdalen Bridge. (Marriott)
Tern Walk	In the bird series of Blackbird Leys road names. Named in 1997.
Terrett Avenue	Sandhills Primary School site. Joseph Terrett was the first head of the school, opened in 1940, a highly regarded teacher who steered the school through its early years, supervising a huge influx of evacuee children from London. He died in 2001, aged 94. Named 31st January 2002.

Tern

Thames Street	After the nearby Thames. From the Celtic Tam-ese or Tam-ouse, meaning a winding or spreading river – when in flood it would, and still can, cover large areas of meadow. Street originally named in 1852, officially in February 1968, when it had been widened as the through route to the Oxpens. Queen Elizabeth II was the first to travel on it, and when told this replied that she was 'glad it served some useful purpose'.
Thames View Road	On the edge of the Rose Hill Estate, with views towards the river. Named in 1969.
The...	Names prefixed with 'The', as in for example The Hamel, are indexed under the main name; for example 'Hamel'.
Thistledown Close	In the plants group of street names in Blackbird Leys, named in May 2002.
Thistle Drive	In the plants group of street names in Blackbird Leys. Named in March 1993.
Thomas Harolde Close	After Thomas Harolde of Barton, who supplied some of the stone for Merton College between 1448 and 1480. Named in 1985.
Thomson Terrace	After James Thomson, Head Gardener at the nearby Littlemore Hospital. Named in about 1947.
Thorncliffe Road	A made up name, thought appropriate at the time. See also Beechcroft Road and Oakthorpe Road. On land bought by the Industrial and Provident Land & Building Society; the developers paid the City to build the roads and recovered the cost from sales. Street built and named in 1894.
Three Corners Road	Blackbird Leys. Probably because of the shape of the road, with three bends. Named in March 1993.
Three Fields	After an old field name. Originally Road no 1 on the Slade Park development, phase 3 and 4. Named 24th January 1977.
Thrift Place	In the wildflower series in Blackbird Leys. Named in 1961, extended in 2001.
Tidmarsh Lane	After Richard Tidmarsh, founder member of the Baptist Church in Oxford and city leader in 1661-90. See *Tidmarsh Lane*.

Tilehouse Close Means 'tile oast or house' after an old field name. Until the 20th century the area was known for the manufacture of bricks and tiles. Spelled Tylehous in 1401 and Tyle Hoste furlong in 1605 (Corpus map). Named in 1970.

Timothy Way After a type of grass for fodder, in the herb and plant series in Blackbird Leys. Named in 1961.

Titup Hall Drive After the local hamlet Titup Hall, and the inn of the same name, renamed in 1854 the Crown and Thistle PH. Titup or Tittup was also a Barton field name. After an old English word 'tittup' meaning to move in a lively fashion, applied here to the horses pulling the Oxford to London coach, that had to increase speed for the ascent of Shotover Hill. This was also the first straight part of the road on which riders could canter. There was once a mounting block at the inn. Coaches would stop here having braved the highwaymen of Shotover Hill, active in the 17th century. The 'Flying Coach' could reach the inn from London in one day. Named in 1952.

Toot Hill Butts After a local field. 'Toot' means a lookout point, and the same meaning appears in Toot Baldon. 'Butt' means to abut or bound, to form a boundary. Spelled Toot Hill Butts in 1804. Named in May 1960, after the suggestion of the Friends of Quarry.

Town Furze After a Barton field name, spelled Town Furze in 1804. Road named in 1938.

Townsend Square After Alderman Mary Georgina, Lady Townsend OBE, Chairman of the Housing Committee, thrice Mayor of Oxford in 1935, 1936 and 1958-9. The street forms a square with the Freelands Hotel (once a private house) and Donnington Lane. Named in 1953. Unusual in being named during the lifetime of the person honoured, but to show appreciation of her service to the City. In retirement she was given the Honorary Freedom of the City. See *Celebrating Current Celebrities?*

Trafford Road After an old Headington Quarry family. Named in 1970, at the suggestion of the Friends of Quarry.

Transport Way On the Watlington Road Trading Estate, supposedly reflecting the history of the site. Tenants objected to this prosaic name which they thought unsuited to the hi-tech companies on the site, but the name was adopted in August 1992.

Tree Lane After a single tree remaining from a clump planted in 1620 at the west end of the lane until 1977, when it succumbed to Dutch elm disease and was replaced by an oak. The Tree Hotel here was on the site in 1714 when called Elm House, later the Tree Tavern and the Tree Inn. Named in directories by 1930.

Trefoil Place In the plants group of road names in Blackbird Leys. Named in March 1993.

Trevor Place Suggested by Messrs Moss, the estate developers, after the first name of one of the Moss family. Named in 1930 or 31.

Trill Mill Court St Aldate's. Built beside the Trill Mill Stream, of significance in the Middle Ages. The mill existed from the 12th to the 17th centuries. The stream was culverted in 1863 but is still navigable underground by the most intrepid of explorers. Named in July 1980.

Trinity Road

Headington Quarry. After the local Holy Trinity Church designed by George Gilbert Scott, built in local stone, the foundation stone laid in 1848 by Bishop 'Soapy Sam' Samuel Wilberforce. When a Methodist chapel had been opened in 1830 the area was described as 'the neglected and destitute quarry hamlet'. (Marriott) Named in 1930.

Trinity Street

Connected with the Blackfriars who lived and worshipped here. The name was revived from a street demolished in the clearance of St Ebbe's, confirmed in 1979.

Troy Close

Horspath Driftway, (although with Headington postal addresses). Named in March 1998. Two troys or turf mazes are marked on a pre enclosure map of Cowley, one of them close to this site.

Tucker Road

After B W Tucker (1901-50) lecturer in Zoology, second President of Oxford Ornithological Society and leading bird specialist. Named in 1959.

Tudor Close

A small development next to Tudor Cottage, an Elizabethan timber framed building, at one time a restaurant. Named in September 1978.

Tudor Cottage, from which Tudor Close takes its name, in about 1998.

Turl Street

Means 'turning gate in wall' referring to a turnstile in the city wall at the north end of the street, onto Broad Street. Spelled The Turle in c1590 and Turl Gate Street in 1661-6. The Turle applied to the north of the junction with Ship Street in 1797 and the south end was Lincoln College Lane. See *Street Names in the Early Days*.

Turn Again Lane

So named because when the old river gate was standing there was no access here except via Littlegate. The lane ended at the Trill Mill stream and a flight of steps down into the water – where one had to turn back. Originally Turn Again lane, then Charles Street, St Ebbe's, but was confused with its namesake in East Oxford, and so reverted officially to the original name in 1972. See *Evolving Names*.

Turner Close   After William Turner 1789-1862, who painted many views of Oxford and taught in the City. He is often called Turner of Oxford to distinguish him from the more famous J M W Turner. The Highways and Traffic Committee also agreed that the name could be associated with Harold Jesse Turner, landowner and a well known Cowley haulage contractor and pig farmer. He helped to start the Cowley Workers' Social Club in 1929 and did charitable work in the area. Named in 1975. See Meyseys Close.

Tyndale Road   After William Tyndale (d.1536) the first translator of the Bible into English and one of the first martyrs in England. Formerly William Street, Cowley St John, named in 1862, renamed in 1958.

U

Ulfgar Road

After Ulfgar or Wulfgar, the Saxon after whom Wolvercote is named, meaning Wulfgar's cottage. It is spelled Ulfgarcote in the Domesday Book of 1086, Wlgarecote in c1130 and Wolgaricote in 1285. Road named in 1937.

Ulfgar Road, April 2010.

Underhill Circus

Barton. Uncertain origins. Possibly after Sydney Francis Underhill, Oxford Mayor in 1910, and Circus, from the circular street plan. Also possibly after a Bishop of Oxford from 1589-1592, John Underhill, born at the Cross Inn, Cornmarket. Alternatively, the City Engineer's file mentioned a family connected with land in Headington. Named in 1945.

Union Street

After the Union Workhouse, in St Clement's parish, later the Cowley Road Hospital, rebuilt in the 18th and 19th centuries, now demolished and redeveloped. In the 18th and 19th centuries, responsibilities for housing and feeding the poor were shared by Cowley and St Clement's parishes, in union. There was also a Union Street in St Ebbe's before its redevelopment. Named probably before 1900.

Upland Park Road

Unknown, probably a made up name – there was a house called 'Uplands' but further south at 269 Banbury Road. Earlier part of the street named in c1928.

Upper Barr

The eastern approach to the Cowley Centre. Named for a local field, in January 1962.

Upper Close

On the site of 1 Godstow Road, Wolvercote, the former home of Christopher Phelps, of Oxford University Computer Services. An earlier owner was Miss J M Scrutton JP (see **Scrutton Close**). Upper Close was the name of the field just across from this site at the time of the Inclosure Award of 1834. Named in 2008 ahead of the completion of the development which the developers for a time had called Godstow Close.

Upper Fisher Row   See Lower Fisher Row and Fisher Row.

Upper (or North) Fisher Row in 1900.

Upper Meadow   Wood Farm. Probably after a field name. Named in May 2004.
Upton Close   Littlemore. After the nearby Lawn Upton House.
Upway Road   After local fields spelled Upway Furlong in 1605 and Upway Down in 1613. Named in 1949.

V

Valentia Road

After Arthur Annesley, 10th Viscount Valentia, High Sheriff in 1874, MP for Oxford 1895 - 1917, enobled in 1917. He lived at Bletchingdon Park and had been awarded the freedom of the City. On his death the title passed to his son, later created Baron Annesley of Bletchington. He was fond of driving coaches and a contemporary description reads: " It was delightful to see his lordship sit on his box, elbows at his side, hands and shoulders well back, his head erect and his eyes well in front – it was a pleasure to see his lordship handle them (the horses). See Annesley Road. Road named 1st October 1928.

Viscount Valentia MP

Van Dieman's Lane

Unknown, possibly related to Van Dieman's Land now Tasmania.

Varsity Place

On the site of the former Varsity Works, which were demolished in 1993. The works were built as a glove factory but were requisitioned in wartime to produce electrical parts for military vehicles operated by the Goodrich Company. Later it was used for manufacturing ice-cream before becoming H & E Engineering, a heating and electrical contractor. Road named in March 1995.

Venables Close

After the Reverend A.R.P. Venables, Curate of St Paul's Church, Walton Street, later Bishop of Nassau. He founded the Boys' School in Great Clarendon Street. Named in 1968.

Venneit Close

After a local meadow, west of the site, across the river, owned by the City from the 16th century. The site was in railway use from the 1850s, as sidings, goods yard and loco-motive depot. Named in c2001.

Verbena Way

In the plant and shrub series of Blackbird Leys road names. Named in 1997.

Vetch Place

In the wildflower series of Blackbird Leys road names. Named in 1961.

Vicarage Close

Off St Nicholas Road, Little-more, presumably named after its vicarage.

Bush vetch   ***Tufted vetch***

Vicarage Lane	See **Vicarage Road.**
Vicarage Road	After New Hinksey Vicarage built in 1887-8 at the west end of the street. Before 1878 it was Post Office Lane, after 1878 Church Street, New Hinksey, renamed in 1955 to avoid confusion with the many other Church Streets in Oxford at that time. The name change was supported by the vicar as the road leads straight down to the Vicarage. See **Vicarage Lane.** See *Oxford's Lost Church Streets*.
Victor Street	After Prince Albert Victor Christian Edward (1864-92), Duke of Clarence, eldest son of Albert Edward, Prince of Wales (later King Edward VII) and Alexandra, Princess of Wales (later Queen Alexandra), and the grandson of Queen Victoria. Albert Street is nearby. Named in c1862.
Victoria Place	Presumably after Queen Victoria. Named in 1862-5.
Victoria Road	In the Twinings development, Summertown. After Queen Victoria. Twining wanted to name the road Queen Victoria Road but the City would not agree. The road is 538 yards long and the building cost, with sewers and street lights was £2,480. Built and named in 1905.
Villiers Lane	Villiers is the family name of the Earls of Jersey; Victor Albert Child-Villiers was Lord Lieutenant of Oxfordshire from 1887 until his death. Named in 1939. See also under Jersey Road.
Violet Way	In the plant and shrub series of Blackbird Leys road names. Named in 1997.

W

Walton Crescent	Named in 1872. See **Walton Street**.
Walton Lane	Named in 1895. See **Walton Street**.
Walton Street	After the old Saxon hamlet of Walton, probably meaning 'tun by the wall' (tun meaning a homestead or small piece of land) situated against the north-west part of the city's medieval wall. Spelled Waltone in 1086, Waltona in c1130 and Waltun in c1174. Known as Walton Street by the 17th century. Walton Manor Farm was near where the iron foundry became established (Ingram 1837). Later known as Lucys', some of which is now redeveloped as housing. Roman implements have been found here. See **William Lucy Way**.
Walton Well Road	Means the 'well of Walton', after a spring or well now capped in a house on the street, recorded in earliest times as Brumman's Well. The well is commemorated in a drinking fountain erected in 1885 at the junction of Walton Well Road and Longworth Road, designed by H.W. Moore and erected by William Ward, coal merchant, in 1885. It was said he had hoped the water would counteract the number of pubs in the area. Road named by 1881.

The fountain in Walton Well Road.

Warbler Walk	In the bird series of Blackbird Leys road names. Named in 1997.
Warburg Crescent	In the naturalists' group of Blackbird Leys roads, after Dr F E Warburg, Vice President of Berks, Bucks and Oxon Naturalists Trust (BBONT) in 1969. (now BBOWT – Wildlife rather than Naturalists'). A nature reserve is also named after him. Named in 1967.
Warnborough Road	After St John's College living at Warnborough, Hants, obtained in 1636. Named in 1878.

Warneford Lane

After the Warneford Hospital which opened in 1826 in Headington as the Oxford Lunatic Asylum and named after the Revd Samuel Wilson Warneford, (1763-1855) a philanthropist and its chief benefactor, also of Birmingham, Gloucester, Leamington and other places (DNB). The hospital had opened as a family establishment, trying to recreate the atmosphere of a country house – for the 41 patients (in 1841) able to pay a moderate fee. At one time it was called the Radcliffe Asylum after Dr John Radcliffe, when his trust gave a donation. It became part of the NHS in 1948. Named in about 1897.

Warneford Road

Named in 1894, probably also after the Revd Samuel Warneford. See Warneford Lane.

Warren Crescent

After Warren House, here in 1832. Named in 1955.

Warwick Street

Perhaps after the county town, as other roads in the area are named after places, e.g. Stratford Street, Chester Street and Bedford Street. However, also possibly after the earls of Warwick, who have held the title since 1100; it was a fashion at the time to name roads for peers. (Fasnacht) Named in 1894.

Water Eaton Road

Part of the old bridleway to Water Eaton village from Summertown, meaning 'homestead by a river'. Named between 1890-94. the village is to the north, and has been in existence since 864 as Eatun, with various spellings over the years, becoming Water Eaton in 1220-30.

Watermans Reach

Folly Bridge.

Watermill Way

Knot known.

Watlington Road

After the 18th century road to Watlington, a village, meaning 'homestead of Waecel's people'. Spelled Waeclinctune in 880, Watelintone in 1086 and Watlintuna in 1246. The derivation is as for Watling Street, an old English name for the Roman settlement of Verulaneum. Named in 1939.

Wayfaring Close

Blackbird Leys. Named in 1997.

Wayneflete Road

After William of Wayneflete, (c1395-1486) formerly Master of Winchester College and Provost of Eton, made Bishop of Winchester by Henry VI, Oxford benefactor and founder of Magdalen College during his tenure as Lord Chancellor of England. He was granted a licence by the King in 1457 to establish a college in Oxford on the site of the 13th century hospital of St John the Baptist, which had been founded by Henry II in the 13th century. Its buildings and endowments became part of the new college. Wayneflete also founded in 1480 the grammar school (now Magdalen College School) to teach Latin to boys. The Wayneflete Building, south of Magdalen Bridge, is also named for him. Road named in c1948.

Webb's Close

Wolvercote. After a local field spelled Webb's Close in 1834. On the University Press development, the name was suggested by the Press. Named in 1967. An extension was also named thus in April 1983.

Weirs Lane

After Weirs Mill, on a branch of the Thames near the north end of the lane, in existence from about 1225, pulled down in c1920. Spelled The Weirs in 1544 and 1766. Runs from Abingdon Road at the west end, into Donnington Bridge Road in the east. Oxford had at least five water mills in the 11th century (VCH). In about 1825 it became a paper mill and continued to manufacture cardboard until the early 19th century. (VCH). By 1937 the City had built 188 houses on the Weirs Lane Estate. Road named in 1900.

Weldon Road	In the musicians' group in New Marston, named after John Weldon (1676-1736), organist at New College and composer of sacred and secular music. Named in 1947.
Wellington Place	St Giles, north of Pusey Street. Named in c1862-5. See **Wellington Square** and **Street**.
Wellington Square	After the Duke of Wellington (1769-1852), Field Marshal, Premier and Home Secretary in 1834, Chancellor of the University 1834-52. In the square was once the Workhouse, also called the House of Industry, built in 1772, which was moved to Headington in 1860. There is a cartouche of the Duke high up on no 3. Built in 1862, named in c1864.
Wellington Street	Jericho - not near Wellington Square but with the same origin. Recorded in Gardner's Directory by 1852.
Wentworth Road	Possibly after Thomas Wentworth, MP for Oxford between 1604 and 1625. The Highways Committee originally named it Sawyer Road, after Colonel Sawyer who owned land to the north of Summertown, but the current name was chosen by the developers, the Urban Housing Company, in 1934. For several years there were two sets of street name plates in the road, which was confusing to all, but the City Council eventually bowed to the inevitable and this name was officially adopted in January 1948. See Carlton Road and *Snobbery and Street Names*.
Wesley Close	After John Wesley (1703-91) Methodist Reader and Fellow of Lincoln College 1726-51. One of nineteen children, he was educated at home by his mother Susanna, and then at Charterhouse before coming to Christ Church in 1720. He became a Fellow of Lincoln College in 1726 and was ordained in 1725. (*Encyclopaedia of Oxford*). His hymns, of which he published 23 collections, are still popular today. He would often compose them on horseback, on his travels around the country. He led his brother Charles' Methodist Society in Oxford between 1729-35 from which time Methodism is commonly dated. Named in April 1959.

Westbury Crescent   After land in Church Cowley called Westburye Lande, meaning 'western hill fort' in 1512 and Westbury Furlong in c1840. Formerly Westbury Crescent North and South in 1930 but renamed in 1967.

Western Road   Grandpont. After the Great Western Railway, the first rail link to Oxford; Oxford's first rail station was a terminus, opened at the west end of the street in June 1844. The trains came from Didcot, on the line of the present Marlborough Road, through Hinksey Park. This station closed to passengers in 1852 and to goods traffic in 1872. The line was extended to Banbury in 1850, for which an embankment was built from earth quarried from what is now Hinksey Lake. Known by this name from1882.

Westfield Close   Cowley Marsh. After a field name, on the Inclosure Map. The City Council had wanted to name these roads after women politicians, as it was thought there was a dearth of women so honoured, but the historical connection was nevertheless made in naming the street on 16th July 1990.

Westgate   Named in advance of its development in 1970, after the old west gate of the City in that area.

West Grove   Sunnymeade. Probably a name made up by the estate developers.

Westlands Drive   North Way Estate. After a local field name, West Landes (on the 1605 Corpus map), part of Colterne pasture. Named in March 1949.

Westrup Close   In the New Marston musicians' group of street names, after Sir Jack Westrup, Professor of Music at the University 1947-1971. Named in June 1979.

West Street   On the west side of the Osney Town square plan. Named in the 1850s.

West View   After the westward view from this sloping site when developed – the view is now hidden by Sheepway Court. Named in c1944.

West Way   The main road leading westward, from the west end of Botley Road to the east end of the Eynsham Road. Named in the 1940s.

Weyland Road   Headington. After Captain Mark Ulick Weyland, Chairman of the short-lived Headington Rural District Council. Named in 1937. See also Mark Road.

Wharton Road   Thomas Wharton Esq was recorded on a plan of Headington attached to the Inclosure Award of 1804 as a local landowner; there was once a Wharton's Charity in Headington, founded in 1852 (VCH). Named in 1935.

Wheatsheaf Yard   After the Wheatsheaf Inn. Although now considered a passage, the term Yard is historically correct as these passages were known as yards in medieval times. When royal permission was given to Jacob, the owner, to sell the houses here to Robert Swinbrook in 1270 the yard was renamed Swinbrooks – it was later sold on to the Hospital of St John. The first recorded evidence of a tavern was in 1662 when Richard Souch was granted a licence and it was known as the Hen

The Wheatsheaf pub sign in 2009.

and Chickens. It was known as the Wheatsheaf in 1761. Long associated with entertainment, it remains a thriving pub today. Gill & Co opposite was one of the country's oldest ironmongers but closed in 2010. Officially adopted as a public highway and named in 1972.

White Hart   Marston. Originally was a group of cottages here, built in 1785 and converted into a pub in 1801. It closed in about 2002. (Honey). Named in 2003.

White House Road   After a whitewashed house on the site of the White House Inn, later renamed the Folly Bridge Inn, at the east end of the street, known as The First White House in 1765, 1773 and 1775. The house once belonged to Brasenose College and was part of Swindells Farm. A nearby field was named White Horse Close. The road was built by Kingerlee of Oxford in 1899-1900 and named in 1899.

White Road   After a well known Cowley family, in the area for generations. James White lived in a large Jacobean house in Temple Cowley. There was a 17th century White's Farm, on the corner of Temple Road, demolished in c1962. Captain John White (d 1934) with the help of his wife did a great deal of research into Cowley history in order to give appropriate names to the many new roads being constructed at the time. Named probably in 1934.

Whitethorn Way   In the shrub series of Blackbird Leys roads. Named in 1960.

Whitson Place   Formerly Bredon Place before 1932, renamed in 1933 after representations by residents. After a local field name spelled Whitson Leaes in 1605 and Whitsun Leaze in c1840. Named in 1933.

Whitworth Place   Jericho. After Robert Whitworth, engineer, one of the surveyors of the final line of the Oxford Canal from Banbury to Oxford (Compton, Oxford Canal)

Wick Close   Wick Farm was nearby, meaning 'dairy farm'. Spelled Wike in 1278-9, Wyke in c1298 and The Wyke in 1676. Wick was one of the medieval hamlets in the parish of Old Headington, Barton being the other. Wick remained as a manorial unit until replaced in the 17th century by Quarry, which had grown up among the quarries. The City Council named it in November 1945.

Wilberforce Street   Renamed in 1959 after Samuel Wilberforce (1805-73) Bishop of Oxford 1845-69 and Winchester in 1869. Founder in 1854 of the theological college at Cuddesdon, now known as Ripon College (Cuddesdon). Because of his ingratiating manner he was nick-named 'Soapy Sam' – he was an eloquent orator in the House of Lords, also as a preacher St Aldate's Church and was influential in pleading the case for a church in Headington Quarry. When Darwin's *The Origin of Species* was being discussed at the University Museum he spoke against the theory of evolution and is alleged to have asked Thomas Huxley "Is it through your grandfather or grandmother that you claim your decent from a monkey?" to which Huxley replied "I am not ashamed to have a monkey as an ancestor". There is no contemporary written evidence of the story, which has nevertheless become famous. Formerly William Street, New Headington in 1930.

Wilcote Road   Barton. After William Wilcote or Willicotes, Lord of Headington Manor from 1399. Named in 1945.

Wilkins Road

After John Wilkins, (1614-72) Warden of Wadham 1648-59, Despite being a hard-line puritan it was said that "he proved to be a man whose learning, toleration and a gift for friendship turned Wadham into what was perhaps the most enlightened college in the University". (CSL Davies & Jane Garnett; Wadham College, 1994). He was a man of tremendous intellectual energy – an example of his eclectic interests was a book he published in 1648 on designs for submarines and flying machines. He founded a decimal system of measurement not unlike the modern metric system and was the first Secretary of the Royal Society. He was a shrewd politician and married Robina Cromwell, sister of Oliver, who owned land in Oxford and whose nephew Richard appointed him Master of Trinity College, Cambridge in 1659, so making him one of only a few people to have headed a college at both universities. He was expelled from the post at the Restoration and as compensation was made Bishop of Chester in 1668. Named in 1933.

William Kimber Crescent

After the Headington Morris dancer and stonemason who had learned the dances from his father and joined the Morris in 1868. Encouraged by Cecil Sharpe, he recorded folk music and passed on his knowledge of folk forms; this was influential in the national revival of Morris dancing. Named in June 1958. See *Celebrating Current Celebrities*.

William Lucy Way

Jericho. After a member of the family that had operated the Eagle Ironworks, founded by William Carter on this site. It had become a limited company in 1897, making railings, manhole covers, lampposts and other ornamental ironwork still seen throughout Oxford. The foundry was one of the first developments in what is now Jericho. It became known as the Eagle Ironworks and in 1854 the company obtained the freehold from St John's College. A Mr Grafton took over from Carter and when he died in 1861, his partner William Lucy took over the running of the foundry. When he died in 1873 the firm became known as Lucy's. The Dick family took over from the Lucy's and now own the firm; Richard Dick was High Sheriff of Oxford in 2009. The Eagle ironworks is featured in Philip Pullman's *Lyra's Oxford*. Redevelopment work started and the estate road named in 2005.

Lucy's Ironworks, surrounded by new development, in about 2005.

Wlliam Morris Close After Lord Nuffield (1877-1963). Named in 2008. See **Nuffield Road.**

William Orchard Close After the 15th century master mason responsible for much of the Wayneflete Building at Magdalen College and for Eton College, a man of substance and of property.   Named in 1968 at the suggestion of Dr A.B. Emden, Principal of St Edmund Hall. An earlier suggestion of the developers was Pumpkin Place, apparently after Pumpkin Cottage once on the site – house buyers here objected and proposed Douglas Close after an old Headington family, but neither suggestion was much liked by the City Council.

Williamson Way After Councillor the Reverend Tony Williamson (b1933) who had just lost his seat on Oxford City Council when the road was named after him in the summer of 1967. He had been Chairman of the Housing Committee of the City although the road was outside the City at the time – this allowed it to escape the City rule that roads should not be named after living people. City Councillor 1961-67 and 1970-88, Lord Mayor in 1982, a worker priest at the Pressed Steel Works for over 30 years, Oxford Diocesan Director of Education 1989-2000, now a Canon of the Cathedral. See *Celebrating Current Celebrities.*

William Street Unknown, possibly after a royal connection. Named in 1878.

Willow Way In the shrub group in Blackbird Leys. Named in 1960.

William Street in 2010.

Wilson Place A re-use of an old St Clement's street name (M Graham)

Winchester Road After the cathedral city. See Canterbury Road. Named in 1878.

Windale Avenue After a local Blackbird Leys field name, Nether Wynesdehale in 1200. Named in 1960.

Windmill Road There were once two windmills in Headington, one of which was at the junction with Old Road. The medieval mill was described as standing in a forest clearing in 1303. Both mills were said to be in ruins by the 19th century but the Windmill Road mill was rebuilt on modern lines and offered for sale in 1823.

Windsor Crescent Unknown. Name suggested by the developer, A C Carter Ltd.

Windsor Street   Unknown

Wingate Close   Unknown. Named in April 1959.

Wingfield Road   Formerly Dover's Row. Named in the 1870s, presumably after the local Wingfield Hospital, established in 1872 for convalescent patients, designed by William Wilkinson, the architect of much of North Oxford. Mrs Wingfield was a benefactor. It became a military hospital in 1914 and by 1924 had been redeveloped as an orthopaedic hospital by Girdlestone. By 1950 it was known as the Nuffield Orthopaedic Centre.

Wolsey Road   After Cardinal Thomas Wolsey (c1475-1530). He had taken a great interest in the building of his Cardinal College on the site of the monastery of St Frideswide, Oxford. In 1525 it came to be called Christ Church and was united with the College in 1546. Many monasteries were suppressed by Wolsey and their revenues taken in order to run his new foundation at Oxford. When Cardinal College was threatened with destruction, Wolsey wrote to Henry VIII "with weeping eyes" to plead for it. Road named in July 1932. See *Snobbery and Street Names* for reference to the Cutteslowe Walls.

Wolvercote Green   See Ulfgar Road for derivation of the name Wolvercote. Formerly Green Road, Wolvercote. In 1958 the residents were asked by the Council if they would like to change it to Wolvercote Green, but as this name had already been adopted in July 1941, the offer caused amusement and the commoners were able to put the Council right on the already existing name.

Woodbine Place   St Thomas. Unknown origin, probably a made up whimsical name. Named in 1874.

Wood Farm Road   After the local farm once on this land, owned by Magdalen College prior to purchase by Lord Nuffield. See **Pether Road** for his connections with Wood Farm. Named in about 1952.

Part of the old Wood House in Iffley.

Woodhouse Way   Iffley. After a 19th century house, mostly burned down in 1964. Its large grounds extended from Tree Lane to Church Way. Known earlier as Rose Mount.

Woodin's Way   After Dr Mike Woodin, a prominent local Green Party politician and proponent of urban regeneration, who died in 2003 aged 38. Named in August 2004.

Woodlands Close	Named in 1957. See **Woodlands Road.**
Woodlands Road	After the wood beside Cuckoo Lane. Named in 1935.
Woodpecker Green	In the bird series of Blackbird Leys road names. Named in 1994.
Woodruff Close	In the flower group of Blackbird Leys road names. Named in 1961.
Woodstock Close	Private road, with flats and houses, developed in 1932. See **Woodstock Road**.
Woodstock Road	After the town to which it leads. Named in 1772. In the 19th century known as the Turnpike Road to Oxford. A ditch beside the road was filled in at first with road scrapings (horse manure) and later with earth excavated from cellars and foundations – trees grew luxuriously here as a result and hence "this part of Oxford, like the Banbury Road, presents features sadly lacking elsewhere" (Hurst, Oxford Topography) The northern end was Woodstock Road, Summertown from 1890-1, the southern end St Giles Road West in c1865. The name means 'a place in the woods' and has been in existence since c1000 (then Wudestoce)
Wootten Drive	Iffley. After Richard Wootten, who held land in Iffley. Named in May 1979.
Worcester Place	Mentioned in Gardner's Directory of 1852. See **Worcester Street.**
Worcester Street	After Worcester College. Formerly Stockwelle Street c1205-10 named after Nicholas de Stockwelle, a Mayor of Oxford in the 13th century and a benefactor of the poor and the church. The name became corrupted to Stockwell when locals had forgotten the Mayor but knew of a a well on the south west corner of Worcester College, also known as Cornish Well, or Corn Well, or Plato's Well in Tudor times to distinguish it from Aristotle's Well, half a mile to the north. The College was established by royal charter in 1714 on the site of the Benedictine Gloucester Hall (then College). Its grounds are some of the most beautiful in Oxford and include a lake.
Wren Road	In the Cutteslowe architects' group of road names. After Sir Christopher Wren (1632-1723) architect of many buildings in Oxford, including the Sheldonian Theatre and Tom Tower at Christ Church. He built 52 churches in London, including St Paul's Cathedral and is one of England's foremost and famous architects. Wren was also a mathematician and physicist and was professor of Astronomy at Oxford. He was Surveyor of Works to Charles II and was knighted in 1673. E C Bentley (1875-1956) wrote the well-known rhyme;

Sir Christopher Wren
Said I'm going to dine with some men.
If anyone calls
Say I'm designing St Paul's.

	It was with fellow alumni of Wadham College that Wren founded the Royal Society. Named in July 1932.
Wyatt Road	In the Cutteslowe architects' group of road names. After James Wyatt (1746-1813), elected RA in 1785. He designed Canterbury Quad and gateway and was architect to the Trustees of the Radcliffe Observatory in 1776 (Ingram) and completed the work there in 1794, after the death of James Keene.

Wychwood Lane	Unknown.
Wykeham Crescent	Cowley. After William of Wykeham (1324-1404) Bishop of Winchester, founder of New College in 1379, also of Winchester School. His motto "Manners Makyth Man" is shared by the College and the School. Name suggested by developers G Wimpey & Co Ltd; officially named in 1961.
Wylie Close	After Sir Francis James Wylie (1865-1952) the first Oxford Secretary of the Rhodes Trustees in 1903, the first year of the intake of Rhodes Scholars, following bequests by Cecil Rhodes. Named in 1955.
Wynbush Road	Name suggested by the Steward of Lincoln College in a letter of 29th July 1946 to the City Engineer, as the name had been found on old title deeds. Named in c1948.
Wyndham Way	Possibly after the Hon Mrs Humphrey Wyndham, President of Oxfordshire Red Cross – Wyndham House in Plantation Road is certainly named after her. Named in June 1950.
Wytham Street	Probably after Wytham village, although the street does not lead to the village and is at some distance from it. The name means 'homestead by the bend', (of the Thames). Spelled Witham in 957, Uuihtham in 968 and Wyhtham in 1291. Street named in 1897.

Y

Yarrow Close	In the plant and shrub series of Blackbird Leys road names. Named in 1997.
Yeats Close	Unknown, but possibly a connection with the Oxford and Bucks Light Infantry. The Regimental Headquarters were once on this site. Named in January 1978.
Yew Close	In the tree group of Blackbird Leys road names. Named in March 1993.
York Avenue	Named in 1930. The north part was formerly Magdalen Prospect named in 1874. See **Margaret Road.**
York Place	St Clement's. Shown on a map of 1889. Presumably from Prince Frederick (1763-1827), the Grand Old Duke of York of nursery rhyme fame, Commander in Chief of the British Army. The name theme matches other contemporary royal names in St Clement's, e.g. **Caroline Street** and the former George Street, now **Cave Street.**
York Road	Named on 1st April 1935, as the continuation of Quarry Fields estate. **See Margaret Road.**

Yarrow

Bibliography

A - Z Maps of the City of Oxford published by Geographers' A-Z Map Company Ltd.

Badcock, John *The Making of a Regency Village* (St Michael's Publications, 1983)

Bloxham, Christine and Shatford, Susanne *The Changing Faces of Headington: Book Two* Robert Boyd Publications, 1996.

Burke's *Peerage.*

G.N. Clark *Open Fields and Inclosure at Marston, near Oxford.* (Basil Blackwell, 1924).

Costin. *History of St John's College.* Oxford Historical Society (OHS) series, 1958.

Cox, George Valentine *Recollections of Oxford* (Macmillan & Co.) 1868.

The Concise Dictionary of National Biography (OUP 1992).

Cross, F.L. *Oxford Dictionary of the Christian Church*

Ditchfield, P.H., (Edited by) *Memorials of Old Oxfordshire.* (London, Bemrose & Sons, 1903).

Bliss, Philip *The Remains of Thomas Hearne* 3 volumes (John Russell Smith, London, 1809).

Davies, S.C.L. and Garnett, Jane *Wadham College* 1994

Ellis, William Patterson, *Liber Albus Civitatis Oxoniensia.* (Oxford Chronicle Co. Ltd, 1909).

Evans, Evangeline *The Manor of Headington* (Report of OHS for year 1928. No 73).

Fasnacht, Ruth *How Summertown Started* (Published by Parish of Summertown 1969).

Fasnacht, Ruth *Summertown Since 1820* (St Michael's Publications 1977).

Gardners' Oxford Directory, History and Gazeteer of County of Oxford. (Peterborough, 1852).

Faulkner, J. Meade *A History of Oxfordshire* (Popular County Histories) (London, Elliot Stock, 1899).

Gelling, Margaret *The Place-Names of Oxfordshire* Parts I and II.

English Place-Name Society Vol xxiii, 1953 and Vol xxiv 1954 (English Place-Name Society; Cambridge University Press, 1953).

Gomme, George Lawrence, (Edited by) *Topographical History of Nottinghamshire, Oxfordshire and Rutlandshire.* Collection from *The Gentleman's Magazine* 1731-1863.

Graham, Malcolm *On Foot in Oxford* from the Local History Collections at Westgate, Oxford. Printed over a period of time from about 1970.

Green, The Rev. John Richard and Robertson, the Rev. G. *Studies in Oxford History, chiefly in the 18th C.* Oxford Historical Society 1901.

Gunther, R.T. *Early Science in Oxford* Volumes I and II *Oxford Historical Society* 1923.

Hearne, Thomas *Remarks and Collections* in eleven volumes. (Oxford Historical Society and the Clarendon Press (OUP, 1886 -1918).

Hibbert, Christopher *The Encyclopaedia of Oxford* Macmillan, 1998

Hinchcliffe, Tanis *North Oxford* Yale University Press 1992.
   The History of the University of Oxford The Nineteenth Century. Volumes VI (OUP 1997)
   and VII (OUP 2000). (Edited by M.G. Brock and M.C. Curtoys) and Vol VIII *The Twentieth
   Century* Edited by Brian Harrison, (OUP 1994)

Hobson, M.G. *Oxford Council Acts* in several volumes from 1666. (OUP 1939 onwards).

Honey, Derek *Encyclopedia of Oxford Pubs, Inns and Taverns* Oakwood Press, 1998

Hurst, Henry *Oxford Topography* (An Essay). (OHS 1899).

Hutten, Dr Leonard (died 1632) *Antiquities of Oxford A Dissertation* First published by
   Hearne in 1730. (See Plummer, Charles *Elizabethan Oxford).*

Ingram, James, D.D. *Memorials of Oxford* 3 volumes. (John Henry Parker 1837)

Kelly's Directory Throughout the 20th C

Lock, Walter, DD *Oxford Memories* Humphrey Milford 1932

Maclagan, Michael, *Notes on the Heraldic Evidence in the Town Hall of Oxford*
   (Unpublished MS).

Mallett, Charles Edward *A History of the University of Oxford* Volume III Methuen, 1927.

Marriot, Paul J. *Oxford Street Names Explained* 1977

Newbigging, Carole *The Changing Faces of Littlemore and Sandford* Robert Boyd
   Publications 1996

Oseney Cartulary 3 volumes (OHS)

Oxford City Documents 1286-1665 (OHS 1891)

Oxford City Council unpublished files in the City Engineer's Department. Box file re street
   names and files re various estates.

Oxford City Council Building Control Services unpublished contents of box files on street
   names.

Oxford Historical Society *Collectanea* In four volumes 1885-1905 Oxfordshire
   Architectural and Historical Society and Oxfordshire Archaeology Annual Reports
   (references dated individually)

Parker, James *Early History of Oxford* (OHS Volume III 1884/5).

Pevsner, Nikolaus and Sherwood, Jennifer *Oxfordshire* Penguin Books, 1974.

Plot, Robert *The Natural History of Oxfordshire* 1677

Plummer, Charles (with Leonard Hutten and Nicholas Robinson) *Elizabethan Oxford*
   (OHS 1886)

Quelch, Stephen *Recollections of Oxford*

Quiller Couch, Lilian (Selected and edited by) *Reminiscences of Oxford* (OHS 1892)

Reynolds, Patrick *A Stroll in Old Iffley* Baldur Press, Iffley, 1991

The Complete History of The Garden Reader's Digest, 1963.

Robertson, Martin *Historical Buildings Survey Report* (Unpublished MS 1971)

Room, Adrian *The Street Names of England* (Paul Watkins 1992).

Salter, H.E., The Reverend *The Historic Names of the Streets and Lanes of Oxford* (OUP
   1921)

Salter, H.E. *Medieval Oxford* (OUP 1936)

Salter, H.E. *Properties of the City of Oxford* (OUP 1926).

Salter, H.E. (Edited by W.A. Pantin) *Survey of Oxford* In two volumes (OHS 1960 and 1969).

Salter, H.E. (Edited by) *Surveys and Tokens (Survey of 1772)* (OUP 1912).

Salter, H.E. (Edited by) *A Cartulary of the Hospital of St John the Baptist:* 3 volumes. (OHS 1914)

Salter, H.E.   (Edited by) *The Oxford Deeds of Balliol College* (OHS 1913).

Spokes Symonds, Ann *Oxfordshire People and the Forgotten War The Anglo-Boer Conflict 1899-1902* Robert Boyd Publications 2002.

Squires, Thomas H. *In West Oxford* (Mowbrays, 1928).

Stapleton, Mrs Bryan   *Three Oxfordshire Parishes* (OHS and OUP 1893).

Stockford, Michael *Growing Up in Wolvercote 1931-1951* Privately published 2008.

Symonds, Richard *Oxford and Empire The Last Lost Cause?* Macmillan, 1986.

Tuckwell, The Reverend W. *Reminiscences of Oxford* (Cassell & Co 1900).

Von Uffenbach, Zacharias Conrad   *Oxford in 1710* (Edited by W.H. and W.J.C. Quarell, MA's) Basil Blackwell, Oxford 1928

Wade, W.M. *Walks in Oxford 2* volumes (1817-21).

White, Captain John and Mrs White Article on *The Street Names of Cowley* published in 1932.

Wood, Anthony *The Life and Times 1632-1695* 5 volumes (Edited by Andrew Clark) (OHS AND OUP 1891 onwards)

Wood, Anthony *Survey of the Antiquities of the City of Oxford* (Edited by Andrew Clark) 2 volumes (OHS and OUP 1889 and 1890).

Note: OHS is The Oxford Historical Society.
        OUP is Oxford University Press.